I0816000

Praise for
The Called Shot: Babe Ruth, the Chicago Cubs, and the Unforgettable Major League Baseball Season of 1932
by Thomas Wolf

Named the Best Baseball Book of 2020 by *Sports Collectors Digest*

Finalist for the 2021 Seymour Medal from the Society for American Baseball Research

"[Wolf] delivers a solid and exciting look at the 1932 baseball season. . . . Baseball fans will delight in this thrillingly told history."

—*Publishers Weekly*, starred review

"Many fans know about Babe Ruth's legendary 'called shot'—when, during the 1932 World Series, he pointed to the bleachers at Wrigley Field and hit a home run in the same direction. But Wolf takes the familiar sports legend (which is true, mostly) and weaves around it an engaging and insightful recounting of all that led up to that moment, and the colorful figures who played important roles in how the game—and America—played out in that dramatic year."

—Chris Foran, *Milwaukee Journal Sentinel*

"Wolf presents a fascinating study, well-researched, and the story of the entire season erupting at that point."

—Andy Esposito, *New York Sports Day*

"Wolf's work is informative, entertaining, and accessible to readers who are not necessarily baseball fans. The book demonstrates those aspects of the game most appealing to its fans (statistics, characters, and its stories), but does so in a way that anyone interested in the social, political, and sporting climate of the first half of the North American twentieth century would enjoy."

—Rachel Franklin, *Aethlon: The Journal of Sport Literature*

"This book has it all. It is well-written, well-researched, and full of surprises."

—Mark McGee, NINE: *A Journal of Baseball History and Culture*

"*The Called Shot* is a satisfying read and provides depth and context to a memorable baseball season. As the reader will discover, the 1932 season was more than just Babe Ruth's most iconic moment."

—Bob D'Angelo, *Sports Bookie*

"[*The Called Shot*] is a fun read and gives great insight on what life was like in Chicago in the early 1930s, . . . what it was like being a Cubs fan, and life in general."

—Al Yellon, *Bleed Cubbie Blue*

BASEBALL IN THE ROARING TWENTIES

BASEBALL IN THE ROARING TWENTIES

The Yankees, the Cardinals, and the Captivating 1926 Season

THOMAS WOLF

University of Nebraska Press | Lincoln

The University of Nebraska Press is part of a land-grant institution with campuses and programs on the past, present, and future homelands of the Pawnee, Ponca, Otoe-Missouria, Omaha, Dakota, Lakota, Kaw, Cheyenne, and Arapaho Peoples, as well as those of the relocated Ho-Chunk, Sac and Fox, and Iowa Peoples.

For customers in the EU with
safety/GPSR concerns, contact:
gpsr@mare-nostrum.co.uk
Mare Nostrum Group BV
Mauritskade 21D
1091 GC Amsterdam
The Netherlands

Library of Congress Control Number: 2025007083

Set in Questa by A. Shahan.

For

SILAS KINEALY WOLF

A future baseball fan

Contents

List of Illustrations ix

List of Tables x

Author's Note xi

Acknowledgments xiii

Introduction: The Roaring Twenties 1

PART 1. THE TEAMS

1. A Dynasty Is Born 7
2. Miller Huggins 12
3. The Cardinals and Rogers Hornsby 20
4. Spring Training in Terrell Woods 26
5. Spring Training in St. Petersburg 32

PART 2. THE SEASON

6. Opening Days 41
7. Babe Ruth and Ty Cobb 46
8. Early Season Blues for the Redbirds 53
9. Grover Cleveland Alexander 58
10. Away from the Ballpark 66
11. Dutch Leonard Has a Story to Tell 75
12. Yankee Pitchers and Tony Lazzeri 83
13. Rube Foster and Black Baseball 94

14. Sesquicentennial Games 102
15. Judge Landis Takes Over 109
16. The Golden Age of Sports 119
17. Final Days 128

PART 3. THE POSTSEASON

18. World Series Games One and Two 137
19. World Series Games Three, Four, and Five 146
20. World Series Games Six and Seven 152
21. The Colored World Series of 1926 161
22. Judge Landis Steps Up to the Plate 168
Epilogue 175

Notes 185
Bibliography 207
Index 217

Illustrations

Following page 74

1. President Calvin Coolidge and his entourage at Griffith Stadium
2. Rogers Hornsby
3. George Sisler, Babe Ruth, and Ty Cobb as spectators at the 1924 World Series
4. Bill "Wee Willie" Sherdel
5. Satchel Paige
6. Waite Hoyt
7. Jim "Sunny Jim" Bottomly
8. Mule Suttles
9. Tony Lazzeri
10. Grover Cleveland Alexander
11. Babe Ruth, Miller Huggins, and Lou Gehrig
12. Rube Foster
13. Bill "Willie" Foster
14. Billy Southworth
15. Bob O'Farrell
16. Dave Malarcher
17. Dutch Leonard
18. Ty Cobb and Shoeless Joe Jackson
19. Tris Speaker
20. Ban Johnson
21. Kenesaw Mountain Landis

Tables

1. Hornsby's and Ruth's 1925 statistics, compared 3
2. The American and National League standings after the July 5 doubleheaders 108
3. Final standings for the 1926 Major League Baseball season 133

Author's Note

The narrative in this book is focused primarily on the Yankees and the Cardinals, the 1926 pennant races in the white Major Leagues, and the Cobb-Speaker scandal, but I want to acknowledge that another baseball Major League existed in 1926, operating in a parallel universe. The best players and teams of the Negro National League and the Eastern Colored League were comparable to players and teams of the white Major Leagues of the era. I have referred throughout the book to these two professional leagues as the white Major Leagues and the Negro Leagues. The definitive history of the 1926 Negro League season is yet to be written, but it is a story every bit as important and historic as the story of the white Major League season of 1926.

Over the years Grover Cleveland Alexander acquired various nicknames: Dode, Alec, Alex, Alkali Pete, Pete, 'Ol Pete. In Nebraska, some still refer to him simply as Grover. For purposes of simplicity and clarity, I have referred to him either by his full name or by "Alex," one of his more prominent nicknames.

Another major figure in the book is Kenesaw Mountain Landis, the former federal judge who served as commissioner of Major League Baseball from November 12, 1920, until his death on November 25, 1944. I have referred to him either by his full name or as Judge Landis.

Acknowledgments

For nearly five years, I've had the pleasure and challenge of immersing myself in the history of the 1920s and the fabulous baseball seasons of that decade. *Baseball in the Roaring Twenties* is focused on the 1926 season, but I hope the story of that year brings attention to other seasons, other ballplayers and pennant races, and other issues facing our national pastime. I am indebted to the researchers, scholars, and writers who have previously studied and written about the marvelous 1920s. It is truly a decade that roared.

Thanks to Rob Taylor and his All-Star team at the University of Nebraska Press for backing this project and providing the editorial and logistical support to bring it to fruition. I also want to acknowledge Amanda Jackson for copyediting this manuscript in preparation for publication. Credit and thanks also to Doug Easton for indexing the book.

A special thanks to my longtime agent, Stacey Glick, who has encouraged my writing projects and shares with me a passion for the game of baseball.

As always, it was a pleasure to work with Cassidy Lent, the library director at the National Baseball Hall of Fame, who cheerfully and promptly answered all my research questions, no matter how minor or odd the queries happened to be. John Horne provided valuable assistance in searching and finding the photographs that appear in this book. Thanks, too, to Bill Simons, a skilled editor and baseball scholar, who has promoted and directed the Cooperstown Symposium for many years.

I benefited greatly from the previous work and perspective of authors and baseball historians who have researched and written about this era. Thanks especially to Steve Steinberg for sharing his thoughts on Miller Huggins and the 1926 Yankees, and to Jacob Pomrenke for several communications about gambling scandals and game fixing in the early twentieth century.

Other baseball scholars who offered unique perspectives and encouragement include C. Paul Rogers III and Dan Taylor. Thanks also to Willie

Steele, Clayton Trutor, Robert Drake, and Steve Wendl for their continuing friendships and mutual interest in the world of baseball.

I appreciate all the researchers and writers who have discovered, documented, and written about the richness of Black baseball and the Negro Leagues to provide a truer and more integrated narrative of the game's history. Special thanks to Phil Dixon for his commentary and links on social media to highlight players and stories from the past.

Thanks to Dave Shaw who provided excellent editorial guidance when the book was just beginning to take shape and have a life of its own. Thanks also to Marjorie Hudson for many helpful conversations about writing and publishing.

Thanks to Marko Fong, Jim Breeden, and Richard Horner who read portions of this book in its early stages and offered comments and critiques that helped to shape and clarify my thinking as I revised and worked to complete the story of baseball in 1926.

Thanks to Don and Mary Anne Knefel, Kirk Griffin, and Sally Hull for decades of friendship and for many conversations about the progress and content of this book as it evolved and took shape over the years.

I want to express my gratitude to family members who supported and encouraged work on this project, including Carol and Des Runyan, Carol and Ted Ballou, Julie Bosworth, and Steven Palumbo.

Thanks also to John Wolf, Grace Dolfi Wolf, Michael Wolf, and David Wolf—all former athletes and keen students of the game of baseball.

I am most appreciative of Patricia Bryan, a discerning critic and my coauthor on two previous books. Patricia provided technical assistance, patiently listened to countless baseball stories and anecdotes, read drafts of every chapter, corrected my grammar, and offered astute and insightful comments about the stories in this book. I am deeply grateful.

BASEBALL IN THE ROARING TWENTIES

Introduction

The Roaring Twenties

The Roaring Twenties stands out as one of the most captivating and consequential periods of the American twentieth century, a decade fueled by reckless optimism and relentless ambition.

In the early years of the 1920s, the nation's newspapers were filled with stories of the Red Scare, the trial of Sacco and Vanzetti, the financial crimes of Charles Ponzi, a recession that lasted eighteen months, the Teapot Dome scandal, and the death of a president.

By the midpoint of the decade, international tensions had eased, and the country was at peace. Seven years had passed since the end of World War I. Americans trusted the future.

The experiment of Prohibition was still being tested. That didn't mean Americans had stopped consuming alcohol. Anyone who wanted to purchase or drink alcohol could find a bootlegger or a speakeasy.

The economy was robust, and Americans enjoyed more leisure time. The unemployment rate stood at 3.2 percent. Real wages had increased. The rich were getting richer, and even the not-so-rich believed they were on the threshold of success. Automobile production increased to satisfy the increased demand for cars. Americans bought radios and went to motion pictures, like *Gold Rush*, starring Charlie Chaplin, or *The Phantom of the Opera*, featuring Lon Chaney.

It was a time of social change, especially for women, who gained the right to vote through the passage of the Nineteenth Amendment. In Wyoming, Nellie Taylor was elected the nation's first female governor. Women smoked in public. Lucky Strike cigarettes began using female celebrities, like Amelia Earhart, in their advertisements. Cigarette smoking was promoted as a way for women to lose or maintain their weight. Skirt hems rose. Mae West wrote and starred in a Broadway play titled *Sex*. In nightclubs and speakeasies, women danced and drank with men, intoxicated by the sounds of jazz bands.

It was an era of celebratory parades. Notable achievements of groups and individuals were honored with noisy processions and cheering crowds.

There was a dark and troubling side to the decade as well. The crime rate increased, partly as a response to Prohibition. There was a rise in hostility toward immigrants. The National Origins Act of 1924 became law, establishing immigration quotas and limiting immigration based on race and nationality. The Ku Klux Klan resurfaced, claiming six million members. Although the KKK continued to preach hatred toward Blacks, Catholics, and Jews, the organization was accepted in many communities as a responsible civic group.

Religion was important in the lives of many, and not just in churches or on Sunday mornings. Evangelists, including the former baseball player, Billy Sunday, and the popular Aimee Semple McPherson, attracted huge crowds to tent revivals. For twelve days in July of 1925, the trial of biology teacher John Scopes consumed the nation's attention, pitting science against religion and climaxing in a theatrical courtroom encounter between William Jennings Bryan and Clarence Darrow.

It was a decade of risk-taking and daring feats. Speculators enriched themselves in a thriving stock market, bet large sums on the outcome of sporting events, and gambled on land values during the Florida land boom. Flagpole sitting, popularized by Alvin "Shipwreck" Kelly, came to be a source of entertainment and amusement, drawing large crowds. Aerial barnstorming shows featured men and women walking on the wings of biplanes hundreds of feet above the ground.[1] A little-known stunt pilot who billed himself as "Daredevil Lindbergh" performed as a wing walker. By the end of the decade, this daredevil would be one of the most famous men in the world.

The era became known as the "Golden Age of Sports." With money in their pockets and more leisure time, fans flocked to racetracks, boxing matches, baseball parks, and college football stadiums. The two most revered athletes of the early 1920s were Jack Dempsey and Babe Ruth, though Dempsey hadn't fought since his title defense against the Argentinian heavyweight Luis Angel Firpo, a two-round bout at the Polo Grounds in New York City in 1923.

As for Ruth, after breaking and setting numerous home-run records in the early 1920s, he had a disastrous year in 1925, plagued by health issues, struggles at the plate, and repeated conflicts with his manager, Miller Huggins. The best player in either league in 1925 was twenty-nine-year-old Rogers Hornsby, the player-manager of the St. Louis Cardinals. In 1925 Hornsby had the highest batting average, the most home runs, and the most runs batted in of any player in either the National or American Leagues. Hornsby's 1925 statistics surpassed Ruth in every single category.

Table 1. Hornsby's and Ruth's 1925 statistics, compared

Player	At Bats	Hits	Doubles	Home Runs	RBIS	Batting Average	Slugging Average
Hornsby	504	203	41	39	143	.403	.756
Ruth	359	104	12	25	66	.290	.543

But Ruth or no Ruth, baseball was still America's national pastime and number-one sporting attraction. The white Major Leagues received most of the attention in the nation's mainstream press, but the Negro Leagues thrived in the 1920s with a large and loyal fan base. The Negro Leagues featured such future Hall of Fame players as Oscar Charleston, Willie Foster, Bullet Joe Rogan, Cool Papa Bell, and Satchel Paige.

In the late fall of 1925, another team sport—college football—was gaining in popularity, and the most famous athlete in America was no longer Jack Dempsey or Babe Ruth, but a twenty-two-year-old football player named Red Grange, who played for the University of Illinois.

While President Calvin Coolidge had little interest in athletes or sporting events, his wife, Grace Coolidge, was one of America's most avid baseball fans, rooting unabashedly for her hometown Washington Nationals.

In the spring of 1926, Grace Coolidge had reasons to be optimistic that the Nationals might win a third straight American League title. Manager Bucky Harris returned, and the core everyday players from their two pennant-winning seasons would also return. The pitching staff, still headed by thirty-eight-year-old Walter Johnson, seemed solid, at least on paper.

Although the Nationals would not repeat as American League champions, the 1926 season would prove to be a transitional year in the history of the sport. For the previous twenty years, the game had been dominated by men like John McGraw, Connie Mack, Tris Speaker, and Ty Cobb. All four of them served as managers or player-managers during the 1926 season, but they were nearing the end of their careers. A new generation of stars was on the rise, all in their first or second full seasons in the Majors: Lou Gehrig, Tony Lazzeri, Paul Waner, Lefty Grove, Bill Terry, Hack Wilson.

In Black baseball, Rube Foster, the organizer of the Negro Leagues, was struck down by mental illness, but his younger half brother, Willie Foster, would be the hero of the 1926 Colored World Series, pitching a 1–0 shutout in the final game of a best-of-nine series that featured eleven games, including two games in the series that ended in ties.

In the white Major Leagues, the 1926 season would feature two exciting pennant races, allegations of a gambling scandal involving Speaker and Cobb, a comeback by Babe Ruth, heroics by thirty-nine-year-old Grover Cleveland Alexander, and a seven-game World Series between Rogers Hornsby's Cardinals and Babe Ruth's Yankees that would end in dramatic fashion in the bottom of the ninth inning at Yankee Stadium. Fittingly, the final play of the 1926 season would directly involve both Hornsby and Ruth.

The extraordinary 1926 baseball season would be a year to remember and to celebrate. This book tells that story.

1

The Teams

1

A Dynasty Is Born

In March of 1903, Ban Johnson, the president of the American League, brokered an agreement with Frank Farrell and Bill Devery to establish a professional baseball team in New York City. The new owners paid $18,000 for the rights to the organization. In addition, they agreed to secure and establish a playing field for the team's home games.

Johnson had his reservations about doing business with Farrell and Devery. They were men of dubious reputation. In one way or another, both had acquired their status and wealth through illegal or quasi-legal activities, sometimes with the help of Tammany Hall politicians.

But Johnson had recently succeeded in arranging a truce with the National League, and the two leagues were now considered coequal Major Leagues. The National League already had two teams in New York—the country's biggest city and most fertile market for baseball—and Johnson wanted a team from his league situated in the city.

An intermediary—Joe Vila, a sports reporter for the *New York Evening Sun*—had introduced Johnson to Farrell and Devery. Once the franchise had been created, the next step was to find players, a manager, and a ballpark.

The time was short. The deal with Farrell and Devery was announced to the public on March 12. The first home game was scheduled to be played on April 30, a mere seven weeks away.

Johnson was committed to seeing that the new ball club had a quality manager and players who could compete against the best teams in the league. Five members of the defunct Baltimore Orioles were signed. Johnson persuaded his friend, Chicago White Sox owner Charles Comiskey, to allow Clark Griffith, a thirty-three-year-old pitcher, to sign a contract with the new ball club and become its manager. Johnson enticed two proven National League stars—Willie Keeler and Jack Chesbro—to join the new team.

Finding a space to build a ballpark was a different challenge. A site—part swamp, part mud, and populated mostly by rocks—was found and agreed upon in late March. It was on high ground in Washington Heights, two blocks east of the Hudson River and just north of the Polo Grounds, where John McGraw's Giants played their home games. Five hundred laborers, earning $1.50 a day, labored to prepare the field. The cost to Farrell and Devery was $200,000. A wooden grandstand was erected that cost another $75,000. The ballpark was officially called American League Park but was also referred to as Hilltop Park.

The first home game was played on April 30, five weeks after construction began on the site. The New York squad acquired a variety of nicknames but was initially called the Highlanders. A few years would pass before the name Yankees was attached to the franchise.

For the inaugural game against the Washington Nationals, Ban Johnson was on hand to celebrate the team he had created and to throw out the first ball. When the first batter of the Nationals came to the plate, a band played "The Star-Spangled Banner." Frank Farrell and Bill Devery were in the crowd of 16,243 that watched the home team win the game 7–2. Jack Chesbro pitched a seven-hitter. Willie Keeler went two for two, walked twice, and scored three runs.

A little more might be said about the new owners.

As a young man, Bill Devery had briefly been a club fighter, but he had no real interest in sports or athletic contests. He had risen from bartender to various positions in the city police department, swiftly moving up from patrolman to precinct captain, where his principal responsibility was visiting illegal establishments—brothels, gambling dens, casinos, taverns, off-track betting facilities—and collecting payoffs that he passed along to Tammany Hall politicians.[1]

Devery was a big man with a protruding stomach, a bushy mustache, and a great deal of personal charm. He was a well-known public figure and well-liked. Over the course of his life, he assembled thirty-six scrapbooks containing cartoons and articles in which he was featured.[2] In his retirement, he liked to bring out his scrapbooks for guests to see. Devery's biographer described him as "a flamboyant and notoriously corrupt police official, a Tammany Hall collection man, and district organizer, and the favorite villain of reform orators and their allies in the press."[3]

At some point early in his career, Devery crossed paths and became friends with Frank Farrell, an adventurous businessman who owned racehorses and was known as "the Pool Hall King" of New York City. He and Devery had some of the same business interests and knew many of the same politicians who ran things in New York City.[4] Farrell's pool halls—he purportedly owned 250 of them—were the headquarters for a variety of enterprises.[5] In *Pinstripe Empire*, Marty Appel's comprehensive history of the New York Yankees, Farrell's business activities are described as follows: "If it hugged the line between legal and illegal, you could probably find it at a Farrell establishment. You could go in, do some opium, win at roulette, spend your winnings on a prostitute, and arrange for a backroom abortion all at once. Or so it was said."[6]

Farrell and Devery: these were the two men welcomed into ownership of a franchise in the America League.

Ban Johnson knew the backgrounds and character of Devery and Farrell when he began negotiating with them and was wary about doing business with them or letting them into his league. But they had the money to invest, and they agreed that a third individual—a coal mining executive named Joseph Gordon—would be brought on as president of the team. Farrell and Devery promised to stay in the background.

Johnson was a big man with rounded shoulders and an oval head. He had a commanding physical presence and was a brilliant and imaginative organizer. He knew how to exercise power and influence. In 1893 he was named president of what was then called the Western League. He took great pride in his tenure as president of the league.

In 1899 the Western League changed its name to the American League. Johnson was instrumental in the league's financial success. He gave umpires more power to control player behavior on the field, and the league cracked down on drinking, gambling, and rowdiness in the stands. He recruited players from the National League by offering higher salaries. Fans appreciated the quality of play and the more civilized behavior in the stands. Attendance at American League games soon surpassed that of National

League contests. Johnson took great pride in his league and what he had done to make it a success.

Devery and Farrell owned the team for twelve seasons with modest success. The team had three second-place finishes, but it was mostly a second division ball club. Fifth and sixth place finishes were common. Chesbro set a Major League record with forty-one wins in 1904, the most outstanding achievement from the days of Farrell and Devery. Attendance lagged, averaging just 4,500 paid admissions per game.

By 1914 Farrell and Devery had lost money on their investment and were at odds with each other. Devery had always considered ownership of the team an expensive hobby. They were ready to sell the ball club.

Once again, Ban Johnson stepped in to facilitate a transfer of ownership. Johnson was disappointed that the team—now known as the Yankees—had failed to succeed in the country's biggest market under the ownership of Farrell and Devery.[7] Johnson went looking for new owners, individuals who were wealthy enough and committed enough to construct a top-flight roster, attract fans, and compete for championships.

Johnson found Jacob Ruppert and Tillinghast "Til" Huston. The press referred to them as "the Colonels."[8]

The two men did not know each other well, but both were rich. Both were also fans of the New York Giants and frequently attended their games at the Polo Grounds. It may have been Giants manager John McGraw, a friend of Huston's, who introduced Huston to Ruppert.[9]

Ruppert was the third-generation owner of the Ruppert Brewery, which he had recently inherited from his father. He was a wealthy man with political connections, having served four terms in Congress. Huston, trained as a civil engineer, was a businessman who had made his fortune in Cuba after the end of the Spanish-American War. No one questioned that the two men had the backgrounds and financial profiles required to own a baseball team.

Ban Johnson met Frank Farrell and Til Huston at the Wolcott Hotel on New Year's Eve 1914 to discuss the deal. Located between Fifth Avenue and Broadway in the Midtown South area of New York, the building had been designed in the French beaux arts style. During its years as a residential hotel, such inventive luminaries as the dancer Isadora Duncan and the writers Edith Wharton and Mark Twain had lived in the building. It seemed an appropriate venue for consummating the creative deal Johnson proposed.

Bill Devery was not present at the meeting. Jacob Ruppert joined the meeting via a telephone connection. The men discussed the financial arrangements and came to a tentative agreement. Twelve days later, at the Wall Street law offices of Elkus, Gleason, and Proskauer, the transfer of ownership was legally completed. Ruppert and Huston agreed to pay $460,000 jointly for the franchise, which included assuming $300,000 in debts.[10]

Ruppert paid his half-share with a cashier's check. Huston reached in his pockets and pulled out a handful of bills. He paid in cash, depositing a stack of one-thousand-dollar bills on the table.

The New York Yankees had new owners and a new direction.

2

Miller Huggins

With encouragement from Ban Johnson, the first thing that Ruppert and Huston did was hire a new manager. They selected Wild Bill Donovan, a former curveball pitcher with 185 wins who was employed as a coach for the Detroit Tigers and nearing retirement.[1]

Donovan managed the Yankees for three years, from 1915 through 1917. The team never finished higher than fourth, and attendance figures were no better than during the years when Farrell and Devery owned the team. Ruppert and Huston agreed that a new manager and a revitalized roster were necessary for competitive and commercial success.

On April 6, 1917, the United States declared war on Germany and entered World War I. Shortly thereafter, Til Huston reenlisted in the army to serve with the Sixteenth Regiment of Engineers. With Huston participating in the war effort in France, it was up to Ruppert to make decisions about the future of the Yankees. Huston had expressed a preference for Wilbert Robinson, the current manager of the Brooklyn Robins, but when Ruppert met with Robinson at the brewery, he came away uncertain that Robinson was the best man for the job.[2]

Ban Johnson had a different recommendation. He urged Ruppert to interview Miller Huggins, the manager of the St. Louis Cardinals. Huggins was younger than Robinson and well respected. He had succeeded in keeping his Cardinals in the first division, despite the league's worst pitching staff and a starting lineup that included only one hitter—twenty-one-year-old Rogers Hornsby—who would finish the season with a batting average above .300. It was known that Huggins was disenchanted with the ownership of the Cardinals.

Ruppert arranged the meeting.

The two men had met a few years before, in a hotel lobby. At that time, the Yankee owner was not impressed. Huggins was a small man, not much bigger than the average sixth grader. He had large ears and high cheekbones. He tended to slouch. The Yankee batboy, Eddie Bennett, was taller than Huggins.

Ruppert's initial impression was not unique. On first meeting Huggins, any serious baseball fan would find it hard to believe that he had played thirteen years in the Major League. The writer Damon Runyon once described Huggins as looking like a character who might be played by the actor Charlie Chaplin.

There were other quirks. Huggins had never married. He lived most of his adult life with his sister, Myrtle, who also never married. Quite simply, Huggins had dedicated his life to baseball and nothing else mattered very much.

It's likely the meeting took place at Ruppert's office on the fourth floor of his brewery, located in New York City's Yorkville neighborhood. It was a vibrant area of the city, largely populated by German immigrants. The sidewalks were crowded. Trolleys on iron rails screeched past pedestrians. When Huggins arrived, he would have noticed the sweetish smell of yeast in the air. Ruppert's brewery was just one of several in the neighborhood.

Ruppert's office exuded opulence. The walls were paneled with rosewood. Expensive area rugs lay upon the carpeting. It is unlikely that Miller Huggins had ever been in a room quite so lavishly decorated and furnished.[3]

Jacob Ruppert was a large, self-confident man, a man of wealth and power who had served four terms as a United States congressman. He had inherited the brewery business from his father, a German immigrant and naturalized citizen. In 1917 it was not a good time in America to be of German ancestry. German Americans were regarded with some suspicion as to their loyalties. The former secretary of state Elihu Root had recently declared that German sympathizers should "be taken out at sunrise tomorrow and shot for treason."[4] Root made it clear that he was speaking not just of common citizens but also of journalists who opposed America's involvement in the war.

Ruppert was not a German sympathizer, though he spoke with a noticeable German accent, which became more pronounced when he was excited.[5] He was a man of distinction in New York and the business world, an immaculate dresser, often photographed in crisp white shirts and stylish clothes.

He drove a Rolls Royce that always shone like it was new. He had the hobbies, and some of the peculiarities, of the very rich. He collected rare books, jade, and exotic animals. He raised purebred Saint Bernard show dogs and entered them in competitions. Although he owned a country house, his primary residence was a luxurious twelve-room apartment on Fifth Avenue.[6]

Like Huggins, Rupert never married. They had one other bond in common. They both had loved baseball since they were young boys, and they both were determined to lead winning baseball teams to world championships.

The two men sat across from each other and talked. Ruppert changed his opinion of Huggins as the Cardinals manager talked about the game of baseball, his ideas about training, strategy, and how to manage a team. Ruppert was impressed and ready to offer Huggins the opportunity to manage the Yankees.

At the end of the 1917 season, Bill Donovan was relieved of his duties. A few weeks later, on October 25, Jacob Ruppert signed Huggins to a contract to manage the Yankees for the next two seasons. The date marked the beginning of a new era for the New York Yankees.

Huggins was born March 27, 1878, in Cincinnati, Ohio. The president at the time of Huggins's birth was Rutherford Birchard Hayes, a fellow Ohioan. The game of baseball was in its infancy, but Huggins liked the sport and was good at it. Unfortunately, his father disapproved. According to Huggins's sister, Myrtle, their father was "a strict Methodist who abhorred frivolity and listed baseball as such."[7] In order to participate in the game as a youth, Huggins played under the assumed surname of Proctor.

While playing in the Minor Leagues, Huggins attended law school, graduating from the University of Cincinnati in 1902. If baseball didn't work out as a career, he could practice law. John McGraw had seen Huggins play and had the chance to sign him but thought he was too small to play in the Majors. McGraw was no giant himself—he was a less-than-towering 5 feet 7 inches—but he dismissed Huggins as "that shrimp."

Huggins made his Major League debut in 1904 when he was twenty-six years old, signing a contract with the hometown Cincinnati Reds. He played six years with the Reds, then seven years with the Cardinals. From the beginning, his natural position was second base. He was a patient hitter who batted in a crouch, offering the smallest of strike zones to pitchers, and led the National League in walks in four seasons. A skilled baserunner, he stole twenty-seven or more bases eight times. Not surprisingly, he was not a power hitter. In thirteen seasons, he never hit a ball over the outfield fences. His nine career home runs were all inside-the-park homers.

In 1913, at the age of thirty-five, Huggins was named player-manager of the Cardinals, replacing Roger Bresnahan. That first season was difficult. His team finished dead last, winning only fifty-one games. A year later, Huggins guided his team to a 81–72 record and a third place finish, thanks to a pitching staff that posted a league-leading ERA of 2.38.

Even with that improvement, Huggins recognized he had to upgrade the roster. He hired Bob Connery, a former Minor Leaguer, as the team's full-time scout, and Connery went looking for undiscovered talent in the lower Minor Leagues.

In 1915 Connery spotted a skinny and raw infielder playing for the class D league Denison Railroaders in the Western Association. The youngster was just eighteen years old, but he had a competitive spirit that appealed to the scout. Connery signed him to a contract for $600. The ballplayer's name was Rogers Hornsby.

Hornsby was nineteen years old when he debuted in the Major League at the end of the 1915 season, playing in eighteen games and collecting fourteen hits. His first extra base hit was a double off Grover Cleveland Alexander, the future Hall of Famer and eventual winner of 373 games. The next year Huggins named Hornsby the team's regular third baseman, and he responded by hitting .313.

Huggins and Connery had unearthed an exceptional talent, and Hornsby was to spend the next eleven seasons with the Cardinals, becoming the most fearsome right-handed hitter in either league. Despite the daily presence of Hornsby in the lineup and with Huggins directing things from the dugout, the Cardinals struggled to win more games than they lost. The 1916 Cardinals finished 60–93. A year later, they won eighty-two games and lost seventy, but finished sixteen games behind John McGraw's Giants.

After the 1917 season, when Huggins left the Cardinals to become manager of the New York Yankees, his first managerial move was to strengthen the team's defense up the middle. The Yankees had a good shortstop in Roger Peckinpaugh. Huggins wanted to pair him with Del Pratt, who had played second base for the last six seasons for the St. Louis Browns. To obtain Pratt, Huggins traded several marginal players and a young pitcher named Urban

Shocker to the Browns for Pratt and forty-two-year-old pitcher Eddie Plank, who had already announced his retirement.

The seven-player deal was consummated on January 22, 1918, with the Yankees also receiving $15,000. Shocker was twenty-seven years old and had posted a record of 12–8 over two seasons with the Yankees. He was not happy about the trade and deeply resented that Huggins had traded him. He had not yet attained the status and stardom that would come later in his career, but he was confident that he would pitch successfully in the Major League. To prove that point, over the next six years with the Browns, Shocker won 126 games.

As for Plank, he had no intention of pitching for the Yankees. For several years he had contemplated retirement and planned to relocate to his farm outside Gettysburg, Pennsylvania. From the farm, he issued a statement: "I will not go to the Yankees next season. I am through with baseball forever."[8]

True to his word, Plank farmed and later gave tours of the Gettysburg battlefield, not far from where he had been born and grown up. Nine years later, he suffered a stroke and died.

With Peckinpaugh and Pratt at short and second, and with Wally Pipp at first and Frank "Home Run" Baker at third, Huggins had a solid infield. If there was a glaring weakness in the lineup, it was in right field.

In 1918 the Yankees right fielder was Frank "Flash" Gilhooley. He hit .276 with just one home run. A year later, the Yankee right fielder was Sammy Vick, who batted .248 with two home runs. Vick was sometimes replaced by George Halas, who later made a name for himself in the National Football League. Halas went 2–22 at the plate in his single Major League season.

The Yankees didn't do badly under Huggins in the war-shortened 1918 season, when they finished third, or in 1919, when they finished second, but things changed dramatically for the franchise on January 3, 1920—coincidentally just fourteen days before Prohibition went into effect—when the Yankees purchased beer-loving Babe Ruth from the Boston Red Sox in baseball's most famous transaction.

Ruth was installed as the Yankees' new right fielder, and in his first year on the job, batted .376 and hit fifty-four home runs to set a single-season record. He led the league in home runs five straight years, and he changed the way the game of baseball was played and the way fans thought about it.

Babe Ruth quickly became the game's biggest star and greatest attraction. Attendance at Yankees home games soared, averaging more than seventeen thousand admissions per game.

You had to see Ruth play to believe what he could do. Sportswriters struggled to find words and phrases—and appropriate alliteration—to describe him. He was "The Bambino" and the "Big Bam." He was the "Colossus of Clout" and "The Sultan of Swat."

Fans simply called him "The Babe."

The transformation of the New York Yankees under Miller Huggins seemed to be complete. From 1920 through 1924, the Yankees finished second twice, won three American League pennants, and captured their first world championship. At the conclusion of the 1924 season, Huggins recognized his mistake in trading away Urban Shocker and made a deal to reacquire him. He offered the Browns several players, possibly even a youngster named Lou Gehrig who was just starting his Major League career.[9] Luckily for the Yankees, the Browns needed pitchers more than an unproven first baseman, so the Yankees got Shocker back in exchange for three hurlers: Joe Bush, Milt Gaston, and Joe Giard.

With an improved pitching staff, the Yankees seemed poised to dominate the American League for the next decade. Then 1925 happened.

Everything fell apart at once. The only bright spot was Bob Meusel who hit 33 home runs and drove in 138 runs. The pitching staff struggled, even the newly acquired Urban Shocker. Gehrig replaced the dependable Wally Pipp at first base. Peckinpaugh and Pratt had been traded and no longer anchored the infield. Frank Baker had retired.

And then there was Babe Ruth. For Babe Ruth, the 1925 baseball season was a disaster, a year to forget.

In February, he reported to the Yankees training camp in St. Petersburg, Florida, out of shape and overweight. From there, things got worse.

The Yankees had trained from 1921 to 1924 in Louisiana, but in 1925 the team moved from New Orleans to a new training facility at Crescent Lake Field in St. Petersburg. No fences had been erected in 1925 between the lake and the playing field, so alligators sometimes crawled out of the lake to sun themselves in the outfield grass.

When Ruth encountered one of these creatures resting in his domain in right field, he told Huggins, "I ain't going out there anymore."

Ruth struggled during exhibition games and fell ill as the team headed north. At Asheville, North Carolina, he collapsed on the train platform. Outside of Washington DC he collapsed again, this time in the train's bathroom, striking his head on the sink. Unconscious, Ruth was carried off the train at New York's Penn Station and whisked by ambulance to St. Vincent's hospital. He was feverish and weak. His body twitched with convulsions. Rumors spread about his condition. In England, the *London Evening News* picked up the story, sensationally and erroneously reporting that Ruth had died. Without checking the facts, they published an obituary.

For forty-seven days, Ruth remained hospitalized at St. Vincent's. Doctors never confirmed, or perhaps figured out, exactly what was wrong with him. Reportedly, he suffered from some combination of the flu and indigestion or perhaps a more severe gastric illness. On April 17, he was operated on for a stomach ulcer. Newspapers indelicately described Ruth's condition as "the bellyache heard 'round the world."

Ruth didn't make his first appearance in the lineup until June 1. As the season progressed, he slumped at the plate, and as the once-great Ruth faded, so did his Yankee team, which escaped the American League cellar only because Ruth's former team, the Boston Red Sox, was even worse.

Off the field, things were just as bad. In the clubhouse, Ruth clashed with teammates and his manager. When pitcher Waite Hoyt insinuated that Ruth didn't hustle after a fly ball, Ruth attacked him. Hoyt was just out of the shower, dripping wet, and naked in front of his locker. The two came to blows before Huggins separated them. As for curfews and showing up on time at the ballpark, Ruth simply ignored his manager's rules. Huggins countered by employing a private investigator to follow Ruth and report back on his activities.[10]

The conflict between player and manager reached a crescendo at the end of August on a road trip to St. Louis. The Yankees didn't have much to play for. They were twenty-six games out of first place. In the first game of the series on Friday afternoon, Waite Hoyt pitched a three-hitter, but the Yankees lost 1–0. Ruth singled, walked, and struck out twice in four at bats. Then he showered, dressed, and disappeared into the evening.

His teammates had a good idea of how Ruth might spend the night before the next day's game. Ruth had once proclaimed, "St. Louis has the best prostitutes in the American League."[11] He had several brothels to choose from. According to Marshall Hunt, a writer who sometimes accompanied Ruth on his nighttime adventures, the Babe particularly liked The House of the Good Shepherd, a brothel operated by May Traynor at 4007 Forest Park Avenue.[12] Her establishment also served meals to its clientele, and Hunt claimed it offered the best steak dinners in St. Louis.[13] Wherever Ruth spent the night, he didn't return to the Yankees' locker room until the next afternoon, arriving ninety minutes late for the Saturday game.

Huggins confronted Ruth in locker room and told him, "You are fined and suspended. The suspension runs the rest of the season."[14] Ruth stormed out, vowing to challenge Huggins's decision.

First, Ruth sought an audience in Chicago with baseball commissioner, Judge Kenesaw Mountain Landis, to protest the fine and suspension, but Landis was on vacation, fishing at Burt Lake in Michigan, so Ruth took the train to New York and complained to Jacob Ruppert, stating his opinion that Huggins was a terrible manager and that the fine and suspension were unwarranted. Ruppert heard him out but supported Huggins. Ruth calmed down. After nine days of the suspension, Huggins reinstated him for the team's final but meaningless games.

For the season, Ruth hit a career-low .290. He finished the year with just 25 home runs, 104 hits, twelve doubles, and 66 RBIs. Not bad for the average Major League outfielder, but certainly not Ruthian.

Baseball scribes were quick to predict that the Babe, soon to turn thirty-one, would never again dominate the sport. The baseball writer Fred Lieb lamented, "It is doubtful that Ruth will again be the superstar he was from 1919 through 1924."

The baseball world was convinced that neither the seventh-place Yankees nor the diminished Babe Ruth would be much of a factor in 1926.

3

The Cardinals and Rogers Hornsby

The franchise that became the St. Louis Cardinals was purchased in 1881 for $1,800 by Chris Von der Ahe, a German-born entrepreneur who knew a great deal about beer and knockwurst but very little about baseball.[1]

Prior to acquiring the baseball team, Von der Ahe operated a grocery store, a meat market, and the Golden Lion saloon. His team was known as the St. Louis Browns and competed in the American Association, which was also identified as the "Beer and Whiskey League" because several of the franchises were supported by breweries and distilleries. At the time, the rival National League did not permit alcohol to be sold or consumed in their ballparks.

Von der Ahe had a talent for promotion. He wanted fans to come to the ballpark and have a good time. The Golden Lion was located right next to the grandstand. He installed handball courts, a cycling track, and water rides for fans to enjoy. He was a man of vision and liked being the center of attention. Soon after gaining ownership, he installed a life-size statue of himself outside the ballpark.[2]

Peter Golenbock describes Von der Ahe's approach to marketing:

> Men like Von der Ahe believed in the very modern notion of doing commerce through baseball. The St. Louis owner saw that baseball was as much a spectacle as it was a game. Before the game, the walrus-mustached Von der Ahe, flanked on either side by fawn-colored greyhounds, would don a top hat and frock coat, and would lead his players, dressed in silk, in a parade into the ballpark. Von der Ahe held horse races and fireworks in his park, built lawn bowling lanes on the grounds, and provided an atmosphere of fun and merriment. The Browns were part of an amusement park atmosphere. Moreover,

Von der Ahe believed that if the baseball fan was enjoying himself, he would buy a lot of beer.[3]

As a team owner, Von der Ahe was stubborn and egotistical, and he was determined to run his baseball team the way he ran his other businesses. He picked his bartender, Ned Cuthbert, to manage the team for the 1882 season. Cuthbert didn't know much more about baseball than Von der Ahe did. The team finished fifth in the six-team league. In 1884 Von der Ahe relinquished some control and handed the job of managing the team to Charlie Comiskey, the twenty-five-year-old first baseman and future owner of the Chicago White Sox. Comiskey was good at the things that Von der Ahe was not: recognizing and acquiring good players and then molding them into a competitive baseball team.[4]

The Browns played for ten seasons—from 1882 through 1891—as part of the American Association, winning the league championship four consecutive years while Comisky managed the team.

After the 1891 season, the American Association disbanded and the Browns joined the National League. Charlie Comiskey deserted St. Louis and signed with Cincinnati. Von der Ahe decided he could manage the Browns in 1892. The team finished next to last in the twelve-team league, winning just fifty-six games and losing ninety-four.

Over the next six seasons, the Browns continued to flounder, never finishing higher than ninth. They hit rock bottom in 1897, winning only 29 games and losing 102. Things got worse for Von der Ahe. He quarreled with his players. His wife sued him for divorce. His business was failing. The other owners of the league wanted him removed.[5]

Bad luck followed. On April 16, 1898, during a game between St. Louis and Chicago, a fan dropped a lighted cigar under the grandstand into a pile of canvas causing a fire that destroyed the grandstand, the saloon, the cycling track, and the water ride. Players from both teams helped fans escape the blaze. More than a hundred people suffered injuries.

Legal troubles ensued. Eventually, the other National League owners banded together to force Von der Ahe out of the league. An auction was held in 1899. The franchise was sold for $40,000 to the Robison brothers, Frank and Stanley. To complete the transition, the team changed its uniform: brown stockings were replaced by red stockings. The team also changed its name. No longer was the team called the Browns. They were now the Cardinals—the St. Louis Cardinals.

The Robison family owned the Cardinals for the next twelve years. They acquired Cy Young, who won 26 games in 1899 and 20 games in 1900, but during their tenure, the team never finished higher than fourth in the National League. Frank Robison sold most of his shares to his brother before he died in 1908. Stanley died three years later, and in his will, majority ownership of the team passed to his niece, Helene Hathaway Robison Britton.[6]

At the time of Stanley Robison's death, it was assumed—and expected—that Helene Britton would sell the ballclub. No woman had ever owned a Major League franchise. But Helene Britton had other ideas. She was thirty-two years old and knew something about baseball. As a young girl she had attended games with her father and sometimes traveled to away games with him. She decided to keep the team and run it herself.

Britton became the first woman to own and run a Major League baseball team. Suitors came, offering to buy the team, but she turned them down.[7] She attended and participated in league meetings. Male owners offered to refrain from smoking cigars in her presence during the meetings. She assured them that she was used to men smoking. The cigars were lit, and the meetings proceeded.

She had ideas about how to encourage and increase attendance. To attract more female fans, she instituted a Ladies Day promotion. Women accompanied by a male escort received free admission.

She initially chose Roger Bresnahan, the team's catcher, to be its manager, and she signed him to a five-year contract. But the relationship became contentious. They argued over money and roster issues. When Bresnahan arranged a trade that would send second baseman Miller Huggins to the Chicago Cubs, Britton squashed the deal. In 1913, for both personal and financial reasons, Britton sold Bresnahan to the Cubs and installed Huggins as the player-manager of the Cardinals.

In 1917, Britton, frustrated by the demands of ownership, sold the Cardinals to a group of St. Louis investors, headed by James C. Jones. Jones convinced Branch Rickey, then employed as an executive with the American League St. Louis Browns, to assume a management position with the Cardinals. Rickey was given control of baseball operations and a small stockholder position. After Huggins left the Cardinals to sign a contract with the Yankees, Rickey hired Jack Hendricks as the new Cardinals manager.

In the war-shortened 1918 season, with Hendricks as manager, the Cardinals won just fifty-one games and lost seventy-eight. Even the twenty-two-year-old Rogers Hornsby, the team's best player, slumped. He hit a meager .281, the worst performance of his career. Hornsby was dissatisfied with the team's direction and made it known that he didn't respect Hendricks as a manager.

In the spring of 1919, Branch Rickey—not yet the legend he would become—made the decision to fire Hendricks and take over as manager himself, while continuing with his role as the team's business manager.

Rickey was a college-educated man who obtained a law degree at the age of thirty. He was a man with deep religious convictions who refused to play or watch baseball on Sundays. He opposed the use of alcohol, supported the Anti-Saloon League, and was a featured speaker on the temperance circuit before Prohibition.[8] Lee Lowenfish, Rickey's biographer, described him as "intense and loquacious," qualities that carried over in his career as a manager and baseball executive.[9]

In Rickey's short and undistinguished Major League career as a player, he appeared in just 119 games over four seasons, posting a .239 career batting average. What distinguished Rickey was that he had a sharp mind and was a shrewd judge of baseball talent. Long before baseball managers and executives relied on statistical analysis, Rickey was devising new ways to evaluate players.

To say he was unlike most of the players he managed would be an understatement. He was extremely intelligent, pious, and long-winded. He liked to talk. In clubhouse meetings or one-on-one conversations with players, he spoke at length, sometimes dropping in biblical references or quotes.

The Cardinals began to play better baseball after Rickey became manager. But even though Rickey was able to turn the Cardinals around, thanks in large part to Hornsby, who was becoming the most reliable and potent offensive weapon in the National League, the team failed to finish above third place during Rickey's tenure.

Early in the 1925 season with the team's record a dismal 13–28, despite Hornsby hitting a solid .368 with twelve home runs, the Cardinals management made a change. Rickey was named a vice president and given a position in the front office. Rogers Hornsby was designated as the new manager, with the dual responsibility of managing the team and continuing to be its most effective offensive weapon.

The transition was complicated as Rickey and Hornsby accepted their new roles. In addition to being the team's manager, Rickey was a stockholder in the Cardinals, owning 1,167 shares, a 12.5 percent share of the team. Once Rickey was informed that he was being replaced as manager, he declared that he wanted to sell his shares. Hornsby saw this as a business opportunity and agreed to purchase Rickey's shares. He was able to do so thanks to some creative financing arranged by Sam Breadon, the team's president.[10]

Once the deal was completed, Hornsby—just twenty-nine years old—was now the youngest manager in the Major League and the youngest shareholder of the St. Louis Cardinals baseball team.

One might ask if the added responsibility of ownership and managing a last-place team would impact Hornsby's day-to-day effectiveness as a player, especially at the plate.

In this instance, the numbers speak for themselves. After Hornsby was named manager in 1925, he hit .415. He would finish the season with a .403 batting average, 203 hits, 41 doubles, 39 home runs, and 143 runs batted in. It was his second triple crown season. He was named the league's Most Valuable Player and acclaimed as the best hitter in baseball. No one else was even close.

With Hornsby managing the team, the Cardinals climbed from last place to fourth place, winning sixty-four games and losing fifty-one. The Cardinals and their fans had every reason to believe that 1926 could be a banner year for the team.

For most of his playing career, Hornsby was the highest-paid player in the National League, and in all of baseball, his salary was second only to that of Babe Ruth. But Hornsby was a terrible manager of his own finances. He lost money on investments and in the stock market, and most notably, he lost money betting on horse races.[11]

Over the years, Hornsby accumulated additional off-the-field problems, both legal and ethical. He was involved in multiple lawsuits, some stemming from automobile accidents, others from unpaid debts, and one from the husband of a woman with whom Hornsby had an extramarital affair.[12]

Hornsby and his wife also had several questionable relationships. They had befriended a local St. Louis gambler named Tony Foley, who was involved with a crime organization called the Bottoms Gang. In the winter of 1925, Foley was convicted for his role in the gang's theft of one thousand gallons of whiskey from a government warehouse, which they later sold across state lines. Foley received a two-year prison sentence.[13]

In the spring of 1926, the Hornsbys invited a new friend, Frank Moore, a Kentucky-based bookmaker, to join them in Texas for spring training. Hornsby paid for Moore's hotel and socialized with Moore and his wife at night. It was a fortuitous business relationship for Moore—at least for a while. The relationship soured when Moore took Hornsby to court over the issue of unreimbursed horse racing bets.[14] Moore asserted that from December 1925 to March 1926, he had placed $327,995 in bets for Hornsby and his wife. The bookmaker claimed that Hornsby owed him more than $45,000.

When the case went to trial, Hornsby was asked, "Are you an amateur gambler?"[15]

Hornsby replied to laughter in the courtroom, "That is for you to decide."

What was no laughing matter was Hornsby's intensity and competitiveness as a player and a manager. On the baseball field and in the dugout when he was a manager, Hornsby was all business.

An incident in June of 1925 illustrates this point. Just a little more than three weeks after becoming manager of the Cardinals, Hornsby's team was playing the Phillies in St. Louis when the home-plate umpire was challenged by the pitcher and catcher of the Phillies over balls and strikes. Philly's manager, Art Fletcher, joined in the heated discussion.

Although the argument had little to do with Hornsby or the Cardinals, at least directly, Hornsby came out of the dugout and inserted himself in the debate. Soon it became a dispute between the two managers. Fletcher and Hornsby exchanged words, and then without any additional provocation, Hornsby punched Fletcher in the face and knocked him down.

Questioned later about why he had acted so abruptly, Hornsby calmly responded, "I wasn't making any progress talking to him."[16]

4

Spring Training in Terrell Woods

In February 1926, Rogers Hornsby took his St. Louis Cardinals team to Terrell Woods, Texas, just a few miles outside of San Antonio, for spring training. Thanks to the strong finish to the 1925 season and several off-season acquisitions, the Cardinals organization and their fans were optimistic about the upcoming season.

The first practice was held on February 22, and Hornsby addressed his squad with a simple message, delivered in his typically blunt way. He told the players, "If there's anybody in this room who doesn't think we're going to win the pennant, go upstairs now and get your money because we don't want you around here."[1]

He also announced one of his arbitrary rules. Pitchers were allowed to play golf, but not everyday players. Hornsby didn't like golf and believed the sport was bad for hitters. "When I hit a ball," he once said, "I want someone else to chase it."

He had opinions about everything and didn't care whether others agreed or not. As for diet, he favored foods high in protein: eggs, whole milk, steak, and ice cream. He didn't like ballplayers to go swimming because he thought it used the wrong muscles. He hated air conditioning in hotels because "it freezes up the body."[2] He didn't think ballplayers should watch movies or read because it was bad for their eyes.

At the age of thirty, he just a few years older than most of his players. Although he had led the Cardinals to a surprising fourth-place finish in 1925, he was still unproven as a Major League manager. His selection as manager of the Cardinals was based on his reputation as a player, which was not uncommon in this era.

Years later, Les Bell, the Cardinals third baseman, reflected on Hornsby's reputation as a manager, "I've heard a lot of ballplayers say he was a tough man to play for. I never found him that way." Bell noted that Hornsby was "a lone wolf" but "all he ever asked of anybody was that they give him all they had out on the field."[3]

Hornsby's overall career record as a manager was mediocre, at best. His teams posted a winning percentage of just .460 in all or part of the thirteen seasons in which he was employed as a manager. His teams finished in the first division just five times and only twice in full seasons.[4]

A more common reaction to Hornsby as a manager was uttered by Freddie Lindstrom, an infielder with the New York Giants in the 1920s and 1930s. "Once you lay aside your bat," he said of Hornsby, "you're a detriment to any ball club."[5]

Gene Karst, the Cardinals public relations man when Hornsby was manager, offered this opinion: "Rogers Hornsby was, in my opinion and in that of many others, the most blunt and tactless guy in the world." Karst also noted that Hornsby didn't like many people. "He was really prejudiced against blacks and Jews, Catholics, and everyone else."[6]

Hornsby took pride in the fact that he was honest and direct with everyone—players, owners, and umpires. "I've never been a yes man," he acknowledged, and his confrontations with owners proved that was true.

Baseball was Hornsby's primary focus for all his adult life. He once said, "People ask me what I do in the winter when there's no baseball. I'll tell you what I do. I stare out the window and wait for spring."

Hornsby also had strong views as to what the Cardinals needed to bolster their roster in the off-season: one or two good right-handed starting pitchers and another outfielder, preferably one who could hit with power. As for the outfielder he wanted, Hornsby said, "Guys who can field, you can shake out of any old tree. Find me guys who can hit."

To improve the roster, Branch Rickey put aside his dislike of Hornsby and made two acquisitions over the winter. He traded a utility infielder to the Cincinnati Reds for right-hander Vic Keen and purchased the contract of Sylvester Johnson from the Pacific Coast League.

Johnson wouldn't contribute in 1926 but would stay in the Majors for nineteen years and win 112 games. Keen was the more promising addition to the roster, though a bit of a gamble. He was young and had achieved two winning seasons for the Cubs, winning twelve games in 1923 and fifteen games in 1924. In 1925 he made thirty appearances for the Cubs, mostly in relief, won just twice, and posted an unimpressive 6.26 earned run average. Rickey and Hornsby were willing to take a chance that Keen could regain his form.

One of Rickey's other key acquisitions was signing former Cubs manager Bill Killefer as a coach. Killefer had thirteen years of experience in the Major League as a catcher, a coach, and briefly as a manager. He was especially good at mentoring young pitchers. Killefer was one of the few people in baseball Hornsby respected and would take advice from.

Acquiring another starting pitcher and an outfielder would have to wait until after the season began. Hornsby and Rickey agreed that those deals would be key to the success of the Cardinals in 1926.

Hornsby arrived at spring training with a young and inexperienced team. He was the only projected everyday player over the age of thirty. In their careers, only Jim Bottomley had ever hit more than twenty home runs in a season—twenty-one, to be exact, in the preceding season. It did not appear that this was a team capable of scoring many runs.

The infield would consist of Bottomley at first, Hornsby at second, Tommy Thevenow at shortstop, and Les Bell at third. Not counting Hornsby, the infield averaged twenty-four years of age, and only Bottomley had more than one year of Major League experience. Defensively, they were a solid group, especially with Bottomley and Thevenow at first and shortstop.

The outfielders were Ray Blades, the oldest of the trio, at age twenty-nine; Heinie Mueller, who had never played more than ninety-two games in a single season; and Taylor Douthit, who had played less than a hundred games in his career. The three outfielders had combined in their careers to hit forty-four home runs, just five more than Hornsby had hit by himself in the previous season.

Hornsby's most reliable player was Bob O'Farrell, a vastly underrated catcher in an era of outstanding backstops.[7] Over the course of a twenty-one-year career, he would lead the league three times in putouts and twice in assists. In the 1926 World Series, he would make the final and definitive defensive play of the series.

His contemporaries understood O'Farrell's value. He would be voted the National League's Most Valuable Player in 1926, the first catcher to win the award.

Hornsby had four starting pitchers on his roster, three right-handers and a southpaw. Two of the right-handers—the newly acquired Vic Keen and Flint Rhem—had outstanding college careers. But they were unproven as starters at the Major League level.

Although Keen had primarily been used as a reliefer with the Cubs in the prior season, Hornsby wanted him as a starter. As the son of a Methodist minister, Keen was a serious and soft-spoken young man. He had entered the University of Maryland with the intention of earning a medical degree. As a pitcher he earned recognition for his performance as a college hurler and his success pitching for semipro teams in the area and for a team in the Blue Ridge League, an independent professional league. In the spring and summer of 1921, he was credited with forty wins in forty-one starts, pitching mostly against local semipro teams. His lone loss was to the Hilldale Athletic Club—known as the Darby Daisies—a Negro League team located just west of Philadelphia that featured future National Baseball Hall of Fame players Judy Johnson and Louis Santop.[8]

Like Vic Keen, Flint Rhem had gotten noticed because of his exploits as a college pitcher at Clemson University, but the two players couldn't have been more different in terms of background and temperament. Rhem came from a prominent and wealthy South Carolina family. He was self-confident and gifted with raw talent. Everyone who saw Rhem pitch could see he was capable of dominating hitters. On the mound, he was imposing, with a lively fastball and sharp curve, averaging fifteen strikeouts per nine innings in college. A local newspaper nicknamed him "Big Smokey."[9]

Off the field, Rhem struggled with self-control and alcohol.[10] Years later, the St. Louis sportswriter Bob Broeg wrote that Rhem "boozed away the greatness expected of him."[11] There was no question that Rhem had raw talent. But at this point in his Major League career, he had won only ten games in two years.

Hornsby needed both Keen and Rhem to develop into effective starters, since he had only two returning pitchers he could count on: Willie Sherdel and Jesse Haines.

Sherdel was a slim, twenty-nine-year-old left-hander from McSherrystown, Pennsylvania, who earned the nickname "Wee Willie" early in his career.[12] Sherdel had grown up near the now-retired Eddie Plank, who had served as a mentor and pitching role model in Sherdel's early years. Sherdel briefly attended Gettysburg College but had little interest in completing a college education. "All I did in school," Sherdel reflected, "was look at [my] watch and count the minutes until . . . I could play baseball."[13] In that regard, he was a lot like Hornsby.

In eight prior seasons with the Cardinals, he won eighty-six games and lost seventy-nine. Sherdel had been used as a spot starter and long reliefer by Branch Rickey. Hornsby moved Sherdel to the starting rotation in late 1925. He finished the year with a record of 15–6, completing 17 of 21 starts. Sherdel was durable and crafty, relying on off-speed pitches and slow curves. His off-speed pitches were described as "a slow ball, then a slower one, and sometimes one that barely comes to the plate."[14] He averaged fewer than three strikeouts per nine innings, but he pitched expertly with men on base.

Sherdel's counterpart and his roommate on road trips was Jesse Haines, a right-hander who pitched his first game for the Cardinals as a twenty-six-year-old rookie in 1920. Going into 1926, his career record was similar to Sherdel's: eighty-three wins, eighty-seven losses. Haines would pitch his entire career—nineteen seasons—with the Cardinals, and he remains the second-winningest pitcher in the team's history. Only Bob Gibson has recorded more wins in a Cardinal uniform.[15] Haines had a fierce competitive spirit—not unlike Gibson's—which was appreciated by his manager.

If it had been up to Haines's parents, he wouldn't have had a professional baseball career at all. They disapproved of the sport and of playing games on Sunday. Haines kept a spare uniform in a neighbor's corn crib so he could sneak away on weekends to play ball. The game was all he thought about, even though the equipment he used was primitive: "[We] played with a hard rubber ball, a dime bat, and a quarter glove." When not playing the game, he was collecting baseball cards. "We collected those little cards with pictures of ballplayers on them," he recalled. "Those cards were about the only way we ever got to see what a player looked like."

Haines utilized a fastball and a curve, but his best pitch was a knuckler. Eddie Rommel had taught Haines how to spin the ball off his index and middle fingers. Thrown from different arm angles, the pitch tended to dip sharply as it reached the plate, reacting more like a spitball than any other breaking pitch.

Spring training was unseasonably wet. It rained almost every day. To give his players as much game competition as possible, Hornsby often scheduled two games a day against Minor League teams in the area, splitting his squad in half, managing one team himself and assigning Killefer to manage the other team.

The Cardinals spring record against Minor League competition was an impressive 25–1, but Hornsby didn't know for sure if he had a second division club or a possible pennant contender. The opening weeks against Major League teams would give Hornsby a better idea of how good his team was and what it needed to get better.

5

Spring Training in St. Petersburg

Babe Ruth stepped off the train in St. Petersburg, Florida, on February 5, 1926, one day before his thirty-first birthday and two weeks before the Yankees would begin spring training. After the debacle of the 1925 season, Ruth considered himself physically fit and ready for his thirteenth Major League season. He intended to stay in shape by playing a lot of golf until his teammates arrived for spring training.

Ruth was a man who lived in the present moment and didn't dwell on the past. If 1925 had been a disaster due to his performance on and off the field, including clashes with his manager and assorted temper tantrums, so be it. This was a new year. The reformed, if not entirely contrite, Babe Ruth was ready for the coming season.

When the 1925 season ended, Ruth gave up a lucrative barnstorming tour and went on a three-week hunting trip in Canada with friends. He claimed to have reenergized himself by tramping through the woods, hiking, and staying away from the indulgences that had led to his physical problems during the prior year.

In December, Ruth engaged the services of Artie McGovern, a former flyweight boxer who ran a gym in Midtown Manhattan and served a diverse clientele. McGovern had built a business on the idea that he knew more about fitness and diet than anyone else. His clients included many of America's most well-known athletes and celebrities, including the heavyweight boxer Jack Dempsey, band leaders John Phillips Souza and Paul Whiteman, and the golfer Gene Sarazen.

McGovern was a few years older than Ruth and about half his size, but he was determined to force Ruth to adhere to a regimen of diet and exercise that would reduce Ruth's weight and tone up his muscles. Ruth didn't listen to many people, especially when it came to his personal habits or inclinations, but he was smart enough to know that he needed the kind of discipline that McGovern offered.

Getting Ruth in shape after his disaster of the 1925 season was a serious challenge. It was well-known that the Babe had a disregard for healthy activities and off-season training. He was thirty or forty pounds over his playing weight of earlier years. He had neither the conditioning nor the muscle tone necessary to regain his stature as the game's most dominant power hitter.

Ruth took McGovern seriously. He adhered to a sensible diet and showed up on time for workouts. He ran and jumped rope. McGovern invited reporters into the workouts to see Ruth toss a medicine ball back and forth. McGovern was blessed with publicity as the city's sportswriters wanted to see what Ruth could do under his tutelage.[1]

Together they recorded a short video of the two boxing, the diminutive and speedy McGovern trading halfhearted punches with the massive Ruth. At one point, Ruth dropped his gloves, let McGovern pummel his midsection, and boasted to the camera, "Who's the heavyweight champion?"[2]

A few days after Christmas, McGovern gave an interview to the press, praising Ruth's commitment to diet, exercise, weight reduction, and general physical fitness. "He is one of the most sincere workers I ever handled," McGovern said.

Spring training was seven weeks away, but McGovern offered this bold prediction on Ruth's fitness for the season, "He is in the best shape of his career right now and he will have his greatest year in 1926."

Miller Huggins and a contingent of Yankee team members left the snow and ice of New York City behind on February 19, departing from Pennsylvania Station on the night train for Florida. In anticipation of warm weather in Florida, many of the assembled Yankees carried golf clubs along with their luggage. A reporter noted that "the party looked more like the Walker Cup golf team than a major league baseball outfit."[3]

It was the second year for the Yankees to train at Crescent Lake Field in St. Petersburg. One improvement: adequate fencing had been erected around the lake, so alligators would not bother Ruth in right field.

Huggins had a lot to prove. Sportswriters openly criticized his managerial skill and suggested his team didn't have the talent to work its way up to the first division. If his team was going to improve after the disaster of the 1925 season, he needed a comeback year from Babe Ruth and significant contributions from younger and untested players. Huggins knew success during the season would require considerable focus and energy on his part.

There was more on his mind than baseball as he contemplated the beginning of spring training. He had been a savvy investor for many years, but he didn't want to be distracted in 1926 by any of his off-the-field business ventures. His biggest and most profitable investment had been in real estate in Florida. In February 1926—a half-year before the Florida land boom went bust—Huggins sold his orange groves and other Florida property to J. C. Creamer of Brooklyn, for $150,000. "I find that baseball and real estate do not go well together," Huggins explained, "and as I love the game, I got out of the real estate field."[4]

Players and sportswriters enjoyed spring training. Huggins scheduled two practice sessions each day for the players. The writers could relax, so long as they wrote a few stories to send back to their editors in New York. There was time for fishing and golf and sunbathing at the nearby beaches. The weather was warm and hospitable. Nightlife was plentiful. The Gangplank, a local nightclub and speakeasy, featured live bands. It was a favorite location and a known hangout for Florida bootleggers. Johnny Torrio, the retired gangster and mentor of Al Capone, owned property in St. Petersburg and sometimes visited with his entourage.[5]

A few players brought their wives and families to St. Petersburg. Only one player arrived with his mother. That was Lou Gehrig. His forty-four-year-old mother stayed at the Del Prado hotel and enjoyed afternoons at Spa Beach. When Gehrig and his mother were together, they conversed in German, his mother's native language.[6]

If this seemed odd to any of Gehrig's teammates, it wasn't discussed openly.

This was the ninth spring training for Miller Huggins as manager of the Yankees. Despite three consecutive American League pennants and a second-place finish in 1924, Huggins was faced with rebuilding the roster in 1926.

He had a solid pitching staff, comprised of three veterans—the lefty Herb Pennock, plus right-handers Urban Shocker and Bob Shawkey—and the twenty-six-year-old Waite Hoyt. The four had already won a total of 562 Major League games. Pitching was the least of Huggins's worries.

The Yankee outfield would feature Babe Ruth in right, the speedy Earle Combs in center, and Bob Meusel in left. All three could hit. As a group, they were adequate defensively. Meusel was sometimes erratic as a fielder but had one of the strongest throwing arms in baseball. Ruth didn't cover as much ground as he had in the past, but he was an underrated defensive outfielder. Combs was solid but not spectacular as a centerfielder.

The catcher was supposed to be Benny Bengough, but he was bothered by a sore throwing arm. His backup, purchased from the St. Louis Browns, was Pat Collins, and it would be Collins who became the regular catcher during the season. Neither provided much firepower. Bengough would finish his career with more than 1,200 at bats and not a single home run. Before coming to the Yankees, Collins had never played in more than eighty-five games in a season and had a career batting average of .237.

If Huggins was going to turn the Yankees around, in addition to a rebound year from Ruth, he was going to have to get production and solid defense from his young and unproven infield.

Joe Dugan would be the third baseman. He was a good fielder and a reliable hitter, but he had suffered a knee injury in 1924 and despite surgery, the knee would bother him and impact his performance the rest of his career.

The first baseman would be Lou Gehrig. He was just twenty-two years of age and had become the starting first baseman for the Yankees midway through the 1925 season, replacing Wally Pipp. At this point in his career, Gehrig had appeared in just 149 Major League games, but he would play in every Yankees game for the next thirteen seasons and the first eight games in 1939 before removing himself from the lineup. He would smash Everett Scott's supposedly unbreakable record of playing in 1,307 straight games and set a new record that would also be considered unbreakable.[7]

As for Pipp, the Yankees decided he wasn't needed as a backup. Over the winter, the Yankees tried to trade him, but no American League team was interested, even though Pipp, at age thirty-two, was still a healthy and productive ballplayer. On February 1, just weeks before spring training commenced, Pipp was sold to the Cincinnati Reds for $7,500.

The biggest uncertainty for Huggins was the double play combination of Mark Koenig and Tony Lazzeri, rookies who had started their careers on the West Coast. Koenig had played briefly with the Yankees in 1925, appearing in twenty-eight games. Lazzeri had impressed scouts who saw him hammering the ball in the Pacific Coast League in 1925—hitting sixty home runs in 192 games, driving in 222 runs, and scoring 202 runs—but he had no experience at the Major League level. In fact, he had never even attended a Major League game.

The natural position for both players was shortstop, and Huggins planned to play Koenig in that position. He had a strong arm, though he was sometimes erratic in the field. Huggins wanted Lazzeri to learn a new position: to be the Yankees' second baseman, the position Huggins had played for thirteen seasons. Throughout spring training, Huggins could be seen tutoring Lazzeri.

Less than a week into spring training, Huggins decided the team was not fully focused on baseball. He banned the playing of golf. During the two-a-day practices, Huggins concentrated on the fundamentals and paid special attention to his youngest players. Traditionally, teams wanted to be solid defensively at catcher, shortstop, second base, and centerfield. Those positions were being handled by young and relatively inexperienced players in 1926—something for Huggins to worry about.

In addition to golf, the weather, the beach, and the Gangplank, Huggins had to design a training schedule that accommodated the various visitors who came to Florida to watch exhibition games. Jacob Ruppert arrived with two aides to get a close look at his employees. Ruppert liked what he saw and offered a cautious observation, foreseeing a first-division finish, but declining to predict a pennant.

Judge Kenesaw Mountain Landis, baseball's commissioner, appeared, though he was more interested in the local golf courses than the Yankees' training camp. One day Landis played in the rain and shot 106.

The most notable visitor was Jimmy Walker, the flamboyant and recently elected mayor of New York City. He had traveled to Florida to get a first-hand look at his hometown Yankees.

Jimmy Walker had a close relationship with Jacob Ruppert. Both were Tammany Hall politicians with an interest in sports. In his days as a state legislator, Walker sponsored bills legalizing boxing and Sunday baseball in the state of New York. The owners of all three New York City Major League teams benefited financially by being able to schedule and sell tickets to Sunday games. Typically, Sunday crowds were the biggest of the week. To celebrate Walker's success in the 1925 mayoral election, Ruppert had thrown a victory party for Walker at the Yankee owner's elegant Fifth Avenue apartment.[8]

Prior to his career in politics, Walker had been an aspiring songwriter who wrote the lyrics to the hit "Will You Love Me in December as You Do in May."[9] Walker never lost his enthusiasm for the world of entertainment. He regularly attended theater productions and vaudeville shows. He married twice, both times to showgirls.

Walker vigorously opposed Prohibition. Under his administration, speakeasies proliferated in the city and enforcement of liquor laws was lax. Walker was often seen as a customer at these illegal establishments. As a symbol of New York City in the Jazz Age, the press gave Walker the nickname "Beau James."[10] The historian Kevin Baker characterized Walker "as a man who lived for little but pleasure."[11]

It's likely that during his visit to St. Petersburg, the mayor visited the Gangplank for some evening entertainment. He posed for pictures with Ruppert at the training facility and watched a Yankees scrimmage. In the game Walker attended, Ruth hit a long home run and sprinted across the outfield to make an excellent running catch.

Satisfied that the team was in good shape, Walker took the train back to New York.

The press was interested in how Ruth was performing after his terrible year in 1925—and the writers were especially curious about what kind of physical shape he was in. One afternoon Ruth went for an ocean swim while reporters watched. A reporter wrote, "Babe swam with more earnestness than skill, but Johnny Weissmuller never looked in better shape."[12]

Ruth wasn't the only Yankee who received humorous attention from the sportswriters, who took time out from their working vacation to come up with clever nicknames for the newest Yankees. Lou Gehrig was described as "the Columbia catapult." Lazzeri was called—among other things related to his heritage—"the swarthy Neapolitan" and "the famed spaghetti farmer."[13]

Huggins took time to give interviews, putting a positive spin on how the team was getting ready, noting that he was encouraged by the development of young players, the team's morale, and Ruth's commitment to practice.

Near the end of training camp, the Yankees played two exhibition games against a strong Cincinnati Reds squad. The Reds had finished third in the National League in 1925, fifteen games behind the pennant-winning Pittsburgh Pirates and 6.5 games behind the second-place New York Giants. In addition to newly acquired Wally Pipp, the Reds had reliable Edd Roush, a future Hall of Famer, in the outfield and a solid roster. The pitching staff was the team's strength: Pete Donohue, Eppa Rixey, the former Yankee Carl Mays, and Cuban-born Dolf Luque. Those four starters put up 66 wins in the previous season. If the pitching held up, the Reds expected to be in the pennant race.

The Yankee bats were somewhat subdued in the games with the Reds, but they won both, 4–1 and 5–4.

In late March, the Yankees left sunny Florida and headed north, playing exhibition games along the way against Wilbert Robinson's Brooklyn Robins.

On March 29, in the first game of the series, Koenig homered once and Gehrig homered twice. The Yankees won. The next day, the Yankees won again, 2–0, and the day after that, they won 10–2. Huggins was impressed with the team's offense. "I have always known it to be a powerful hitting club." And then he added, "The source of greatest satisfaction to me is the way our defense is improving in the infield"—by which he meant that Koenig and Lazzeri were working out as he had hoped.[14]

A snowstorm in Nashville caused a game to be canceled. Brooklyn manager Wilbert Robinson lamented that it was too cold to play golf. On April 2, the Yankees won again with Lazzeri hitting a grand slam and a triple. A few days later, the Yankees embarrassed Dazzy Vance, Brooklyn's best pitcher, beating the Robins 11–5.

The winning streak continued, all the way to New York. Most of the remaining games were won by lopsided scores: 9–5, 16–9, 14–4, 14–7. When the final game was played on April 12, the series ended, and the Yankees had swept all twelve games from the Robins.

It was only mid-April. Huggins was pleased. He thought his team was ready.

2

The Season

6

Opening Days

Opening day was celebrated in the nation's capital with Vice President Charles Dawes on hand to throw out the ceremonial first pitch.

Starting with President William Howard Taft in 1910, it had been customary for the sitting president to attend the game and take part in opening day ceremonies. The ceremony included the inauguration of the new season with an opening day toss. Taft was a baseball fan, and Nationals owner Clark Griffith, along with American League president Ban Johnson, thought that Taft's presence at the ballpark would be good for the game and help to increase paid admissions.[1]

Whether or not it was simply a good business decision, it united, in an important symbolic way, the national game with the presidency. For Taft's appearance in 1910, the Nationals provided the three-hundred-pound president with a large and specially designed spindle-back, wooden chair. In 1911, when Taft performed the ritualistic first pitch, he threw the ball to the Nationals' starting pitcher, Walter Johnson, then a twenty-two-year-old rising star. That day Johnson pitched a one-hit shutout of the Philadelphia Athletics, leading the hometown Nationals to a 3–0 win.

President Coolidge had performed the opening day tradition in 1924 and 1925 accompanied by his wife, Grace, a devoted and serious student of the game and a dedicated fan of the hometown Nationals. Coolidge missed the game in 1926 since his father had recently died and the president was observing a period of mourning. Coolidge—with Grace at his side—would resume his attendance at opening day games in the last three years of his presidency.

Vice President Dawes was more than an adequate replacement for Coolidge. Although his role was ceremonial and he doesn't figure elsewhere in the story of the 1926 season, it is worth noting that he was one of the most distinguished and accomplished individuals to ever serve as vice president.

His ancestors came to America on the Mayflower. Before entering politics, he earned a law degree from the University of Cincinnati and was successful as a businessman and banker. During World War I, he served in the army and rose to the rank of brigadier general. In government, he held the position of director of the budget. He was awarded the Nobel Peace Prize for his work on the Dawes Plan, which settled issues related to reparations that Germany had to pay after the war. Following his service as vice president, Dawes functioned as America's ambassador to Great Britain. He wrote nine books in his lifetime and was accomplished as a musician and composer.

It's unknown if Vice President Dawes liked the game of baseball.

Nevertheless, Dawes was at Griffith Stadium on April 13, 1926, for opening day ceremonies and to throw out the first ball. Twenty-three thousand fans attended the game. After performing his assigned duty, Dawes watched Walter Johnson, now thirty-eight years old, of the Nationals outduel Eddie Rommel, the celebrated knuckleballer of the Philadelphia Athletics. The two pitchers matched scoreless innings until Joe Harris singled in Bucky Harris in the bottom of the fifteenth inning to give the Nationals a 1–0 win. Johnson struck out nine and allowed just six hits. The fifteen innings were played in two hours and thirty-three minutes.

In St. Louis, manager Rogers Hornsby sent Flint Rhem to the mound on opening day.[2] A crowd of seventeen thousand attended the game at Sportsman's Park.

Rhem delivered a shaky but successful performance, pitching a complete game. The Cardinals got off to a solid start, leading 6–0 after five innings, and hung on as Rhem faltered in the late innings. For the game, Rhem surrendered nine hits, walked five, and struck out two. The final score was 7–6. The hitting star of the day was Jim Bottomly who drove in four runs. Manager Hornsby continued his fine work with the bat, carrying over from his stellar 1925 campaign. Hornsby reached base on each of his four at bats, collecting two singles, a walk, and a double.

The New York Yankees traveled to Boston to open their season with an afternoon contest against the Boston Red Sox. It was a frigidly cold day in

Boston with chilling winds that made both teams wish they were back at their spring training sites.

The game was a battle between the two worst teams in the league in 1925. The Red Sox were predicted to be cellar dwellers again in 1926. The Yankees, coming off an impressive spring training, hoped to make it to the first division.

Earlier that day, Babe Ruth had some business to attend to in downtown Boston. Warrants had been issued for his arrest on the charge that he owed Massachusetts state taxes for 1923 and 1924. Ruth contended that he was a resident of the state of New York during those years, not Massachusetts, though he did own property in Sudbury.

That morning Ruth borrowed a car and drove to the statehouse to discuss the tax issues with the commissioner of corporations and taxation. Seeing no open parking spaces, and assuming it would take just a few minutes to clear up his legal problems, Ruth parked the car in the street and locked it.[3]

While Ruth was inside, explaining his position to the commissioner—in a meeting that lasted two hours—Ollie Brennan, a city patrolman, noticed Ruth's car blocking traffic, wrote him a ticket, and placed it on his windshield. When Ruth emerged from the meeting and discovered the ticket, he was incensed.

A crowd gathered as Ruth pled his case to Officer Brennan. After a few minutes of conversation, Brennan agreed to tear up the ticket. Reporters clustered around Ruth and asked him for a statement. Photographers wanted him to pose for pictures. The usually amiable and accommodating Ruth, still fuming, refused.

He got in his car and drove to Fenway Park to prepare for the ballgame.

Bob Shawkey was the opening day pitcher for the Yankees. Howard Ehmke hurled for the Red Sox. The game was attended by twelve thousand warmly dressed but shivering fans, who were treated to a slugfest. The teams combined for twenty-three runs and pounded out twenty-six hits, with the Yankees eventually victorious by a score of 12–11.

Shawkey got the win, despite giving up seven runs in just over five innings of pitching. Urban Shocker and Sam Jones finished the game in relief. Ruth vented his anger on a parade of Red Sox pitchers, collecting a single, two doubles, two runs batted in, and a stolen base.

At about the same time that Babe Ruth was dealing with his legal problems in Boston, three New York City undercover police were stationed at the Polo Grounds in New York. The police had a hunch that Paul Hilton, known as the notorious "radio burglar," would show up at the opening day game of the Giants.

Hilton had been sought by the police after a three-month crime spree of home invasion burglaries in the borough of Queens. Hilton had acquired his nickname because he was especially fond of stealing radios. He was suspected of more than thirty robberies. During several robberies, he encountered police. He was also wanted on the charge of assault. He had shot three officers, including one who died.

The radio burglar had a long history of run-ins with the law. He had served time in several correctional facilities, including the men's prison at Elmira, where he had played third base on the institution's baseball team.[4] In the past, Hilton had also used the alias Frank Merriwell, a fictional character who appeared in several baseball novels written by Gilbert Patten. The police suspected that Hilton might show up for the opening day game between the Robins and the Giants.

A little before game time, Hilton was spotted near a ticket window and approached by two detectives. After a brief struggle, watched by dozens of fans, Hilton was pinned to the ground, where the police "beat him until he ceased his resistance."[5] At the time of Hilton's arrest he was carrying a loaded pistol, three penknives, a rosary, and a Saint Christopher's medal. Soon after his arrest, he admitted to the burglaries and the shooting of the three police officers.

Hilton was taken away and jailed. He was questioned and asked why he stole radios. He replied, "I like music."[6]

Back at the Polo Grounds, a game was played. The Brooklyn Robins managed to break their preseason losing streak at the expense of John McGraw's Giants. The Robins scored a run in the third and two in the seventh. Jesse Petty, a thirty-one-year-old right-hander with just nine career victories, pitched the best game of his career, shutting out the Giants on one hit, a double in the sixth inning by Frankie Frisch. Petty struck out two and walked three but never was in trouble of losing his shutout bid.

Elsewhere on opening day in the American League, player-manager Tris Speaker's Cleveland Indians defeated player-manager Ty Cobb's Detroit Tigers 2–1 behind the nine-hit pitching of George Uhle. Neither Speaker nor Cobb contributed to their respective team's offense. In the other American League opener, the hometown Chicago White Sox beat the St. Louis Browns, 5–1.

In National League games, it took the Cincinnati Reds ten innings to beat the Chicago Cubs, 7–6, and spoil Joe McCarthy's debut as the Cubs' manager. The hometown Philadelphia Phillies beat the Boston Braves, 6–3.

With the conclusion of the day's games, the 1926 season was underway.

7

Babe Ruth and Ty Cobb

In the American League, the New York Yankees started the season just as Miller Huggins had hoped—and perhaps even better than he expected.

On May 6, the Yankees, with a record of 13–7, were tied for first with the Chicago White Sox. The defending American League champions, the Washington Nationals, trailed the Yankees and White Sox by a half game in the standings.

The Yankees were doing it with their bats. The team had scored more runs than any team in either league. Third baseman Joe Dugan was leading the league with a .434 average, and Babe Ruth was not far behind with a .417 average. Huggins acknowledged the obvious when he told a reporter, "This is the hardest hitting club I've ever had."[1]

Huggins went on to say, "I'm not worrying about the pitchers. If we continue hitting and develop defensive strength at short and second the team will go far."[2] The manager's concern was with Koenig, the cannon-armed but erratic shortstop, and Lazzeri, the rookie learning a new position.

So far, Lazzeri had been performing adequately. Koenig was another story. He had been charged with ten errors in the first twenty games. His errors in one of the Boston games cost the Yankees a win. Throughout his Major League career, Koenig's fielding would be problematic. In the 1926 World Series, he would be blamed—perhaps unfairly—for a defensive lapse that would impact the outcome of a game and the series. Late in his career, after being demoted to the Minors, he switched positions and tried to earn a Major League roster spot as a pitcher. Koenig didn't succeed as a pitcher, but late in the 1932 season, he would be recalled from the Minors and play a significant role in propelling the Chicago Cubs to the World Series.[3]

On May 7, the Detroit Tigers came to Yankee Stadium for a four-game series. The Tigers were led by their player-manager Ty Cobb, now thirty-nine years old. Cobb's Tigers were in fourth place with a record of 9–11. It was a weekend series, and the four games would attract over one hundred thousand fans to Yankee Stadium. Although Cobb didn't know it—no one did—this would be the last time he competed in a Tiger's uniform against Babe Ruth and the Yankees in Yankee Stadium.

Cobb was—without question or much argument—baseball's best player from 1907 to 1918. Over that twelve-year period, he led the league on multiple occasions in every offensive category except home runs. He was the league leader in hits (seven times), doubles (three times), triples (four times), runs scored (five times), runs batted in (four times), batting average (eleven times), and stolen bases (six times). He was fearless on the basepaths and the game's most intense competitor. His contemporary, George Sisler, said "The greatness of Ty Cobb was something that had to be seen, and to see him was to remember him forever."[4]

Cobb and Ruth had a long-simmering feud. The two ballplayers, representing two different eras and two different philosophies of how the game should be played, were contentious adversaries. Cobb was also jealous of Ruth's popularity. When the Yankees played in Detroit, huge crowds turned out to see Ruth. This incensed Cobb, who had been idolized by Detroit fans for nearly two decades.

Born eight years apart, they were men with contrasting backgrounds but with certain similarities in their respective backstories.

Cobb's father was a distinguished member of his community and a teacher; his mother came from a respected Georgia family. In 1908 Cobb's father was shot and killed on the porch roof of his own home. The circumstances were odd. His wife, Amanda Cobb, admitted to firing two shots, claiming that she thought her husband was a prowler. She was charged with murder and acquitted.

Ruth's parents were of German ancestry and spoke German at home. His father ran a saloon. Like Cobb's father, Ruth's father suffered a violent death. Following an argument in his saloon, George Ruth became embroiled in a fight with a customer outside the bar. The men fought; George Ruth fell backward, hit his head on the curb, and died.

Both Cobb and Ruth married young. Cobb was twenty-two years old when he married; his wife, Charlotte, was just eighteen. Ruth was nineteen when he married Helen Woodford, a sixteen-year-old waitress. Cobb's marriage was rocky but lasted thirty-nine years before ending in divorce. Ruth's wife died in a house fire in 1929. Both men married a second time.[5]

In his early days with the Red Sox and the Yankees, Ruth showed flashes of temper, more often directed at umpires or teammates than opponents. In 1917 he attacked home-plate umpire Brick Owens, punched him, and wrestled him to the ground. A few years later, he threw dirt on umpire George Hildebrand, and after he was ejected and mocked by fans in the stands, he went after the two fans who had taunted him. In separate incidents, he had brief fights with teammates Wally Pipp and Mark Koenig in the Yankee dugout.

But compared to Cobb, Ruth was as mild mannered as a Sunday school teacher. Cobb, acutely sensitive to criticism and quick to take offense, lived his life with a chip on his shoulder, a quick temper, and a reputation for settling all grievances with his fists. As Grantland Rice wrote: Cobb was born "bubbling with violence."[6]

In *Cobb: A Terrible Beauty*, Cobb's most recent biographer, Charles Leerhsen, describes more than a dozen examples of Cobb's anger and attacks on teammates, opposing players, hecklers, umpires, a groundskeeper, a grocer, and others who confronted Cobb in some way or irritated him with their comments. He was indicted once, in 1907, for an assault on a young man named Charlie Putnam, who had made an imprudent remark to Cobb. That altercation was settled out of court. Cobb attacked Ed Siever, a teammate and pitcher who had the temerity to criticize Cobb's effort as a fielder. Cobb knocked Siever down in a hotel lobby, then kicked him in the face. Cobb went after opposing players, too, fighting Joe Engels, a pitcher with the Nationals in the opposing team's clubhouse. In a more storied confrontation, Cobb fought Giants infielder Buck Herzog in a Dallas hotel room. The two pushed back the furniture and brawled as teammates watched Cobb, who outweighed Herzog by nearly fifty pounds, knock Herzog down several times. The confrontation with the grocer had to do with a piece of spoiled fish the grocer had sold to Cobb's wife. Cobb confronted the merchant with a pistol, then put the weapon aside and went outside to fight the proprietor's brother-in-law. The police were called and took Cobb and the brother-in-law to the police station, then released them. The merchant later said of Cobb: "He's dangerous when he gets mad. I think he's unsafe."[7]

When they competed, Cobb often mocked and taunted Ruth, calling him names. Once Cobb made Ruth furious by pantomiming that he was a gorilla or an ape—a not-so-subtle suggestion that Ruth was more of an animal than a civilized human.

Remarkably, in all the years Cobb and Ruth played against each other—more than a decade—they only had one brief near-fight. On Friday, June 13, 1924, the Yankees were leading the Tigers 10–6 in the top of the ninth inning in a game at Navin Field. Ruth was upset about some brushback pitches that he'd had to duck away from, and he thought he saw Cobb signal his pitcher, Bert Cole, to throw at Bob Meusel. When Cole's next pitch hit Meusel in the back, Meusel tossed his bat at Cole and headed toward the mound. Ruth charged out of the Yankee dugout; Cobb raced in from centerfield. Somewhere around second base, Ruth and Cobb briefly collided, where they were soon engulfed by a swarm of players and umpires, some fighting, others trying to restore order. Ruth was dragged away by the diminutive Miller Huggins, an umpire, and a couple of teammates. Before things settled down, fans joined in, leaving their seats and climbing over railings to take part in the melee. The Yankees retreated to their locker room. While nearly a thousand fans battled the police and Tigers security forces, the umpires declared the Yankees winners by forfeit.[8]

By May of 1926, Cobb was in his twenty-second season as a Major Leaguer; Ruth was in his fourteenth year. Cobb's style of play—emphasizing bunting, hit and runs, stolen bases, baserunning—contrasted with the game as Ruth had redefined it. Ruth's ability to hit home runs had changed the way the game was played and the way fans enjoyed it.

It was evident to both men—and to baseball owners—that fans had come to prefer Ruth's style of play to Cobb's. Ruth's ascendence as the biggest star in the game angered and frustrated Cobb, but owners and players alike benefited as the game grew in popularity and fans bought tickets to see Ruth play. That was simply the reality.

In the opening game of the series on a Friday afternoon, twelve thousand fans turned out to see a game that lasted eleven innings and took three hours and seven minutes to play. It was the second-longest game of the season for the Yankees, who triumphed 7–6. Waite Hoyt pitched for the Yankees, Ken Holloway for the Tigers.

The Yankees scored two runs in the bottom of the first. With Gehrig on first base and two out, Ruth hit a long home run to right field. The Tigers got a run in the top of the fourth, and the Yankees responded with two in the bottom of the inning, thanks to Lazzeri's lead-off double; a pair of walks; a single by the pitcher, Hoyt; and a ground out. Lazzeri doubled in another run in the fifth inning. The Tigers got three runs back in the sixth, thanks to some wildness on the part of Hoyt who gave up three walks and two singles. Cobb tied the game with an RBI single in the seventh, his only hit of the afternoon. Koenig put the Yankees back ahead with a double in the bottom of the inning. In the ninth, with the Tigers trailing 6–5, Cobb reached on a force out, stole second, and scored on Frank O'Rourke's single. The Yankees finally gained the victory in the eleventh inning by executing a version of small ball that Cobb loved. Lazzeri walked, Dugan's sacrifice bunt moved him to second, and Lazzeri scored on a single by Collins. Pennock, in relief of Hoyt, was credited with the win. It had been an exhausting and thrilling baseball game.

Game Two of the series on Saturday afternoon went to the Tigers, 7–5, before a crowd of thirty thousand. The Tigers got off to a 7–0 lead, with Cobb delivering a two-RBI single in a five-run rally in the third inning. Ruth homered again, this time in the fifth, with two outs and two teammates on base. The series was tied, one game apiece. If fans wanted more, they were about to get it. The third game of the series would prove to be a classic.

On Sunday morning, May 9, bold headlines appeared on the front page of the *New York Times*, alerting readers to the status of the attempt by Richard D. Byrd and Floyd Bennett to fly over the North Pole.

Americans were obsessed with aviation, and Byrd's ambitious and dangerous flight rightfully earned its place as the top story in world news. Byrd and Bennett would make the trip and return safely, acquiring more headlines, promotions, medals, and acclaim, though in future years, questions were raised about whether they had made it all the way to their objective: the North Pole.

For baseball fans in New York City, the afternoon of Sunday, May 9, meant Game Three of the four-game series between the Tigers and Yankees, Cobb versus Ruth. The day started with the Yankees in first place by half a game over the Washington Nationals.

A crowd of fifty-five thousand packed Yankee Stadium. It was the largest crowd to witness a game at Yankee Stadium since August 24, 1924, when Cobb's Tigers pitched Dutch Leonard against Bullet Joe Bush on a sunny Sunday afternoon. In that game two years earlier, Cobb and Ruth both homered, but the final tally had the Tigers on top, 7–2.

The Sunday game on May 9 would prove to be a memorable slugfest in which Ty Cobb got the better of Babe Ruth.

The starting pitchers were rookie Augie Johns for Detroit, and the veteran Bob Shawkey for New York.[9] Both pitchers were knocked out before the end of the second inning.

In the top of the first, the Tigers got three runs off Shawkey on four singles and a sacrifice fly. Cobb contributed one of the base hits. The Yankees got a run back in the bottom of the inning on Lou Gehrig's triple that drove in Earle Combs.

The two teams combined to score eleven runs in a very entertaining second inning. The Tigers stretched their lead to six runs by scoring four in the top of the second. Shawkey got the first two batters out, but then gave up a walk to Johnny Bassler, a double to Johnny Neum, and a single to Al Wingo. With Ty Cobb coming to the plate, Miller Huggins replaced Shawkey with Urban Shocker. On Shocker's first pitch, Cobb homered into the right-field stands.

Trailing 7–1, the Yankees came to bat in the bottom half of the inning. Augie Johns had been given a six-run lead but couldn't hold it. Twelve Yankees batted in the inning. Lazzeri led off with a walk. The next four batters singled. Cobb replaced Johns with Rip Collins. Earle Combs hit a sacrifice fly. Gehrig singled to keep the rally alive. Ruth lined out to right. Meusel singled. Lazzeri, up for the second time in the inning, also singled. Dugan, also up for the second time, doubled. The inning ended with Pat Collins striking out.

A quick recap: Yankees scored seven runs on eight hits, a walk, and a sacrifice fly. All the starters contributed to the scoring, except for one: Babe

Ruth, who flied out in his one at bat in the inning. The Yankees' 8–7 lead didn't last long. The Tigers got two runs in the fifth; the Yankees tied it in the bottom of the inning.

In the top of the sixth, with no one on base, Cobb faced Myles Thomas, the pitcher who had relieved Shocker. Cobb hit his second home run of the day. To add insult to injury, both of Cobb's homers sailed over the head of Yankee right fielder Babe Ruth and landed in the right-field stands—a section of Yankee Stadium fondly known as Ruthville, where fans gathered to celebrate the Babe's frequent blasts.

Cobb's homer put the Tigers ahead for good. They added four more insurance runs in the ninth. The final score was 14–10 in favor of the Tigers. Hooks Dauss, with five innings of relief, got the win.[10]

Cobb's stat line for the game: five plate appearances, one walk, two singles, two home runs, three runs scored, four runs batted in. At the end of the day, Cobb had raised his season batting average to .426.

On Monday, the series concluded with a 13–9 win by the Yankees before a smallish crowd of seven thousand. Herb Pennock got the win. Cobb singled and drove in two runs. Ruth hit a solo home run.

For the series, Ruth went 4–14, a .286 average, with three home runs and six RBIs. Cobb was 7–16, a .438 average, with two home runs and twelve RBIs.

It was the start of a sixteen-game winning streak for the Yankees. They would not lose another game for nearly three weeks. By late May, the Yankees would have an 8.5 game lead in the American League pennant race.

8

Early Season Blues for the Redbirds

The Cardinals opened the 1926 season with an eight-game homestand, four games against the Pirates, then four against the Cubs. Hornsby hoped to get his team off to a fast start in what figured to be a highly competitive National League season. No single team, not even the defending champion Pirates, appeared to have the firepower and pitching to dominate the National League.

After squeezing past the Pirates with a score of 7–6 in the first game of the season, the Cardinals got jolted the next day, losing 10–3. More significant than the loss was an injury suffered by starting pitcher Jesse Haines, the veteran knuckleballer. In the top of the third inning, Pirates catcher Earl Smith smashed a line drive up the middle that struck Haines on the instep above the right ankle. Haines crumpled to the ground, limped off the field, and was transported to the hospital for x-rays. The ankle was not broken, but Haines would be unable to pitch for the next ten days and would contribute only a few relief appearances over the next two months. Now Hornsby had to worry about how to replace Haines in his pitching rotation.

The Cardinals closed out the Pirates series with two wins, a 2–0 victory behind a stellar five-hit shutout hurled by Vic Keen—Hornsby singled in both runs—and then a 3–2 triumph in the final game of series.

Then the Cubs, under new manager Joe McCarthy, came to town for a four-game series. The 1925 Cubs finished in last place with a 68–86 record, 27.5 games behind the pennant-winning Pirates. Over the course of the season, they employed three managers: George Gibson, Rabbit Maranville, and Bill Killefer. All three compiled losing records.

The choice of McCarthy as the new manager was unconventional. He had never played or coached at the Major League level. What stood out to general manager William Veeck was McCarthy's success at class AAA Louisville and his reputation as a shrewd judge of baseball talent. Veeck and

McCarthy agreed that the problem with the Cubs was simple: they didn't have enough good players.

Based on McCarthy's recommendations, Veeck purchased the contracts of Hack Wilson, Riggs Stevenson, and Charlie Root from their Minor League clubs and added them to a roster that included Charlie Grimm and Gabby Hartnett, two solid players at the beginning of their Major League careers. The acquisitions would pay off immediately. In 1926 Wilson would bat .321 and lead the team in home runs with twenty-one. Although limited due to injuries, Stephenson would hit .338. Root would lead the pitching staff with eighteen wins.

The best-known player on the roster that McCarthy inherited was Grover Cleveland "Pete" Alexander, the thirty-nine-year-old right-hander who already was responsible for 315 Major League wins. Alexander had been with the Cubs for seven full seasons.[1] Prior to his tenure with the Cubs, he had won more than thirty games for the Philadelphia Phillies in three consecutive seasons before entering the army in 1918. After the war, he had performed solidly with the Cubs. But McCarthy wanted younger players, and he thought Alexander's advanced age and well-documented drinking problem would limit his effectiveness.

Alexander started the season with the Cubs, but he wouldn't be on the roster for long.

The first two games of the Cubs' series went to the Cardinals by scores of 3–2 and 10–5 behind solid pitching performances by Bill Sherdel and Flint Rhem. But the Cubs got a split in the series with a 5–4 win in fourteen innings and a 7–0 shutout behind the five-hit pitching of Wilbur Cooper.

Hornsby's pitching staff was still unsettled. He needed one or two more reliable starters while awaiting the return of Haines from his injury. Offensively, the Cardinals had scored more than four runs just twice, and only Hornsby and Heine Mueller were batting over .300.

After this opening homestand, the Cardinals had a ten-game road trip to look forward to. It was too early to panic, but Hornsby had reasons to worry.

By mid-May things were worse. On May 13, a day when the Cardinals were blasted 12–1 by the New York Giants, a quarter of the season was in the books, and the Cardinals record was 12–17, good for seventh place, just 2.5

games ahead of the floundering Boston Braves, and 7 full games behind the league-leading Brooklyn Robins.

The problem was twofold—and blatantly obvious: hitting and pitching. Hornsby was batting .358—not bad in a normal year, but 45 points lower than in 1925. No one else was above .300. Mueller had cooled off and was at .265. Les Bell was hitting a respectable .294. Centerfielder Taylor Douthit was in a severe slump with just four hits in thirty-five at bats so far in the season. The shortstop Tommy Thevenow, a terrific gloveman, was hitting .188.

Vic Keen and Flint Rhem, the two college boys, paced the pitching staff with a combined record of 9–2. No one else had emerged as a healthy and competent starter. Even Bill Sherdel had struggled and had a record of 1–4. Haines was due to return to the starting rotation at full strength soon, though, and that was a positive.

Things improved when the lowly Boston Braves came to town, and the Cardinals swept them behind pitching performances of Keen, Rhem, and Sherdel. The Phillies followed the Braves for a four-game series.

After average crowds of 3,500 for the first three games of the Phillies series—the Cardinals lost the first game but won the next two—a crowd of 11,000 churned through the turnstiles for the Saturday game, billed as "Rogers Hornsby Day." Despite the team's struggles thus far in the season, the fans had not forgotten what Hornsby's tenure with the Redbirds had meant for the franchise and the fan base.

Hornsby had won batting titles in six consecutive seasons, including triple crown years in 1922 and 1925. From 1921 through 1925, Hornsby averaged twenty-nine home runs a season and posted a cumulative batting average of .402. No one else had ever averaged .400 or better over five consecutive seasons. Fittingly, after the 1925 season, Hornsby was voted the league's Most Valuable Player by a committee of baseball writers.

The celebration began with a raucous procession from the fairgrounds to Sportsman's Park. Crowds lined the streets as Boy Scout troops, civic groups, baseball fans, marching bands, and a drum corps marched through the city. The parade included baseball dignitaries: Judge Landis and National League president John Heydler.[2]

At Sportsman's Park the flag was raised, and the parade concluded with the playing of the national anthem. Then the ceremony moved to home plate, where Hornsby was presented with a check for $1,000 and a gold medal.[3] The stoic Hornsby managed to crack a sly smile of appreciation.

Bill Sherdel started and pitched a complete game for the Cardinals, allowing nine hits but only two runs. Weak-hitting Tommy Thevenow knocked in two runs in the third, and Ray Blades hit a three-run homer in the seventh to pace the win. The Cardinals won 9–2.

The Cardinals had climbed back to .500. Their record was now 18–18, and they'd moved up in the standings to fifth place, though still seven games out of first place. The streaking Cincinnati Reds now held the top spot in the league.

Things were falling into place for the Cardinals. But before Hornsby could relax a bit and enjoy perusing the daily racing form between games, he needed to strengthen his lineup. He firmly believed that if the Cardinals were going to be true contenders for the National League pennant, he needed to upgrade the outfield and acquire a veteran starting pitcher.

Three weeks later, Giants manager John McGraw contacted Sam Breadon and Branch Rickey about a possible trade involving outfielders. McGraw wanted Heinie Mueller and was offering Billy Southworth in return. Southworth's best position was right field, but McGraw had Ross Youngs in right field. McGraw played Southworth in center, which was not his preferred position. In addition, McGraw and Southworth had a somewhat tenuous relationship.

Mueller had been personally scouted and signed by Branch Rickey in the summer of 1919 after showing up at a tryout camp in St. Louis. At the time, Mueller was just nineteen and brimming with self-confidence. He announced that he could "run like Ty Cobb, hit like Home Run Baker, and field like Tris Speaker."[4] Mueller had speed and promise, and he was a decent outfielder, but after five full seasons in the Majors, he had just twelve career home runs. At the time of the 1926 trade, he was hitting .267 and reminded no one of Cobb, Baker, or Speaker. Mueller was seven years younger than Southworth, and McGraw wanted a centerfielder, so the trade made sense for the Giants from a positional standpoint.

Southworth was thirty-three years old. He had started his professional baseball career as a catcher, then an outfielder, for the Portsmouth Cobblers of the Ohio State League, a semipro team in central Ohio. Before landing on the roster of the Cardinals, he had short stints with Cleveland, Pittsburgh, the Boston Braves, and the Giants. His three years with the Braves were his most productive, batting over .300 in each season.

Hornsby and the Cardinals viewed Southworth as an upgrade, at least offensively, and at the time of the trade, Southworth was having one of his best years at the plate, hitting .326. Hornsby had Taylor Douthit in center and Ray Blades in left, and good backups in Chick Haley and Wattie Holm, so Southworth fit into the lineup smoothly.

It turned out to be an excellent trade. In 1926 Southworth had his best and most productive year in the Majors, producing key hits during the second half of the season. Years later, Les Bell, the Cardinals third baseman in 1926, said the swap of Southworth for Mueller was "the worst trade John McGraw ever made."[5]

9

Grover Cleveland Alexander

On June 22, 1926, just eight days after the Billy Southworth trade, Branch Rickey acquired Grover Cleveland Alexander from the Cubs for the waiver price of $4,000. It was to be the most consequential acquisition of Rickey's early career.

Working under three different managers, Alexander had been the Cubs' best pitcher the previous year, posting a record of 15–11 and an earned run average of 3.39, the eighth best ERA in the National League in 1925. It was evident that Alexander could still pitch and win games. But it was also widely known that since his return from military service, he had a drinking problem that sometimes impaired his readiness to work as a starting pitcher.

It's not that Alexander didn't try to mend his ways. Following the 1925 season, he checked himself into the Keeley Institute, a privately managed facility in Dwight, Illinois, that specialized in the rehabilitation of alcoholics. The Cubs paid the bills for his therapy. The Keeley Institute offered a four-week-treatment plan that included four injections a day of bichloride of gold.[1] Alexander stayed for three months, but his drinking habits returned soon after leaving the facility.

In February, Alexander and his wife, Aimee, joined the Cubs for spring training on Catalina Island, the island off the coast of California that was owned by Cubs owner William Wrigley.[2] Alexander—who was two months older than the new manager—clashed with McCarthy from the beginning, saying at one point, "I'm not going to take orders from any bush manager."[3]

A few days into spring training, Alexander developed a sore arm and injured his ankle. X-rays of his ankle were inconclusive. At first, it seemed it might be broken, but it turned out to be a bad sprain. He spent several days in the hospital with Aimee at his bedside. She later recalled that McCarthy drove past the hospital on his way to the ballpark every day but made no effort to visit her husband.

Once out of the hospital, Alexander went about getting into shape at his own pace, as he had in the past. This frustrated the new manager. McCarthy took exception to Alexander's self-designed workout plans, stating publicly that the players all seemed in good shape "with the exception of Alex."[4]

But when the season started with a three-game series against a strong Cincinnati Reds team, Alexander was ready to pitch. He got the start on April 16 in Cincinnati, losing 2–1 to Red Lucas in a well-pitched game by both starters that lasted just an hour and fifteen minutes. Five days later, he faced the Reds in Chicago, opposed by Pete Donohue, and Alexander earned his first win, 4–2. On April 27, he lost another close game, this time to Pittsburgh, 2–0, as Johnny Morrison of the Pirates held the Cubs to just two hits.

For three games in April, Alexander posted stellar numbers. In twenty-five innings pitched, he allowed just five earned runs. His teammates provided little support: only five runs in the three games. As he had throughout his career, he was a brisk and efficient worker on the mound; no game he started in April lasted longer than an hour and thirty-seven minutes.

May was a different story. He won games on May 2, a 6–5 win over the Cardinals, and on May 8, a 6–4 win over the Giants, but he didn't pitch well in either game. The May 8 victory against the Giants—Alexander's 318th career win—was the last game he would win as a Cub.

Two weeks later, Chicago Cub fans staged a Grover Cleveland Alexander appreciation day at Wrigley Field and presented him with a new Lincoln sedan as a gift. McCarthy gave Alexander the start that day against the cellar-dwelling Boston Braves, but he floundered, giving up thirteen hits and seven runs in a game the Braves won 7–1.

Things were going downhill. Alexander's arm hurt. He wasn't sure he could pitch effectively. He was drinking too much. He didn't pitch again during the homestand. And in early June, when the Cubs went on a road trip to the east—Pittsburgh, New York, Boston, Brooklyn—he stayed behind in Chicago, scheduled to rejoin the team in Philadelphia. He showed up late. McCarthy could tell that Alexander had been drinking and was in no condition to pitch.

Joseph McCarthy was no teetotaler. He was a whiskey drinker himself and liked a glass of good scotch. He tolerated players who drank to excess—Hack Wilson and Pat Malone, to name two of Alexander's teammates on the Cubs—if they came to the ballpark ready and able to play ball after a night on the town.

McCarthy decided that Alexander was unreliable and expendable. Despite the seven full seasons he had pitched for the Cubs and how much fans in Chicago appreciated him, McCarthy was in the process of reshaping the roster and a veteran pitcher with destructive habits didn't fit with what he wanted to create in Chicago.

The Cubs were staying in the Hotel Adelphia in downtown Philadelphia. On June 15, 1926, McCarthy typed out a message for Alexander on hotel stationery. The first part of the message was simple and direct: "This is to officially advise you that you have this day been indefinitely suspended without pay for violating rules of training, drunkenness, and not appearing in uniform."[5]

The message was delivered to Alexander. His days with the Cubs were over.

A week later, Branch Rickey and Rogers Hornsby took a chance and signed him off waivers.

Alexander was thirty-nine—old for a pitcher who didn't take care of his body. But he was not done yet with baseball.

Grover Cleveland Alexander was born February 26, 1887, in a farmhouse in Elba, Nebraska, a speck of a town located in the west-central part of the state, eight miles from St. Paul, the county seat, and nearly six hundred miles from the nearest Major League ballpark. He was named for Stephen Grover Cleveland, the president of the United States at the time of his birth.

Rural Nebraska in the late 1800s didn't offer much in the way of entertainment or diversion from farm work. Passengers on stagecoaches and wagon trains came through the area on occasion, and in the summers, a traveling circus might appear for a brief time.[6] Most farm boys like Alexander toiled long hours on family farms and eventually went into farming to make their living. However, there was baseball, and fans in rural areas fiercely supported their town teams.

In the summer of 1908, Alexander was twenty-one years old and earning $1.75 a day digging post holes for the Howard County Telephone company. He was supplementing his income by pitching for local town teams on Sundays, getting paid five dollars a game, when he was discovered by the shortstop of a traveling team from Oklahoma. The shortstop said he had connections with a manager of a semipro team in Galesburg, Illinois, and that Alexander was good enough to make his living as a professional ballplayer. At first reluctant to leave his family and home, in January of 1909, he signed a contract to play for the Galesburg Boosters, a team in a class D league.[7]

That summer, after pitching several innings of relief in an exhibition game against the local Knox College team, Alexander assumed a starting role for the Boosters and later hurled a no-hitter and an eighteen-inning shutout in July. Then on July 28, he suffered a serious head injury; he was knocked unconscious by a throw from the opposing team's shortstop.[8] The ball struck him solidly in the head, causing a traumatic brain injury. He was unconscious for thirty-six hours, and when he awoke, he suffered from double vision, a condition that persisted for several months. He didn't pitch again until the spring of 1910.

After stints in the Minors with Indianapolis and Syracuse, he finally made it to the big leagues in 1911. He was a soft-spoken young man with strawberry-blond hair and the look of a lanky farm boy. His uniform appeared to be one size too large, and his ballcap looked one size too small. He wore the cap at a crooked angle. He was generally quiet and moved slowly, never seeming to want to go anyplace in a hurry.[9]

As a twenty-four-year-old rookie with the Philadelphia Phillies, he won twenty-eight games and lost thirteen, establishing a new record for most wins in a rookie season. No rookie has ever bettered it. The Phillies finished fifth that season. Over the next six seasons, he averaged twenty-seven wins a season, collecting thirty or more wins in three consecutive seasons, 1915 through 1917. Despite Alexander's pitching brilliance, the Phillies won the National League in only one year.

In 1915 the Phillies faced the Boston Red Sox in the World Series, losing the series, four games to one. Alexander won Game One, beating Boston's Ernie Shore, 3–1. In the ninth inning of that contest, he pitched to Babe Ruth, who entered the game as a pinch hitter. It was the first time the two future Hall of Famers faced each other. Ruth grounded out to Fred Luderus, the Phillies first baseman.[10]

The Red Sox swept the Phillies in the next four games. Alexander was the loser in Game Three, a contest that ended 2–1. Dutch Leonard, the winning pitcher for Boston, pitched superbly, retiring the last twenty batters he faced.

The baseball world was profoundly impacted by world events in 1917 and 1918. The United States declared war on Germany on April 6, 1917, and seven weeks later, on May 18, President Woodrow Wilson signed the Selective Service Act into law, allowing the country to draft healthy young men between the ages of twenty-one and thirty into the army. As required by law, Alexander registered for the draft on May 25.[11]

The 1917 season was played under a cloud of uncertainty. The country mobilized for war as the conflict raged in Europe. Major League Baseball went ahead with its 1917 season, and for the third year in a row, Alexander posted thirty wins, finishing the season with a record of 30–13. He led the league in nearly every important category: games started, complete games, earned run average, innings pitched, strikeouts, and shutouts.

The inescapable fact, though, was that Alexander and other ballplayers were about to be drafted. The first Major Leaguer to be called up by his draft board was Philadelphia Athletics' shortstop Lawton Witt. He had been summoned to appear for a physical on August 2, eight weeks before the end of the season.[12]

Not all ballplayers who were called up passed their physical. Cincinnati Reds third baseman Henry Groh failed his physical when doctors noticed that his fingers were crooked and didn't bend properly, the result of various injuries on the ballfield.[13]

William Baker, the owner of the Philadelphia Phillies, had to make some tough decisions. His team had finished second to the New York Giants in 1917, but Alexander, his best player, was likely to be drafted, possibly before the start of the 1918 season. He was also the highest-paid pitcher in the National League, with an annual salary of $12,500. He was coming off a sensational season. But his future was unclear.

At the league's winter meetings in New York at the Waldorf Hotel, Baker struck a deal with Chicago Cubs owner Charles Weeghman. On December 11, Baker traded Alexander and Bill Killefer to the Cubs for Mike Prendergast, a pitcher; Pickles Dillhoefer, a catcher; and $55,000 in cash. Baker anticipated that the cash would make up for lost revenue in ticket sales once the season started without Alexander to keep the team in contention.[14]

The owner made the argument to the press and fans that the deal was mostly a matter of financial prudence. But he also suggested that the twenty-nine-year-old Alexander—who had won ninety-four games over the past three seasons—might not continue to perform at that level because he was "one of the boys who do not keep themselves in the best of condition."[15]

Even considering the large amount of cash in the deal, it was one of the most lopsided trades in baseball history. Alexander was already acknowledged as one of the game's greatest pitchers—only Christy Mathewson had ever won thirty games in three successive seasons. Killefer was a valued nine-year veteran. At the time of the trade, Prendergast's career record was twenty-eight wins and thirty-eight losses. Dillhoefer had been to bat ninety-three times in the Major Leagues and had gotten exactly twelve hits.

As expected, Alexander was called for a physical by his draft board and designated 1-A on January 16, 1918. After a brief holdout, he joined his new teammates on Catalina Island for spring training.[16]

It would be a short season for Alexander. He was the opening day pitcher for the Cubs, losing a 5–4 decision to the Cardinals, then winning his next game, 9–1, over the Reds. In his farewell appearance at Wrigley Field, he pitched a two-hitter—Rogers Hornsby got both hits—in a 3–2 win over the Cardinals.

On April 27, Alexander reported for military duty. He was philosophical and unemotional about what lay ahead for him. "I am ready to go. No one will have a chance to call me a slacker."[17]

Knowing that he would soon be overseas, Alexander took care of some personal business. On May 31, he married Aimee Arrants, a fellow Nebraskan he'd met on a blind date several years earlier. She followed him to New York, where he went through basic training for his combat role in the military. One afternoon, he got a pass to take his bride to a baseball game at the Polo Grounds.[18]

Alexander trained on Long Island with the Army's 342nd field artillery regiment and shipped out to France in midsummer. For seven weeks during October and early November, his regiment was engaged in heavy combat on the front lines, eventually participating in the Meuse-Argonne Offensive. Then—suddenly—the war ended. An armistice was signed on November 11, 1918. Soldiers could look forward to coming home.[19]

Eight white Major League ballplayers and three Negro League players died in military service during the war. Three died in combat; two died in training accidents; six died of other causes, including pneumonia and the Spanish flu.[20]

Alexander survived. But he was not unscathed. He was now deaf in his left ear; his right ear had been damaged, too, when he was hit by shrapnel. He had injured muscles in his right arm from pulling the lanyard that launched rockets. His biographer, John C. Skipper, concluded, "He came home shell-shocked and susceptible to two demons that plagued him for the rest of his life—alcoholism and epilepsy."[21]

A contributing factor to the epilepsy may have been the traumatic brain injury he suffered in Galesburg ten years earlier, when he was knocked out by a thrown ball during a routine infield play. Alcoholism was the more obvious and defining condition that he had to deal with for the rest of his life.

A few years later, Alexander reflected, "In France, I had hard liquor for the first time. I had drunk beer all my life but that was all. Overseas, everybody knew he was going to battle continually, and no one knew whether he would be alive tomorrow or not. So a lot of men who had never drunk before drank over there. But fortunately for them, it didn't get a hold of them like it did of me."[22]

Four months after the armistice, in March 1919, Alexander was on a ship headed back to America. He joined his new Chicago Cubs teammates on Catalina Island for the beginning of spring training. It would take less than eight weeks for him to get in shape to pitch.

His first start was on May 9, and the Cubs lost 1–0 to the Reds. He was in good form, though he walked five batters, which was uncharacteristic. He lost his first five decisions but finished 16–12 for the season.

It was the beginning of seven productive years as a Cubs pitcher, during which he won 138 games and lost 83.

And then in June 1926, at the age of thirty-nine, Grover Cleveland Alexander was traded to the St. Louis Cardinals.

No one was more pleased with the trade of Alexander from the Cubs to the Cardinals than his new manager, Rogers Hornsby. He had wanted another starting pitcher, and he got one who had already accounted for 318 wins. The only active pitcher with more wins was the Nationals' Walter Johnson who had 396.

There is a bit of irony in the fact that McCarthy, the whiskey drinker who later in life struggled with alcohol himself, was eager to rid his team of Alexander, while Hornsby, who neither smoked nor drank, was confident that

Alexander could help his team.[23] Hornsby was aware of Alexander's off-the-field behavior, but Hornsby trusted his own instincts and his sense of having watched and played against Alexander for more than a dozen seasons. It is worth remembering, too, that Hornsby's coach, Bill Killefer, had been Alexander's catcher when both were with the Phillies and that Killefer had been his manager for part of the 1925 season in Chicago. Killefer confirmed Hornsby's judgment that Alexander could help the Cardinals in the pennant race.

On June 27, 1926, just five days after arriving in St. Louis, and thirty-six days since he had last pitched, Hornsby gave Alexander his first starting assignment as a Cardinal, when the Cubs came to town for a four-game series. The Cardinals were in second place, two games out of first, with a record of 37–28; the Cubs were fifth, seven games behind, with a record of 31–32.

Alexander pitched the first game of a Sunday doubleheader. Against his old team, he pitched as well as he had in April when he was with the Cubs, tossing a ten-inning complete game. He gave up just four hits: singles in the second, third, and seventh and a two-run homer by Charlie Grimm. Billy Southworth scored the winning run on an infield single by Ray Blades in the bottom of the tenth to give the Cardinals a 3–2 win. James Crusinberry of the *Chicago Tribune* reported that Alexander was able to "reap revenge for having been sold down the river."[24]

As Alexander left the field, he passed a scowling Joesph McCarthy. He smiled and tipped his cap at his former manager.

The Cubs won the nightcap 5–0 as Sheriff Blake tossed a one-hitter. The only hit by the Cardinals was a two-out, seventh-inning single by Billy Southworth. But the real drama was in the top of the ninth inning. After Sparky Adams, the Cubs' second baseman, popped out to Rogers Hornsby, home-plate umpire, Charlie Moran, awarded first base to Adams due to catcher's interference. The Cardinals' fans didn't see it that way and unleashed a barrage of glass pop bottles and seat cushions. Players and umpires found cover in the dugouts while thousands of objects were tossed onto the field. The game was delayed for fifteen minutes while groundskeepers removed the debris.

The *Tribune* reporter wryly commented that "the event stamps St. Louis fans as undisputed bottle throwing champions of baseball."[25]

More importantly, though, Alexander had his first win as a member of the Cardinals, and Hornsby had found the additional starting pitcher he needed to win a pennant.

10

Away from the Ballpark

The 1926 baseball season was played at the midpoint of America's fourteen-year experiment with Prohibition—the country's most divisive social issue during the decade.

Advocates for Prohibition in the late nineteenth and early twentieth centuries included social activists, such as Jane Addams and Susan B. Anthony, as well as organizations, such as the Anti-Saloon League (ASL) and the Ku Klux Klan (KKK). Cartoons in the early 1900s featured the militant Carrie Nation storming into saloons, terrorizing patrons, waving a Bible in one hand and swinging a hatchet with the other hand.

One of the most notable and effective crusaders for Prohibition was former Chicago White Stockings baseball player Billy Sunday, the most popular evangelist of the early 1900s. Sunday was known for his speed and daring on the basepaths. His career batting average was a modest .248, but he stole 236 bases in eight seasons, including 84 in his final year of professional ball.

Sunday might have been an average ballplayer, but he was a mesmerizing and energetic public speaker, renowned for his dramatic performances and sermons. On stage, he would race from side to side, leaping in the air or sliding like a runner stealing a base. He sometimes arranged baseball games in connection with his appearances and used his reputation as a ballplayer to charm and entertain the audience.[1]

Like other evangelists of the era, Sunday stressed a literal interpretation of the Bible and attracted large crowds to his tent revivals, where he preached against sin, the evils of alcohol, and the temptations of modern life. He told his listeners, "Whiskey and beer are all right in their place, but their place is in hell." His message extolled the virtues of traditional values, in contrast to the changing times. His most famous sermon was titled "Booze or Get on the Water Wagon."[2]

Sunday supported the work of Carrie Nation and the ASL and other reformers who wanted to crush the alcohol industry and permanently put an end to the production and consumption of intoxicating beverages. His appeal from the pulpit and during tent meetings contributed to the long national campaign demanding Prohibition. When the Eighteenth Amendment, created by the Volstead Act, became part of the United States Constitution at midnight on January 16, 1920, Billy Sunday was in Norfolk, Virginia, to conduct a revival. That evening, to an attentive crowd of ten thousand, Sunday spoke enthusiastically and optimistically about what Prohibition would mean for America:

"The reign of tears is over. The slums will soon be only a memory. We will turn our prisons into factories and our jails into storehouses and corncribs. Men will walk upright now, women will smile, and the children will laugh. Hell will be forever for rent."[3]

In fact, while the Eighteenth Amendment forbade the manufacture, sale, and transportation of intoxicating liquor, it did not prohibit the drinking of alcohol, and the results were far different than what Sunday predicted.

In *Last Call: The Rise and Fall of Prohibition*, Daniel Okrent observed that "the original Constitution and its first seventeen amendments limited the activities of government, not of citizens. Now there were two exceptions: you couldn't own slaves, and you couldn't buy alcohol."[4]

There were, however, exemptions. Citizens were allowed to store any quantities of wine or alcohol they had in their own homes before Prohibition went into effect. Religious organizations could serve wine as part of their religious services. Pharmacists operating out of drug stores could provide liquor to customers who obtained prescriptions from their physicians.[5]

These exemptions generated changes in behavior. Enterprising saloon owners decided to switch professions and become pharmacists. Wealthy individuals established wine cellars in their homes and filled them with bottles of expensive wines, since it was perfectly legal for them to possess wine, host parties in their homes, and serve alcohol to their guests.

Even during Prohibition, heads of households were permitted to produce two hundred gallons a year of fermented fruit juice—in other words: wine. The production of grapes increased, and fertile land in the grape-growing region of California's Napa Valley skyrocketed in value. Even inferior grapes were highly marketable.[6]

Societal changes were pronounced. Defiance of Prohibition was immediate and widespread, especially in cities like New York and Chicago, and most notably in immigrant and ethnic communities.[7] Federal tax revenues declined.

Some positive results from Prohibition were later noted. Alcohol consumption dropped by an estimated 30 percent, arrests for public intoxication fell, and fewer deaths were attributed directly to alcohol. But law enforcement was problematic. Criminal organizations were formed to produce, transport, distribute, and sell alcohol, and in large cities, rival gangs battled each other and the police for control of the illegal liquor trade.

In the end, Prohibition caused more problems than it solved.

Although Prohibition remained a contentious political and social issue for nearly fourteen years, the Eighteenth Amendment had only a minimal effect on professional baseball.

Owners couldn't sell alcohol to fans at the ballparks, but teams could sell popular snacks like soda, peanuts, Cracker Jacks, sausages and hot dogs. In the post-war Prohibition years, attendance climbed sharply, so there were more customers in the stands. In 1919, the last full season played before Prohibition went into effect, paid attendance at white Major League games was 6,532,439. In 1920 paid attendance rose to 9,120,875, an increase of 39.6 percent.[8] Attendance at Yankee Stadium—thanks to the arrival of Babe Ruth—doubled from 1919 to 1920.

During the season, ballplayers traveled from city to city by train and spent more waking hours away from the ballpark than they did at the ballpark. Road trips could last as long as three weeks. Most of a player's free time was in the evenings. If a player wanted to gamble, he could find card games. On off days, he might go to racetracks and bet on the horses. He could also place bets with local bookies. At night, if players wanted to listen to music and socialize, they could visit easily locatable speakeasies, where liquor was readily available. If a ballplayer wanted a drink, finding alcohol was not a problem. It was estimated that by the end of the 1920s, New York City alone had thirty-two thousand illegal drinking establishments.[9] The ten other Major League cities had similarly lax enforcement of the Eighteenth Amendment.

Players who wanted more sophisticated entertainment sought out jazz clubs and live theater.[10] In Boston, Red Sox owner Harry Frazee produced and bankrolled new shows throughout the 1920s—including a play financed by the sale of Babe Ruth to the Yankees.[11] In Chicago, ballplayers could drink and listen to contemporary jazz at the Cotton Club, located in Cicero and operated by Al Capone's older brother Ralph.

The theater capital of America, of course, was New York City. With three teams located in the urban sprawl of the city, there was usually at least one out-of-town baseball team visiting from early April through September. In 1926 alone, more than 150 shows opened on Broadway, including forty musicals. Theater productions included Oscar Wilde's comedy *The Importance of Being Earnest* and Maurine Dallas Watkins's musical *Chicago*.[12]

One of the surprise hits of the season was the play *Sex*, a comedy-drama written by and starring Mae West, who played the lead role of a sex worker. The show opened on April 26, 1926, and ran for 375 performances before it was shut down on the grounds that it was obscene. West was prosecuted on morals charges and served eight days of a ten-day sentence in a workhouse on Welfare Island, where she was treated as a celebrity, resided in the warden's private quarters, and dined with the warden and his wife. Publicity from the show and her arrest helped to advance her career.[13]

There's no data on how many ballplayers happened to see West's performances during the summer of 1926, but 325,000 tickets were sold before the play ended with West's arrest in February 1927.

When a baseball season ended, many players kept playing to earn extra money, either on barnstorming teams or in off-season leagues. Some headed to Cuba, a popular destination for wealthy Americans in the era. Cuba had racetracks and casinos and no restrictions on the use of alcohol.

And Cubans loved baseball, especially American ballplayers.

New York Giants manager John McGraw had been taking Giants players to Cuba since 1911 for preseason spring training and postseason exhibition games as part of what was called the "American Series."[14] McGraw also had financial interests in the country. He and Giants owner Charles Stoneham co-owned the Oriental Racetrack, a property that included a restaurant, a casino, and a hotel.[15]

At the conclusion of the 1920 baseball season, McGraw, as he had in the past, arranged for a team of All-Stars, mostly his own Giants players, to play games in Cuba. But in 1920 the biggest star in the world of baseball—Babe Ruth—didn't play for the Giants; he played for McGraw's American League rival, the New York Yankees.

To increase interest in the series of games, McGraw and Cuban entrepreneur Abel Linares arranged for Babe Ruth to join the Giants team for a series of games in Havana and Santiago de Cuba, the country's two biggest cities.

Ruth would be well paid for his appearances—$2,000 per game. He would earn as much to play in ten of these postseason games as he earned playing eight months of baseball for the Yankees.[16]

And the Babe would get to immerse himself in the nightlife of Cuba, with opportunities to spend money and gamble.

No public figure personified the pure exuberance and decadence of the Roaring Twenties as authentically as Babe Ruth. If Billy Sunday represented one direction America was heading, Ruth represented the opposite direction.

Looking back on his generation and the aftermath of the era, the novelist F. Scott Fitzgerald wrote that the 1920s were an "age of excess," with the whole country "going hedonistic, deciding on pleasure."[17] Fitzgerald might have been thinking of Ruth as he wrote those words.

Throughout the decade of the twenties, Ruth had money and spent it lavishly. He gambled, losing small amounts to teammates during friendly bridge games and losing substantial amounts at racetracks. He drove recklessly, crashed cars, and walked away from the wreckage. His appetites were legendary. He drank to excess, smoked expensive cigars, and ate too much. He chased women, and women chased him. In one oft-mentioned incident, reporters witnessed Ruth being chased through several train cars by a jilted lover—allegedly the wife of a Louisiana politician—who pursued the Babe while wielding a butcher knife. In at least one retelling of the story, the Babe was naked.[18]

Numerous stories attest to Ruth's careless spending habits, his eating and drinking, his frequent and often indiscriminate copulating. The tales have been told and retold in myriad interviews, articles, and books. Some stories have surely been exaggerated and embellished, and it's impossible to verify all the details, but one suspects they are mostly true. There were plenty of witnesses.

Ruth arrived in Cuba in late October 1920, a little more than nine months after Prohibition became the law of the land in the United States. He was accompanied by his young first wife, Helen.[19]

The Babe was coming off the greatest season for a batter in the history of professional baseball. He led the American League with fifty-four home runs—George Sisler was second with nineteen. Ruth outhomered *every team in both leagues*, except for the National League's last-place Philadelphia Phillies, who collectively hit 64. Ruth also led his league in runs scored (137), runs batted in (158), walks (148), and slugging average (.847). He was fourth in batting average (.376).

It's no wonder Cuban baseball fans wanted to see him in action.

In Cuba, the fanfare and adulation were real, and so was the anticipation of what Ruth might do in the games he played, but for Ruth, the trip ended badly. He performed adequately in the games he played, but he didn't like the new Almendares Park in Havana, insisting that the fences were too distant from home plate, making many of his longest drives just routine putouts. During his time in Cuba, Ruth only managed to hit two home runs.[20]

To further bruise his ego, in a notable game on November 6, 1920, Ruth went 0–3 at the plate and was overshadowed by Cuban star Cristobal Torriente, who homered three times. Ruth pitched briefly in the game, facing Torriente and giving up a double to the slugger. The outcome of the game: the Almendares Blues won 11–4. Most of the fans had come to see Ruth, but Torriente's performance thrilled the Cubans in the stands. It was reported that after the game, the fans "threw cash, change, and gold watches onto the field" and presented Torriente with four hundred cigars.[21]

Away from the ballpark, Ruth took full advantage—to his detriment—of the nightlife offered in Cuban cities. Sloppy Joe's Bar, a famous Havana night spot, was just a block away from his hotel. McGraw's racetrack and casino were nearby. Helen stayed mostly in the Hotel Plaza while her husband sampled the Cuban nightlife.

Ruth liked to gamble, and in the few weeks he was on the island, he gambled frequently but with little success. He lost money betting on outcomes at jai alai, playing craps at the casino, and wagering on horse races.[22] One unnamed teammate of Ruth's claimed the Babe lost nearly $7,000 in a single night at McGraw's casino. Another report implied that he'd been conned by professional gamblers into making high-dollar bets on horse races that had been fixed, resulting in greater losses for Ruth.[23]

The amount of money that Ruth lost in a matter of days in Cuba is unknowable. Suffice it to say, he lost more than he earned. All in all, the Cuban tour of 1920 was a low point in Ruth's off-season adventures.

Back in the States for the 1921 season, Ruth had another sensational season, posting numbers comparable to his 1920 season, leading the league in most categories: home runs (59); runs scored (177); runs batted in (168); walks (144); slugging average (.846). He batted .378, third best in the American League. The Yankees won the pennant, but lost in the World Series to McGraw's Giants, five games to three. Ruth's availability for the series was limited due to an abscess on his left elbow that became infected. But soon after the series ended, he went on a barnstorming trip with his teammate, Bob Meusel.[24]

Ruth was now the biggest celebrity in New York City, likely in the whole country. His presence drew crowds. After the barnstorming ended in late October, he signed up for a vaudeville tour and was paid $2,500 a week.[25] The tour began at the New York Palace in mid-November. Buster Keaton and Helen Keller sent telegrams of congratulations and wished him good luck on opening night.[26]

His act involved singing a few songs, telling some jokes, and pretending to be a mind reader. A reviewer described Ruth's baritone voice "as sweet as a furnace shaker in action."[27] It was not a compliment, but the audience cheered the Babe's performance. They didn't care what Ruth's voice sounded like.[28]

Then Ruth's vaudeville show went on the road. In Chicago, Rogers Hornsby purportedly gave a party for Ruth in a suite at the Congress Hotel. Hornsby invited "a group of girls" to the party; the women were instructed to wear flimsy paper dresses or gowns. Ruth supplied $4,000 worth of liquor, delivered by the hotel's wine agent.[29]

The Congress Hotel story originated with Marshall Hunt, a frequent companion of Ruth's, and the tale, with some additional salacious details, has appeared in several biographies of Ruth. Hunt doesn't provide the date of the party or other details about the vaudeville tour, which ended in February, in time for Ruth to join his teammates for spring training. It's probably one of those Ruth stories that stretches the truth. There's no mention of the party in Hornsby's biographies. In fact, that late fall and early winter, Hornsby was playing and managing a team in the California Winter League, where he led the league in home runs. He returned to his home in St. Louis just before New Year's Eve. Hornsby didn't smoke or drink and seldom socialized with other players. He and Ruth played in different leagues and were not friends, though their careers would collide in the 1926 World Series. It's hard to imagine Hornsby planning a raucous gathering to celebrate Ruth's vaudeville tour.

True or not, or even if only half true, the party Hunt described—with copious amounts of alcohol and scantily clad women—seems credible in the context of Prohibition and Chicago in the early 1920s. Even the fact that a prominent hotel in downtown Chicago would employ a "wine agent" during Prohibition appears consistent with the times.

Another Ruth party story—this one recounted in no less than four different Ruth biographies—describes a night that started in Wilmington, Delaware, and ended in Philadelphia. Although details vary, dialogue is likely invented, and facts are sometimes ignored in the published accounts, the gist of the story is that Herb Pennock was invited to a swanky lawn party, perhaps hosted by a member of the Dupont family, and that Pennock brought along Ruth and two of his Yankee teammates, Joe Dugan and Bob Meusel. Drinks were served. Ruth demonstrated his batting technique by swinging a piece of celery. After a while, Ruth developed a fixation on one of the female servers. His companions became worried and urged him to leave to avoid trouble. One of the guests—a Philadelphia boxing promoter—coaxed Ruth away from the party by assuring him that even better opportunities for romance existed at a place he knew in Philadelphia. The promoter took the Yankees to a brothel run by Rose Hicks on Broad Street in Philadelphia.[30] The night wore on. Ruth was spotted sitting in a comfortable chair being shampooed with champagne by two young women. Ruth's teammates finally got him to return to their hotel around five o'clock in the morning.

Ruth summed up the evening, saying, "Anybody who doesn't like this life is crazy."[31]

The next afternoon, the Yankees played the Philadelphia Athletics. Ruth was in the lineup and said he felt fine. He had astonishing powers of recovery. Ruth hit two home runs in the game. The Yankees won 11–6.[32]

Yankee management didn't seem to care about Ruth's promiscuity and his partying and his side trips to brothels. They didn't worry too much—at least before 1925—about his eating and drinking. He had demonstrated considerable physical resilience and the capacity to show up at the ballpark and perform at a high level, no matter where he'd been or what he'd done the night before.

But Ruth's gambling habits did concern Yankee management. They knew about the staggering losses during the Cuba trip in 1920. They knew that a bookie was suing him for $7,700.[33] Jane Leavy writes in *The Big Fella* that Yankee general manager Ed Barrow hired a detective agency to follow and report on Ruth's betting.[34] Ruth had some big wins at the racetrack, but more often big losses.

In the spring of 1924, Ed Barrow contacted Judge Landis and asked the commissioner's office to intercede—to write Ruth "a good stiff letter" and urge him to control his spending and betting. Leavy notes, "Letters of reproach and denial were exchanged with appropriate and unenforceable promises of reform."[35]

The concern was genuine. What ballplayers did away from the ballpark was reflected in the public's perception of the game. As Kevin Baker wrote in *The New York Game* about baseball in this era, "Gambling was everywhere. It was what men did for recreation, as ubiquitous as drinking."[36] The conspicuous mingling of professional gamblers with ballplayers, especially prominent players, potentially compromised the integrity of the game.

Baseball had done its best to renew a bond of trust with fans since the 1920 trial of the eight Black Sox players and their expulsion from the game. Judge Landis and baseball owners did not need another scandal.

Fig. 1. President Calvin Coolidge and his entourage at Griffith Stadium on April 22, 1925, for the opening day baseball game. Coolidge threw out the ceremonial first pitch to officially open the season. [Left to Right: Andrew Mellon, Grace Coolidge, President Coolidge, Frank Kellogg, Washington Nationals manager Bucky Harris, John Sargent.] Harris and Ewing Photographs. Library of Congress.

Fig. 2. Admired and respected as one of baseball's greatest players, Rogers Hornsby won seven National League batting titles and hit .400 or better three times. Hornsby was known for a powerful level swing and the ability to hit with power to all fields. National Baseball Hall of Fame and Museum, Cooperstown, New York.

Fig. 3. ABOVE: George Sisler, Babe Ruth, Ty Cobb—pictured here as spectators at the 1924 World Series between the Washington Nationals and the New York Giants. National Photo Company Collection. Library of Congress.

Fig. 4. Bill "Wee Willie" Sherdel relied on a variety of curves and off-speed pitches to win 165 games—153 as a member of the Cardinals—over a fifteen-year Major League career. He is the career leader for the Cardinals in wins by a left-handed pitcher. National Baseball Hall of Fame and Museum, Cooperstown, New York.

Fig. 5. ABOVE: Satchel Paige was famous for his pitching brilliance, crowd appeal, charisma, longevity, philosophical witticisms, and classic matchups against white Major Leaguers in postseason barnstorming games. Paige dominated Black baseball as an athlete and box office attraction for two decades. National Baseball Hall of Fame and Museum, Cooperstown, New York.

Fig. 6. OPPOSITE: Waite Hoyt was a prominent member of the powerful Yankee teams of the 1920s. Outside of baseball, he was a man of many talents: vaudeville entertainer, mortician, raconteur, and radio broadcaster. National Baseball Hall of Fame and Museum, Cooperstown, New York.

Fig. 7. ABOVE: Nicknamed "Sunny Jim" for his positive outlook on life and cheerful disposition, Jim Bottomly hit .310 for his career. He set a Major League record on September 16, 1924, for most RBIs in a single game when he knocked in twelve runs during a game against the Brooklyn Robins. National Baseball Hall of Fame and Museum, Cooperstown, New York.

Fig. 8. A powerful hitter throughout his career, Mule Suttles led the Negro Leagues in home runs in 1926 with thirty-two homers in eighty-nine games. That season Suttles also hit twenty-eight doubles and nineteen triples while batting .425. National Baseball Hall of Fame and Museum, Cooperstown, New York.

Fig. 9. RIGHT: In the 1920s and 1930s, Tony Lazzeri played alongside Yankee greats Babe Ruth, Lou Gehrig, and Joe DiMaggio, earning the respect of his teammates as a leader in the clubhouse and a clutch performer on the field. National Baseball Hall of Fame and Museum, Cooperstown, New York.

Fig. 10. Grover Cleveland Alexander's best years were with the Philadelphia Phillies and Chicago Cubs, but he achieved his greatest fame as the pitching hero of the 1926 World Series, winning two games and saving one. Despite considerable off-field struggles with epilepsy and alcoholism, Alexander won 373 Major League games, a tie for third in Major League history with Christy Mathewson. National Baseball Hall of Fame and Museum, Cooperstown, New York.

Fig. 11. Miller Huggins—seated here between Babe Ruth and Lou Gehrig—managed the Yankees from 1918 through 1929, winning six American League pennants. Small in stature, Huggins was a large reason the Yankees dominated the league in the 1920s. National Baseball Hall of Fame and Museum, Cooperstown, New York.

Fig. 12. A dynamic individual both on and off the field, Rube Foster was a superb pitcher and a forward-looking executive as president of the Negro Leagues in the 1920s. National Baseball Hall of Fame and Museum, Cooperstown, New York.

Fig. 13. Bill "Willie" Foster, the much younger half brother of Rube Foster, was a dominating left-handed pitcher who hurled the Chicago American Giants to dramatic postseason wins in 1926 and 1927. National Baseball Hall of Fame and Museum, Cooperstown, New York.

Fig. 14. Billy Southworth had a long and successful baseball career as a player, manager, and scout. His clutch hits in the regular season and World Series propelled the St. Louis Cardinals to a championship in 1926. National Baseball Hall of Fame and Museum, Cooperstown, New York.

Fig. 15. An excellent defensive catcher, Bob O'Farrell played in an era with many outstanding backstops. In 1926 he was recognized as the league's Most Valuable Player. Bain News Service. Library of Congress.

Fig. 16. Studious and well respected as a player and manager, Dave Malarcher led the Chicago American Giants to victories in the Colored World Series in 1926 and 1927. National Baseball Hall of Fame and Museum, Cooperstown, New York.

Fig. 17. Dutch Leonard was widely recognized as an outstanding pitcher and a difficult teammate. For his career, he finished with an earned run average of 2.77 and a won/lost record of 139–112. In 1914, Leonard posted a record-low earned run average of 0.96 in 224.2 innings. National Baseball Hall of Fame and Museum, Cooperstown, New York.

Fig. 18. Prior to the arrival of Babe Ruth, the premier left-handed hitters in Major League Baseball were Ty Cobb and Shoeless Joe Jackson, pictured here in 1913 when Jackson was a member of the Cleveland Indians. Cobb's career batting average was .367. Jackson, over thirteen seasons, batted .356 before he was banished for life in 1920 due to his alleged involvement in the Black Sox scandal. Library of Congress.

Fig. 19. Tris Speaker—“the Grey Eagle”—excelled in all facets of the game and had excellent playing careers in both Boston and Cleveland. He also enjoyed success as a manager. One of the game’s best defensive centerfielders, Speaker exhibited speed on the basepaths and retired with a career batting average of .344. National Baseball Hall of Fame and Museum, Cooperstown, New York.

Fig. 20. LEFT: During his long and distinguished career as a baseball executive, Ban Johnson cared deeply about the integrity of the game. National Baseball Hall of Fame and Museum, Cooperstown, New York.

Fig. 21. Kenesaw Mountain Landis was commissioner of baseball from 1920 to 1944. As a fan, he intently watched games from a field-level box seat, leaning forward with his chin on the railing. National Baseball Hall of Fame and Museum, Cooperstown, New York.

11

Dutch Leonard Has a Story to Tell

In the spring of 1926, Hubert Benjamin Leonard, a former Major League pitcher known professionally as "Dutch" Leonard, had a lot on his mind. He was a man prone to dwelling on the past. He lived east of Fresno, in central California, but he was contemplating a train ride to Chicago, where he wanted to have a talk with Ban Johnson, the president of the American League.

Leonard owned a large farm where he grew grapes, prunes, and figs. He had invested wisely and now, at the youthful age of 34, he had become a wealthy man with a large house and a swimming pool. He was especially proud of his sizable collection of phonograph records. He was married to a dancer who performed in vaudeville shows on the New York stages under the name Muriel Worth. She had an act with her dance partner, Lew Brice, brother of his more famous sister, Fanny.

Dutch Leonard had last pitched in the Major League on July 19, 1925, a game he won against the New York Yankees. Soon after that victory, and although he had a record of eleven wins and just four losses, he was released by his manager, Ty Cobb, and his employer, the Detroit Tigers. No team claimed him off waivers, not even the Cleveland Indians, who were skippered by his former teammate, Tris Speaker.

Leonard was a bitter man. He blamed both Cobb and Speaker for effectively ending his Major League career.

In his career, spanning more than a decade, Leonard had been an outstanding left-handed pitcher who played for the Boston Red Sox and later for the Detroit Tigers. With the Red Sox, he was part of an illustrious pitching staff that included Babe Ruth, Smokey Joe Wood, Carl Mays, and Ernie Shore.

Leonard was proud of his career record. He had won 139 games and lost 112. He had thrown two regular-season no-hitters. In 1914 he posted an earned run average of 0.96 in 224.2 innings, the lowest ERA ever recorded for a full season in the Major Leagues. He had pitched and won two World Series games: one in 1915, the other in 1916. He had earned two World Series rings.

One day in the spring of 1926, Leonard opened a desk drawer and pulled out two letters he'd received in the fall of 1919. One of the letters was from Ty Cobb, the other was from Smokey Joe Wood. He had kept the letters for almost seven years, and now he wanted to show them to Ban Johnson.

Dutch Leonard had a story to tell.

The story went like this. At the end of the 1919 season, the Cleveland Indians were in Detroit to play two games against the Tigers near the end of the regular season. The Chicago White Sox had already clinched the American League pennant, and the Indians had secured second place. The Tigers were battling the Yankees for third place. Whichever team finished third would share in postseason money, so the games between the Tigers and Indians were meaningful to the Detroit players but meant nothing to the Cleveland players.

In the first game of the series on Wednesday, September 24, 1919, the Tigers won 4–1, as Dutch Leonard pitched a six-hitter. After the game, according to Leonard, he met under the Navin Field grandstand with Indians player-manager Tris Speaker, Tigers player-manager Ty Cobb, and Indians pitcher Smokey Joe Wood. The four men knew each other well. Leonard had been teammates with Speaker and Wood when the three of them played for the Red Sox.

In the postgame conversation that Leonard alleges, Speaker said that he was certain his team—the Indians—would lose the next game. "Don't worry about tomorrow's game," Speaker said, "we have second place clinched, and you will win tomorrow."[1] Leonard claimed that the four players then decided that since the outcome of the game was certain, they should place bets on the Tigers to win. Leonard said that he would bet $1,500 and claimed that Cobb indicated he would bet $2,000. Wood and Speaker would wager $1,000 each—notably, Wood and Speaker intended to bet that their own team would lose.[2]

The four ballplayers needed someone to place the bets. Cobb suggested Fred West, a park attendant at Navin Field, a man Cobb trusted. Since the total bet would be too large for Detroit bookmakers to handle, West would collect the money from the four players and try to place the bets with a bookmaker he knew in Chicago.

After the meeting, Leonard, whose season was over, boarded a train and traveled to Independence, Missouri. Only Cobb and Speaker played in Thursday's game. Wood had stayed in Detroit, but he didn't play in the game. A small and mostly disinterested crowd attended. Cobb went 1–5; Speaker collected three hits, including a pair of triples.

The Tigers won, as Speaker had guaranteed; the final score was 9–5. Elmer Myers pitched for the Indians, Bernie Boland for the Tigers. Speaker and Cobb both let their starters pitch complete games, but it was hardly a pitcher's duel. Players on both teams were anxious for the game and the season to be over.[3] The combined outcome: thirty-one hits and fourteen runs. It was a lot of offense, but the game was completed in only sixty-six minutes.

A few weeks later, Dutch Leonard received letters from Wood and Cobb, indicating what had happened with the bets that Fred West tried to place. As it turned out, West could only bet a small portion of the money he carried with him. Chicago bookies were unwilling, on such short notice, to accept the full amount that West tried to wager at 10–7 odds.

Wood's undated letter:

CLEVELAND, OHIO, FRIDAY

Dear Friend Dutch:
Enclosed please find certified check for sixteen hundred and thirty dollars ($1,630.00).

The only bet West could get down was $600 against $420 (10 to 7). Cobb did not get up a cent. He told us that and I believe him. Could have put up some at 5 to 2 on Detroit but did not, as that would make us put up $1000 to win $400.

We won the $420. I gave West $30 [as a tip], leaving $390, or $130 for each of us. Would not have cashed your check at all, but West thought he could get it up at 10 to 7, and I was going to put it all up at those odds. We could have won $1750 for $2500 if we could have placed it.

If we ever have another chance like this we will know enough to try to get down early.

Let me hear from you, Dutch. With all good wishes to Mrs. Leonard and yourself, I am

Joe Wood

Cobb's letter:

AUGUSTA, GA., OCT. 23, 1919

Dear Dutch:

Well, old boy, guess you are out in old California by this time and enjoying life.

I arrived home and found Mrs. Cobb only fair, but the baby girl [Beverly] was fine and at this time Mrs. Cobb is very well, but I have been very busy getting acquainted with my family and have not tried to do any correspondence, hence my delay.

Wood and myself were considerably disappointed in our business proposition, as we had $2000 to put into it and the other side quoted us $1400, and when we finally secured that much money it was about 2 o'clock and they refused to deal with us as they had men in Chicago take up the matter with and they had no time, so we completely fell down and of course we felt badly over it.

Everything was open to Wood and he can tell you about it when we get together. It was quite a responsibility and I don't care for it again, I can tell you.

Well, I hope you found everything in fine shape at home and all your troubles will be little ones. I made this year's share of world series in cotton since I came home and expect to make more.

I thought the White Sox should have won, but I am satisfied they were too overconfident. Well, old scout, drop me a line when you can. We have had some dandy fishing since I arrived home.

With kindest regards to Mrs. Leonard, I remain,

Sincerely,
Ty

It is not shocking that these four ballplayers wanted to bet on the outcome of a late-season game, though Cobb was not known as a gambler, and Wood comments that "Cobb did not get up a cent," indicating that Cobb may have intended to bet on the game but didn't come up with the money until it was too late to participate in the scheme.

Prior to the Black Sox World Series–fixing scandal of 1919, it was permissible for players to bet on games, even games their own team played in. As baseball historian Jacob Pomrenke commented, "As long as there has been baseball, there has been gambling on baseball."[4]

Tris Speaker's biographer, Timothy Gay, has written that "Fans in the early part of the Twentieth century loved to wager on baseball games with the same relish they bet on prizefighting, horse racing, sculling, and anything that moved."[5]

What was not tolerated was fixing or knowing the outcome of a game before it was played. The odds improved considerably for bettors if they knew, or thought they knew in advance, who would win a particular game. But as Pomrenke wrote, "Fixing games, betting on games, and bribery offers were common practices in baseball's Deadball Era in the early 20th century."[6]

In the early days of baseball, friendly wagering between fans or players was common. As opposed to other sports—boxing, horse racing—baseball offered creative ways to bet on various outcomes. A *New York Times* article noted that baseball fans "bet on balls and strikes . . . foul balls, errors, wild throws, and outs. Some even bet the pitcher would use a certain windup on the next ball or Whatshisname would try to steal second and be caught. They bet on anything and bet any amount from a dime to hundreds of dollars."[7]

Owners and baseball executives recognized that betting among customers in the ballpark enhanced the fan experience and contributed to a rise in attendance and paid admissions. As baseball increased in popularity before World War I, bettors fell into two broad categories: casual bettors and professional bettors.[8] Men and women—mostly men—also placed bets on baseball games off-site with bookies and in gambling havens like saloons and pool halls.

The proliferation of professional gamblers in the stands caused serious concern among baseball management. The owners couldn't do much to regulate or stop off-site betting, but they had theoretical control of their own facilities and responsibility for what went on in the stands. The owners aspired to promote the sport as "uplifting, clean, and honest," but betting in the stands by professionals suggested that baseball was "actually strongly tainted by gambling."[9]

A disturbance at Boston's Fenway Park in 1917 illustrates the problem. On June 16, 1917, the Chicago White Sox played a game against the Boston Red Sox. Eddie Cicotte pitched for the White Sox; Babe Ruth pitched for the Red Sox. At that time, Boston was considered one of the centers of baseball gambling; hometown gamblers tended to sit together in the right-field bleachers. A prominent Boston gambler, Sport Sullivan, was known to hang out in saloons and hotels where he could meet and establish relationships with visiting ballplayers.[10]

The professional gamblers in Fenway Park had bet heavily on the Red Sox to win, but the White Sox had the lead. Before Ruth could retire the White Sox in the fifth inning, a light rain began to fall. Sensing that it was best for Boston—and for the gamblers betting on the Red Sox—about three hundred fans poured out of the stands and onto the field during that inning. They didn't attack or approach the players or the umpires; they just stood around, deliberately delaying the game, waiting for the rain to cause a cancellation of the contest. After a few minutes, the fans were chased off the field to seats in the lower grandstand. At that point, the gamblers in the right-field bleachers left their seats and climbed over railings to reach the field. Then the recently relocated fans in the grandstands joined them. Soon a full-blown riot ensued. Players had to fight their way off the field. Some players pushed or fought their way through the crowd. Buck Weaver, the White Sox captain, grabbed a bat and swung it at anyone in his way. Eventually, both teams made it safely to their locker rooms. The incident is now referred to as the "Fenway Park Gamblers Riot."[11]

Most owners tried—though often in vain—to crack down on ballpark betting by posting signs that read, simply, NO GAMBLING, and by hiring security guards and detectives to look for and evict known gamblers. While owners wanted to expel professional gamblers, the owners didn't want to discourage friendly wagering between fans.

It would take the Black Sox World Series and more effective administrative oversight to curtail and control baseball gambling.

In June 1926, Dutch Leonard traveled by train from Fresno to Chicago.[12] He took the letters from Wood and Cobb with him.

Leonard went first to see Ban Johnson, but Johnson wasn't at the American League office when Leonard arrived. Next, Leonard went to the Chicago hotel where the Washington Nationals—in town to play a series with the White Sox—were staying. Leonard showed the letters to Nationals manager Bucky Harris and club secretary Edwin Eynon. Then Leonard went to Detroit and showed the letters to Harry Heilman, one of the Tigers' players, and club president Frank Navin. Leonard told the men that he was thinking about selling the letters to the newspapers.

By this time, Ban Johnson was aware that Leonard was in the Midwest and was looking for him. Both Edwin Eynon and Frank Navin had been in touch with Johnson and urged him to meet with Leonard.

Leonard and Johnson met at Johnson's office. The two men sat down and talked. Leonard showed Johnson the letters. He told Johnson his story about how the game in 1919 was fixed and how the four players intended to profit by betting on the Tigers to win.

The game in question, as Johnson surely knew, was played just six days before the start of the scandal-ridden World Series of 1919 between the Chicago White Sox and the Cincinnati Reds—the most egregious and well-known example of ball games being fixed. It had shaken the world of baseball and the trust that fans had in the integrity of the game. Another scandal arising from the same season—if Leonard's allegations were true—would be devastating to baseball.

To protect baseball and American League owners, Johnson decided to act. He called upon his friend and legal counsel, Henry Killilea, a sixty-three-year-old attorney with extensive experience in the game. Killilea had been a Minor League player, a part-time owner, and a team executive, as well as a consultant to Johnson on baseball legal matters.

Johnson and Killilea negotiated a deal with Leonard.

Leonard said he would go public with his allegation and sell the letters to the newspapers unless he received $20,000. It was blackmail, but Leonard had leverage because he possessed the letters, and his story was credible enough to concern Johnson. Leonard saw the money as fair compensation for the salary he'd been denied when blackballed out of baseball by Cobb and Speaker.

Johnson and Killilea viewed the deal for what it was to them: a hush-money payment.

In exchange for not outing two of baseball's biggest stars, Leonard would give up the letters and agree to keep quiet about his accusation that the game they bet on had been fixed. The payoff also satisfied Leonard's desire to taint the reputations of Cobb and Speaker—at least in Ban Johnson's eyes.

Leonard gave up the letters, took the money, and traveled back to California.

Months later, in an interview with journalist Damon Runyon, Leonard was more explicit about his motives, saying, "I've had my revenge."[13]

12

Yankee Pitchers and Tony Lazzeri

In the summer of 1926, the most famous woman in America was not Grace Coolidge or Mae West but a Canadian-born faith healer and evangelist. Her name was Aimee Semple McPherson.[1]

Born in 1890, on a farm in rural Ontario, Sister Aimee, as she was called by the devoted members of her congregation, preached three times a day, seven days a week, in the Angelous Temple at the Foursquare Gospel Church in Los Angeles. The facility, completed in 1923, had a seating capacity of 5,300. It was usually filled with followers who came to hear her sermons and enjoy her performances.

McPherson's rise to fame and power was dramatic and unconventional but not without controversy.

At the age of twenty-five, McPherson left her second husband, took her two young children, and drove off in a Packard touring car to begin a career as an evangelical preacher. She painted the words "Jesus is Coming Soon—Get Ready" on the side of her car, to advertise her crusade. At tent revivals and established churches, she entertained and inspired people. In addition to her in-person events, she reached her admiring audience by presenting programs and sermons on the radio. Much of her message was conventional—she opposed the teaching of evolution and supported Prohibition—but the theatrical style of her rallies and sermons captivated people.[2]

Within a few years, she was drawing huge crowds—comparable to the crowds drawn by the evangelist Billy Sunday, the popular ex-baseball player. She spoke and sang and performed faith-healing demonstrations at her rallies. In San Diego, thirty thousand people turned out to hear her preach. Marines, stationed nearby, were summoned to help restrain the crowd.

She lived with her children and her mother, Minnie Kennedy, in Los Angeles. As McPherson traveled, her fame grew. Her admirers saw her as a charismatic figure. The demands on her time and energy increased.

When home in Los Angeles, she relaxed by going to Venice Beach on Santa Monica Bay for an ocean swim. She liked to swim far out, past the end of the pier and the breaking waves. Then she would return to the beach and sit under a beach tent and work on her next sermon.

On May 18, 1926, in the late afternoon, Aimee McPherson went for a swim and didn't return to the beach—at least, no one saw her come back to shore.

It was feared that she had drowned. Divers searched for her body. When her followers heard that she had gone missing, they gathered on the beach. One diver died trying to locate her body. An anguished bystander threw herself into the ocean and died.

Sister Aimee McPherson was initially presumed dead.

McPherson's biographer, Daniel Mark Epstein, described the reaction of her followers in hyperbolic terms: "Such a deep and universal expression of grief had not been seen since the assassination of Lincoln. It would not be seen again until the death of FDR."[3]

The county coroner, however, declined to issue a death certificate because her body had not been recovered and the news of her disappearance had generated numerous rumors that included purported sightings of her in various places. Her most ardent followers believed that God had lifted her entire body off the earth to heaven. Some thought she had died but would be resurrected. Others suspected her disappearance was a hoax or publicity stunt. At least two ransom notes arrived and were dismissed. The Angelous Temple offered a $25,000 reward for her safe return. But over time, hope faded.

On June 20, Minnie Kennedy officiated at a twelve-hour memorial service at the temple to honor her daughter. Twenty-thousand people attended. A collection plate was passed, and more than $30,000 was donated to the temple.

On June 23—thirty-six days after Aimee McPherson had gone missing—the evangelist reappeared in Douglas, Arizona, a town on the Mexican border. She told a story of being kidnapped off Venice Beach by three Americans who held her hostage in a shack in the Mexican desert. Five weeks after the abduction, she said she managed to escape and walk nearly twenty miles across the desert to the border town of Agua Prieta, Mexico, where she then crossed into Arizona. Once rested up from her ordeal, she returned to Los Angeles, where she was greeted by a band and an enormous crowd of supporters, including the city's acting mayor and members of the city council. McPherson's biographer, described the scene: "As the band played, the beloved evangelist was carried from the train on a wicker throne woven with red roses."

Newspapers from coast to coast reported on McPherson's ordeal and reemergence. It was the most sensational news story of the year—at least, so far.

On June 24, the day that newspapers reported the reemergence of Aimee McPherson, the Yankees were losing a ten-inning game to Boston at Fenway Park. Waite Hoyt took the loss in relief of the starter Herb Pennock. Just two days earlier, Hoyt had pitched a five-hitter against the Washington Nationals, allowing just a single run in the ninth inning, which ruined his bid for a shutout.

Hoyt, along with Pennock and Urban Shocker, had been the most dependable hurlers for manager Huggins. At this point in the season, Hoyt had a record of 11–5, Shocker was 9–3, and Pennock was 12–4.

Waite Hoyt was a local product, born in the fall of 1899 in the Flatbush area of Brooklyn. His father had played semipro baseball and made a living as an entertainer, a vaudeville performer with a pleasing baritone voice. Hoyt's first experience with baseball as a child was playing with other performers in the alleys between buildings in the Manhattan theater district.

His potential was recognized early. Hoyt was big for his age, standing almost six feet tall. He attended Erasmus Hall High School, and by the end of his sophomore year he had gained a reputation as an outstanding pitcher with a lively fastball, pitching for community teams and for his high school. Local sportswriters called him "Schoolboy."[4] At the age of fifteen, he signed his first professional contract with the New York Giants. At the time, Hoyt was believed to be the youngest player ever signed to a Major League contract. In the spring of 1916, after pitching back-to-back no-hitters for his high school team, he dropped out of school—at the age of sixteen—and started his professional career with Lebanon in the Penn State League.

It took Hoyt three years in the Minors before making it onto a Major League roster. Then in 1919, McGraw sold his contract to the Boston Red Sox, where Ed Barrow was the manager. Hoyt earned his first Major League win at the end of July, pitching a twelve-inning complete game at Fenway Park against Ty Cobb and the Detroit Tigers, winning 2–1. Cobb managed a triple in five at bats against the rookie and taunted Hoyt throughout the game. "Cobb called me every name in the book," Hoyt recalled years later.

Although the Red Sox finished fifth that season, Hoyt was part of a pitching staff that included Carl Mays, Sad Sam Jones, Herb Pennock, and Babe Ruth. Within a few years, all five of them would be sold or traded to the New York Yankees. Boston's owner Harry Frazee—a theatrical producer—sold off his best players whenever he needed cash to finance a new production.

In Hoyt's two seasons with the Red Sox, he posted a mediocre record of 10–12. In his first five years with the Yankees, Hoyt was 84–61.

Hoyt's pitching talent was unquestioned. So was his love of nightlife. On long road trips, some lasting three weeks or more, players had their evenings free. Hoyt knew the best places to go, especially in a city like Chicago, where Al Capone supplied nightclubs and speakeasies with all the alcohol their customers desired.

One night in Chicago, Hoyt was out on the town, dining at a restaurant with his roommate, Joe Dugan, and teammates Herb Pennock and Bob Meusel. Dugan told the bartender they were New York Yankee ballplayers and asked him—jokingly—whether they could meet Al Capone.[5] The bartender took the request seriously and disappeared to a back room. When he returned, he said, "There'll be a car here in twenty minutes."[6]

A black limousine appeared, right on time. The four players—not certain as to what was going to happen next—got in the limousine and were driven to the Lexington Hotel, at 2135 South Michigan Avenue, Capone's new headquarters. One of Capone's men met them and gave them instructions. They were to ride the hotel's freight elevator to an upper floor where they would be let out. They were instructed to make sure their hands were always visible. A bodyguard outside Capone's suite would frisk them and then let them in.[7]

The suite was furnished like an office with filing cabinets and adding machines.[8] Capone was seated behind a large desk in front of a bay window that faced Michigan Avenue. Three pictures had been hung on the wall. One of George Washington, one of Abraham Lincoln, and one of Al Capone. Joe Dugan stepped forward to shake Capone's hand and said, "Three great men: George, Abe, and Al."[9]

Capone laughed and then ordered one of his men to bring bottles of champagne to the room.

Capone was a baseball fan and often attended White Sox games at Comiskey Park. As a youth in Brooklyn—before he moved to Chicago to take over Johnny Torrio's criminal enterprises—Capone played on a semipro baseball team with his older brother Ralph and his cousin Charlie Fischetti. They called themselves the Al Capone Stars, and their games were often reported in local papers, like the *Brooklyn Citizen* and *Brooklyn Times-Citizen*. Al played first base and pitched.[10]

Years later, Capone's grandniece Deirdre Marie Capone wrote that her great-uncle once mused about owning the Chicago Cubs.[11]

The champagne was delivered. Capone and the four Yankees drank and talked for an hour before the players were driven back to their hotel. No one recorded the conversation.

Herb Pennock had been traded to the New York Yankees on January 30, 1923, after seven seasons with the Red Sox. Pennock was a tall, thin, slow-working left-hander, who relied on two kinds of curves—an overhand curve and a sidearm curve—as well as a screwball.[12]

He had been raised as a Quaker in rural Pennsylvania. He had unusual habits and hobbies for a professional ballplayer. He collected antique furniture and was careful with his money, investing in a fox pelt farm and greenhouses that grew chrysanthemums.[13] He was quiet and did not swear. He was generally relaxed around teammates, except on days when he was pitching and would become focused and intense. On the mound, he was deliberate and threw with such a relaxed and easy motion that it looked as if he was casually pitching batting practice. His success was due to his ability to change speeds on his breaking ball and locate his pitches.[14]

That first season with the Yankees, he won nineteen games, lost six, led the league in earned run average, and won both his starts in the 1923 World Series. It was the first World Series championship for the Yankees. He was just as good in 1924, posting a record of 21–9, and even in the disaster year of 1925, he managed to win sixteen games with an era of 2.96, second best in the American League.

Urban Shocker was one of the last legal spitball pitchers. The pitch had been outlawed in 1920 but he was one of seventeen players grandfathered in and allowed to use the pitch for the rest of their Major League careers. He needed it. It was his best pitch. Frank Ellerbe, Shocker's teammate on the St. Louis Browns, said, "He had the best control of that spitball of anybody I ever saw."[15]

Shocker's other effective pitch was what he called his "slow ball," which would break sharply down, like his spitter, but at a different speed. He credited the movement on that pitch to a permanently crooked middle finger, a result of a foul tip he failed to handle properly when he was catching in the Minor Leagues.

In his seven years with the Browns, Shocker was one of the best pitchers in the American League, with a league-high twenty-seven wins in 1921 when the Browns finished second to the Yankees. When he returned to the Yankees in 1925, he was thirty-four years old and a well-respected veteran who had thrown more than two hundred innings in six consecutive seasons, including more than three hundred innings in both 1921 and 1922. He was considered as durable as any pitcher in the Majors.

What few people in baseball knew was that Shocker had developed a serious health problem. Shocker began to feel ill in the spring of 1925. He had chest congestion and trouble breathing. He lost ten pounds. Shocker's biographer, Steve Steinberg, speculates that Shocker was experiencing the beginnings of congestive heart failure, likely brought on by a mitral valve prolapse, an untreatable condition in the 1920s.[16]

To sleep, Shocker had to rest in an inclined position or by sitting up. His roommate on the road was the Yankee's twenty-three-year-old batboy, Eddie Bennett, who had suffered a serious spinal injury as a child. "It was a convenient pairing," Steinberg wrote, "the batboy with a back deformity that left him hunched over and the athlete who could not lie in a flat position in bed. They were kindred spirits, both suffering from debilitating diseases."[17]

Shocker was in better condition at the end of spring training, and Huggins chose him to be the opening day pitcher for the Yankees in 1925 against the Washington Nationals. Shocker responded by tossing a complete game, allowing seven hits and a single run, as the Yankees opened the season with a 5–1 win.

From there, the season went downhill for the Yankees. The Nationals swept the next three games—Shocker was the loser in relief two days after his opening day victory—and by the end of the month, the Yankees were in sixth place. In 1925, Shocker finished with a record of 12–12, pitched 244 innings, appeared in forty-one games and started thirty of them.

He turned thirty-five in August. He expected to pitch several more years for the Yankees. Whatever health issues had affected him in the spring of 1925 seemed to be under control.

It wasn't just good pitching that had propelled the Yankees to the top of the standings in 1926. The offense was doing its part, too, from the top of the batting order—Combs and Koenig—to the bottom—where catcher Pat Collins was having the best year of his career. The run-producing middle of the order featured Gehrig, Ruth, Meusel, Lazzeri, and Dugan.

Fully recovered from the physical ills of the prior season, Ruth was batting a lusty .388 and leading the league with 23 home runs and 79 RBIs. The young first baseman, Gehrig, who would become one of the game's most feared power hitters, had produced just four home runs, but was hitting .349. Meusel and Dugan were batting .357 and .364, respectively. Koenig and Combs were hitting close to .300.

And then there was Tony Lazzeri. Born in San Francisco twenty-eight months before the earthquake of 1906, and just eight months after his parents traveled from Italy, the Lazzeri family joined the largest immigrant community in the city. Lazzeri grew up in a tough ethnic neighborhood and left school at the age of fifteen to work with his father at the Main Street Iron Works. His early ambition was to become a professional prize fighter. In later interviews, he said he'd been in numerous fights outside the ring as a youth. "I guess I was a pretty tough kid. The neighborhood wasn't one in which a boy was likely to grow up a sissy, for it was always fight or get licked, and I never got licked."[18]

Before he made his mark as a fighter, he gained a reputation as an outstanding baseball player on Bay Area ballfields. In 1922 Duffy Lewis, player-manager of the Salt Lake City Bees, offered Lazzeri a tryout and then signed him to a contract worth $250 a month. Lewis, once an outfielder for the Boston Red Sox, saw great potential in Lazzeri, who had recently turned eighteen years of age. Lewis was right. Four years later, Lazzeri was the starting second baseman for the New York Yankees.[19]

For a player who had never seen a Major League game until he played in one, Lazzeri was remarkably poised and confident as a rookie. Halfway through the 1926 season, he was second on the team in home runs, with nine, and third behind Ruth and Meusel in RBIS, with fifty-four.

Lazzeri's power was hoped for after his spectacular season in the Pacific Coast League (PCL), where he hit 60 home runs and batted .355 in 192 games.[20] But few expected him to adjust to big league pitching quite so efficiently and so quickly. Although he hit sixth in the order, he was generating the kind of power usually associated with the number three and four batters. In addition, he was becoming a favorite of Yankee fans.

A year earlier, Lazzeri had been under contract to the Salt Lake City Bees and attracting attention from Major League teams as he set PCL batting records during the 1925 season. The Cubs had a working agreement with Salt Lake City, so they were interested, as were the Cincinnati Reds. But those teams were wary of signing Lazzeri for several reasons. Scouts and sportswriters who covered the PCL noted that his home run and power hitting statistics were likely enhanced by the friendly ballpark he played in, as well as the thin air in Salt Lake City. Several earlier signees from the PCL had failed to live up to their potential after making the transition from the West Coast to the Major Leagues.[21]

But the two most significant reservations had to do with his health and his ethnicity. Lazzeri suffered from epilepsy, and while he had never had a seizure on the ball field, teams knew about his condition and were concerned that the affliction would impact his performance. Furthermore, epilepsy carried a stigma with the public. People feared the condition was contagious or was evidence of mental illness. In some states, epileptics were forbidden to marry.[22]

The other issue was Lazzeri's Italian heritage. Only a handful of Italian Americans had ever played in the Major Leagues. During the decade of the 1920s, just sixteen Italian Americans would appear on Major League rosters.[23] In the post–World War I period, Americans had become increasingly hostile to foreigners, especially Catholics, who wanted to immigrate to America. Ethnicity mattered. So did religion. The Ku Klux Klan and other nativist groups, mostly Protestant, were on the rise and supported strict limits on immigration. The National Origins Act of 1924 placed severe restrictions and quotas on immigration, especially for people from Southern and Eastern Europe. The stereotype of Italian immigrants was that they were crude and uneducated, radical in their political beliefs, and prone to violence and criminal activity. Discussing "the power of the Mafia myth," the scholar Richard Gambino wrote that "[Italian Americans] must be either spaghetti-twirling, opera-bellowing buffoons in undershirts . . . or swarthy, sinister hoods in garish suits, shirts and ties."[24] Lazzeri's biographer, Lawrence Baldassaro, noted that in the 1920s, the most well-known Italian Americans in the country were the convicted anarchists Nicolo Sacco and Bartolomeo Vanzetti and the crime boss Al Capone.[25]

While some teams saw Lazzeri's background as problematic, Ed Barrow, the business manager of the Yankees, was willing to take a chance on Lazzeri, if the Yankee scouts confirmed his promise.[26] First, he sent two trusted Yankee scouts, Paul Krichell and Ed Holly, to the West Coast to watch Lazzeri play and assess his ability. The scouts returned with a mixed report. Holly confirmed that Lazzeri could hit, but Krichell expressed concerns regarding the fact that Lazzeri struck out a lot. They also noted the issue of his epilepsy.[27]

Barrow sent Krichell back for a second look and asked Bob Connery, the scout who discovered Rogers Hornsby, to accompany Krichell. Connery was impressed. He advised Barrow: "I don't care what he's got. Buy him. He's the greatest thing I've ever seen."[28]

Barrow was fifty-seven. He was a big man, physically powerful, autocratic, and self-confident. For more than thirty years, he had been involved in the business aspects of baseball. Born in 1868 in the back of a covered wagon on a hemp farm near Springfield, Illinois, he grew up in rural Nebraska and Iowa. As a youth, he played baseball and learned to box.

He knew how to recognize baseball talent. In 1896, when Barrow briefly owned an interest in the Paterson, New Jersey, team in the Atlantic League, he signed a young prospect named Honus Wagner. A year later, he sold Wagner's contract to the Louisville team and made a nice profit on the transaction.[29]

By his late twenties, Barrow had moved into management and was named the president of the Atlantic League.[30] Many years before Bill Veeck appeared on the national scene, Barrow found creative ways to market and promote the teams in his league. He recruited heavyweight boxers—John L. Sullivan and James Jeffries—to umpire at some of his league's games. Another boxer,

Jim Corbett, sometimes played first base during exhibition games. A woman named Lizzie Arlington was hired to pitch in a few exhibition games.[31]

In 1903 Barrow jumped to the Major Leagues and took a position as the manager of the Detroit Tigers. He held that position for two years, then spent more than a decade working in the Minor Leagues as a manager or executive. In 1918 Harry Frazee, the owner of the of Boston Red Sox, hired Barrow as the team's manager. The Red Sox had a good roster and a young pitcher named Babe Ruth. In Barrow's first season, the Red Sox won the American League pennant and beat the Chicago Cubs in the World Series, four games to two. Ruth won both games he pitched, allowing just two earned runs in seventeen innings.

The next year, Barrow shifted Ruth from the mound to the outfield to take advantage of his offensive potential. Ruth responded by hitting twenty-nine home runs, a new single-season record. But relations between Barrow and Ruth were often contentious. In an angry encounter before a game, Ruth threatened to punch Barrow in the mouth. Barrow calmly ordered everyone except Ruth to leave the clubhouse—and told Ruth, if he wanted to settle the matter with his fists, he'd be willing to fight, one-on-one. Ruth—wisely, for once—backed down, put on his uniform, and joined his teammates on the field.

In the off-season after the 1919 season, when Frazee thought about selling Ruth to the Yankees, Barrow strongly objected, telling his employer that it was a huge mistake to sell or trade Ruth. Frazee went ahead. Ruth was sold to the Yankees. In 1920 the Yankees finished second in the AL as Ruth hit fifty-four home runs; the Red Sox finished fourth. A year later, the Yankees hired Barrow away from the Red Sox and empowered him to run baseball operations.

With Barrow in the front office, Huggins directing things from the dugout, and Ruth in the lineup every day, the Yankees won three consecutive AL pennants from 1921 through 1923 and finished third in 1924. After the debacle of the 1925 season, though, Huggins and Barrow agreed they needed to reshape the roster.

Barrow was willing to take a chance on Tony Lazzeri because he was impressed with Lazzeri's toughness. Barrow knew that Lazzeri had started out wanting to be a boxer. He didn't seem to be the kind of player who would shy away from a challenge or wilt in the face of pressure.

Lazzeri wasn't cheap. Barrow paid $50,000 to purchase his contract. The Yankees also transferred the rights to five Minor League players to Salt Lake City.[32]

Barrow had two reasons to think the deal made sense. First, adding a power hitter to the Yankees lineup, especially if Ruth was unable to come back from his poor performance in 1925, was critical if the Yankees were going to be able to contend for another championship.

Just as importantly, at least from a business and promotional perspective, Barrow knew that one million Italian Americans lived in the five boroughs of New York City. If the scouts were right and Lazzeri was a success, it could mean more ticket sales and increased visibility for the franchise.

The Italian ballplayer Lazzeri might be very good for business.

13

Rube Foster and Black Baseball

In the spring of 1926, a nineteen-year-old pitcher made his professional debut with the Chattanooga White Sox in the Negro Southern League. The player had large hands, skinny legs, and an odd corkscrew windup. He stood 6 feet 3 inches tall and weighed 140 pounds. At this stage of his career, he had mastered only one pitch, a fastball he nicknamed Long Tom.[1] He could deliver this pitch with a variety of motions and delivery angles: underhand, overhand, and side arm. On the mound and in person, he exuded confidence and charisma. Fans, both Black and white, flocked to ballparks to see him pitch. He would become the most famous pitcher of his era.

His name was Satchel Paige.

At the time Paige was starting his professional career, Black baseball in America had been thriving, despite considerable hardships, for more than half a century. Most professional Black teams in the late 1800s and early 1900s were travel teams, barnstorming through the country, including the segregated South, traveling by car, bus, and train, playing hundreds of games a year against both Black and white teams, town teams, and semi-pro teams. In the winter months, Black players and teams participated in leagues in Mexico and Cuba as well as the integrated and highly competitive California Winter League, which attracted white Major Leaguers, Cubans, and Hispanic ballplayers.[2]

For understandable financial and organizational reasons, continuity in Black baseball was difficult. Record keeping, except for game reports that appeared in local newspapers, was sporadic. Without any contractual language binding players to teams for more than a season or a single barnstorming tour, players were free to negotiate the best terms or contracts they could from whichever organization was willing to pay them. The result was a lack of stability and constant player movement from one team to another.

During these years, several attempts were made to form Black-only leagues. These leagues either failed to materialize or once organized, fell apart as teams dropped out or couldn't continue to operate for financial or logistical reasons.

Still, by the early 1900s, Black baseball was firmly established in America—a parallel universe to the white Major Leagues. What Black baseball needed was someone with the imagination and organizational talent to address the issues facing Black players and teams.

As it turned out, the individual who would transform Black baseball was already becoming one of the outstanding pitchers of his generation. His name was Andrew "Rube" Foster.

In 1906, the year Satchel Paige was born, Rube Foster was in his ninth year of professional baseball, pitching that season for the Philadelphia Giants. He was a large, round-faced man, who bore a physical resemblance to heavyweight boxing champion Jack Johnson. More than six feet tall and weighing well over two hundred pounds, the pipe-smoking Foster was an imposing figure on the mound. Off the field, he usually carried a loaded pistol.

Born in Calvert, Texas, in 1879, Foster was the child of sharecroppers who had been born into slavery. His father served as a minister of the local African Methodist Episcopal Church and lived by a strict set of rules, which included a prohibition against drinking and other frivolous activities. Not surprisingly, Reverend Foster discouraged his son from pursuing a career in baseball.

Andrew Foster—not yet nicknamed Rube—learned the game as a young boy and developed into an outstanding player. He dropped out of school after the eighth grade to concentrate on baseball.[3] As a teenager, Foster began his professional career in organized ball with the Waco Yellow Jackets, an independent semipro team.

As a pitcher, he had a dominating fastball and a breaking ball that broke in on right-handed batters and away from left-handers. Although individual statistics are hard to verify from the years he played, there is evidence that Foster was arguably the best pitcher in Black baseball during the first two decades of the twentieth century. His brilliance as a ballplayer was unquestioned, and he was acknowledged as having a keen baseball intelligence.

In 1902 Foster was signed by Frank Leland, owner and manager of the Chicago Unions. After a brief stint with the Unions and one season with an integrated semipro team in Otsego, Michigan, Foster signed a contract with the Cuban X Giants, a spinoff of the original Cuban Giants and one of the leading teams on the East Coast. Foster won forty-four straight games with the Cuban X Giants. A year later, Foster changed teams again and signed with the Philadelphia Giants. During the 1905 season, Foster claimed to have won fifty-one of the fifty-five games he pitched for the Philadelphia Giants.

Foster earned his nickname early in his career when he pitched a post-season exhibition game against Rube Waddell of Connie Mack's Phillies, hurling his team to a 5–2 win. Historians have not been able to pinpoint the exact year the game took place, but it is widely accepted that Foster outpitched Waddell and dominated a lineup that included white Major Leaguers. Years later, after he beat Waddell, Foster proudly stated, "They gave me the name of the colored Rube Waddell."[4]

By this time, Foster had also attracted the attention of a baseball immortal: John McGraw, manager of the New York Giants. Legend has it that McGraw approached Foster with a request: that the Black pitcher tutor McGraw's young, white pitcher Christy Matthewson and teach him how to throw the breaking ball that Foster used so effectively. In the years to come, as Matthewson established himself as one of the game's greatest pitchers, he was known for his "fadeaway," a pitch very much like what Foster had developed a decade or more earlier.

Over the next twenty years, Foster was the dominant figure in Black baseball. Though he excelled as a pitcher until he was in his late thirties, pitching was just the beginning of his career and the influence he exerted in the game. In the years to come, Rube Foster would succeed as a manager, an organizer, a promoter, a league executive, and—most importantly—a visionary.

Foster returned to Chicago in 1907 and reestablished his connection with Frank Leland. Foster and Leland eventually terminated their working agreement, but Foster remained in Chicago, which was to be his base for the rest of his life. He took over the team then known as the Leland Giants and renamed it the Chicago American Giants, assembling and managing a dynasty, a team that would dominate Black baseball for more than a decade.

He improved the roster by recruiting future Hall of Famers: the pitcher Smokey Joe Williams, the outfielder Pete Hill, and the shortstop John Henry "Pop" Lloyd.[5] In later years, the brilliant Oscar Charleston and the Cuban star Cristobal Torriente joined the team.[6]

In the early spring of 1908, the American Giants went on the road, playing semipro teams in the Deep South and Texas. Rube's team "traveled in style in private Pullman cars hooked onto the regular train."[7] The road trip covered 4,500 miles, and the Giants swept through the competition undefeated, drawing huge crowds anxious to see Rube Foster and his teammates.[8] The *Indianapolis Freeman* reported that Rube Foster "is without a doubt the most popular ballplayer in the country."[9]

Foster wasn't content in just beating other Black and semipro teams. He believed his team could compete with the best teams in the white Major Leagues. To prove his point, Foster challenged the Chicago Cubs to a three-game series. The games were played in October 1909, after the World Series. The Cubs were no pushovers. They had won three straight National League pennants in 1906, 1907, and 1908. In 1909, despite winning 104 games, they finished second to the Pittsburgh Pirates.

Unfortunately, Foster was unable to play in the games as he was recovering from a broken leg suffered in a game earlier in the summer.[10] All three games were close, but the Cubs won all three contests. Mordecai "Three Finger" Brown was the winning pitcher in two of the games for the Cubs. Although the American Giants failed to score a victory, they demonstrated that their team—like other teams in the top echelons of Black baseball—had the talent to compete with teams in the white Major Leagues.[11] A year later, the American Giants traveled to Cuba and played games against top Cuban teams and a squad made up of players from the Detroit Tigers, including Ty Cobb. Cobb's team won four out of five contests, but Cobb was thrown out stealing twice by American Giants' catcher Bruce Petway. Several American Giants players—Petway, Home Run Johnson, and John Henry Lloyd—outhit Cobb. After the series in Cuba, Cobb declined to play postseason or barnstorming games against Black teams.

In 1911 Foster entered into a partnership with John Schorling, the white son-in-law of Chicago White Sox owner Charles Comiskey.[12] Schorling made a deal with Foster for the American Giants to play their home games in South Side Park, just a few blocks away from the new Comiskey Park on Chicago's South Side where the White Sox would play their games.

In games that historians attribute to the Chicago American Giants, the team posted a record of 78–27 that year. In 1912 their record was 112–20. The 1914 squad, the most dominant Black team of the era, won 126 games and lost just 16. The season included a forty-four-game winning streak. In the winter of 1915–16, the American Giants traveled west and won the California Winter League championship.

From the time he took control of the Leland Giants and guided their transition to the Chicago American Giants, Rube Foster had two grand ambitions: one was to see Black players welcomed into the white Major Leagues; the second was to establish a league for Black teams so that teams could play a regular season schedule like the white Majors.

Foster believed barnstorming would remain an important activity and source of income for players and owners, but he thought an organized league would provide additional benefits in terms of recognition and stability for the teams who participated. Over the next several years, Foster continued to pitch, but increasingly devoted himself to managing the team and handling the business affairs of the American Giants.

In 1914 the Federal League was formed to compete with the two existing white leagues, and Foster saw this as an opportunity for not only a third major league to succeed but also for the top white leagues to expand their rosters by adding talent from current Black teams. He was confident that the talent on Black teams was comparable to the talent on white Major League teams, and he was optimistic that segregation at the Major League level was going to end soon. So certain that integration was on the horizon, Foster declared, "They'll let us in soon. . . . And when they let the Black men in, watch how many present-day stars lose their positions."[13]

Foster might have been right about what would happen if the Major Leagues integrated. But white owners and players were not ready to support integration at the Major League level. The success that Foster's teams had playing against white Major Leaguers also prompted American League president Ban Johnson, a friend and admirer of Foster, to oppose exhibitions of fully rostered Major League teams against Black teams, in the United

States or in Cuba. In Johnson's words, losses to Black teams "would surely hurt [my] league."[14]

The Federal League folded after two seasons, and a year later, the nation entered World War I. Baseball carried on, but rosters were depleted as "work or fight" rules required players to join the war effort, either as soldiers or as workers in vital industries. When the war ended, the country experienced the Red Summer of 1919, which provoked social tensions and concerns about communism. The Ku Klux Klan was on the rise in many parts of the country, and the summer saw increased violence against Black Americans. Numerous lynchings in the South were reported.

Civil unrest also broke out in many northern cities, most notably in Chicago. The initial incident occurred at Chicago Beach, just a few miles from Schorling Park. A Black youth was accused of swimming in what was seen to be a "whites only" area of the lake at the unofficially segregated beach. The young boy was attacked by white men who threw stones at him, and the youth drowned. Two weeks of sporadic violence ensued. More than one thousand Black families had their homes destroyed. Thirty-eight people, Black and white, were killed in a series of racially inspired attacks.

The Chicago disturbances effectively ended any hopes that Rube Foster might have had about the white Major Leagues integrating anytime soon, but he still believed in the idea of a league of Black teams that would play a season-long schedule and compete for a league championship.

On February 13 and 14, 1920, Foster organized a meeting with his counterparts in Kansas City to discuss plans for a Black major league. An agreement was reached. The league would consist of eight teams, all in the Midwest. At first the league called itself the Western League, though they would soon rebrand themselves as the Negro National League (NNL). Rube Foster was selected as the league president.

To ensure some degree of competitive balance, the assets of each team—the players and their contracts—were divided up. Two of Foster's best players—Pete Hill and Oscar Charleston—were assigned to new teams, Hill to Detroit, Charleston to the Indianapolis ABCs. The league drew up a schedule. Ball games commenced on May 2 with a contest between the Chicago Giants (not the Chicago American Giants) and the Indianapolis ABCs.[15]

Each year a league champion was crowned. In 1920 Foster's Chicago American Giants were declared the league's champion. The American Giants repeated in 1921 and 1922. In 1923 the Kansas City Monarchs won the title, paced by Bullet Joe Rogan and John Donaldson, two pitchers in the prime years of their careers.

That same year, a second league of Black teams was formed, consisting of teams in the east. They named themselves the Eastern Colored League (ECL). The Hilldale Darby Daisies of Darby, Pennsylvania, just west of Philadelphia, won that year's championship.[16]

In 1924 and 1925 the champions of the two leagues played a best-of-nine series that was promoted as the "Colored World Series." In 1924 the Kansas City Monarchs defeated the Hilldale Darby Daisies, five games to four. A year later, Hilldale won decisively, five games to one. As president of the Negro National League, Rube Foster took pride in the fact that under his management the two leagues had agreed to the postseason competition, mirroring the form and success of the white Major Leagues.

No one had worked harder than Rube Foster to build credibility for his league and to obtain the top players for his team. He continued to lobby for direct competition between Negro League teams and white Major League teams. Early in 1926 at a meeting in the Chicago Beach Hotel, Foster proposed an idea to American League president Ban Johnson and John McGraw, manager of the New York Giants. McGraw had been a friend to Foster and had previously supported the integration of the white Major Leagues.

Foster's idea was that his Chicago American Giants would play exhibition games against the white Major League clubs that traveled through Chicago to play regularly scheduled games against the Cubs or White Sox. When the visiting teams had an off day, Foster suggested, that day could be used to host a game between the Chicago American Giants and the visiting white team. The games, Foster argued, would draw large crowds and attract interest in both the white and Black communities.

The plan was ambitious and a bit audacious. It never came to fruition. It's unclear how receptive Johnson and McGraw were to the idea. It's also possible that Judge Landis stepped in and quashed the idea.

The Kansas City Monarchs had been the dominant team during the 1925 NNL season, posting a record of 59–23. The St. Louis Stars had finished second, and Foster's American Giants had finished a distant third, 10 games behind the Monarchs and 6.5 games behind the Stars.

In the off-season, Foster made several trades to rebuild and strengthen his lineup going into the 1926 season. He traded the popular Cristobol Torriente to the Kansas City Monarchs for outfielder George Sweatt.[17] Torriente had slumped in 1925. After three seasons where he hit .344 or higher, in 1925, he hit only .264, a hundred points lower than the previous season.

Foster acquired Rube Curry from Hilldale. Curry was a young pitcher with a bright future; he had posted a record of 11–1 for Hilldale in 1925 but was dissatisfied with the contract he was offered. Foster also signed Sanford Jackson, Charlie Williams, and Pythias Russ from the now-defunct Memphis Red Sox.

Kansas City would be the preseason favorite in the NNL. Player/manager Jose Mendez had an excellent pitching staff, still headed by Bullet Rogan. Torriente would replace Sweatt in the outfield. The team's best hitter was shortstop Dobie Moore, nicknamed the "Black Cat" for his fielding prowess. The St. Louis Stars would be contenders again, with Mule Suttles and Cool Papa Bell leading the offense. The Detroit Stars had finished strong in 1925 and were led by outfielder Turkey Stearnes.

With a revamped roster, Foster expected that his American Giants could compete against strong competition for a pennant in 1926.

14

Sesquicentennial Games

On Sunday, July 4, 1926, President Calvin Coolidge turned fifty-four years old. He celebrated with his wife, Grace, by going to church and eating a quiet dinner at the White House.

The next day, the president and first lady traveled from Washington to Philadelphia, where Coolidge was to give a speech in commemoration of the 150th anniversary of the signing of the Declaration of Independence. He would also visit Independence Hall and Christ Church before returning to the White House. It was the first presidential visit to Philadelphia since 1918.

Coolidge was the most introverted man to ever occupy the Oval Office. One presidential scholar described him as "the first president to be renowned for torpor."[1] A friend called him "splendidly null."[2] The columnist Walter Lippman wrote that Coolidge had "a genius for inactivity."[3] Coolidge didn't particularly like crowds or meetings or long conversations or people in general. He was quick-tempered and had a sharp tongue.[4] His most endearing trait might have been a sly sense of humor. He slept eleven or twelve hours a day and believed that the less government did, the better off the country would be. And yet, he gave many speeches during his nearly six years in office and held frequent press conferences, though he often responded to questions with short or single-word answers.

Although the Republican Party faced tough opposition in the upcoming midterm election and possibly the loss of control in the House of Representatives, Coolidge had no intention of personally supporting or campaigning for members of his party who were up for reelection. The day after his speech in Philadelphia, he intended to take a long summer vacation to a remote area of the Adirondacks in upstate New York. It was suggested in the press that the stress of the presidency was reason enough for Coolidge to take his long vacation and that the president needed rest and exercise.

Coolidge planned to stay at White Pine Camp on Osgood Lake, where he could recuperate.

A *New York Times* reporter speculated that the extended time away from Washington and the seclusion offered by White Pine Camp "will furnish the incentive to chopping wood, rowing a boat, taking brisk walks, or other forms of exercise calculated to make him fit for the next Congressional session."[5]

It was hard for most who knew the president to imagine him with an axe in his hand.

The Coolidges arrived at the Broad Street Station in Philadelphia at 11:00 a.m. and traveled in a motorcade to the site of the exposition, billed as the Sesquicentennial International Exposition, a world's fair. The exposition and fair had opened on May 31, but it would not be a success. Seven weeks after President Coolidge's appearance, *Variety* magazine would call the exposition "America's Biggest Flop."[6] A year later, the exposition would be in receivership.

The skies were dark, and a light rain fell steadily, though it didn't seem to diminish the turnout or dampen the enthusiasm of the crowd. The president modestly responded to the crowd by occasionally tipping his hat. Grace Coolidge, dressed all in white and wearing her signature leghorn hat, smiled broadly and waved vigorously to the people along the parade route. It was estimated that as many as two hundred thousand Philadelphians stood on rooftops and lined the streets to cheer the arrival of the Coolidges. Small children in white frocks clutched damp American flags and waved them as the procession passed by.

A crowd of thirty-five thousand politely greeted the president at the Sesquicentennial Exposition site in downtown Philadelphia. When Mrs. Coolidge appeared, the crowd cheered. She waved to the crowd and took a seat on the podium. An awning protected the speakers from the rain as the drizzle became a downpour, drenching those who stayed to listen to the president's address.

President Coolidge began his speech with this sentence, "We meet to celebrate the birthday of America." The president mentioned Thomas Jefferson, the widely acknowledged primary author of the Declaration of Independence, but only briefly. In Coolidge's speech, he mostly gave credit for the ideas in the document to the Protestant clergy of New England, the region in which he was raised.[7]

President Coolidge may not have known, and certainly wouldn't have cared, that the hometown Philadelphia Athletics were scheduled to play a doubleheader at Shibe Park that day against the league-leading New York Yankees, or that all sixteen Major League teams were playing doubleheaders on the anniversary of the signing of the Declaration of Independence. President Coolidge had little interest in athletes or sporting events.

But Grace Coolidge would have been aware of the games being played in Philadelphia between the Yankees and the Athletics, and she would have been keenly interested in the outcome of the games at Griffith Stadium in Washington DC between the Nationals and the Boston Red Sox.

Grace Coolidge was a knowledgeable baseball fan, fiercely devoted to her hometown Washington Nationals. She followed her team and the pennant races daily. As a student at the University of Vermont, she had learned the intricacies of baseball scorekeeping and filled in her scorecard during the games she attended. She raised two boys who often left baseball bats, balls, and gloves strewn about on the living room floor of the duplex where the Coolidges lived before they moved to Washington. She would sometimes join her sons in backyard baseball games. When attending games at Griffith Stadium, she participated as an enthusiastic and attentive fan, eating peanuts, cheering for the Nationals, and keeping a scorecard where she recorded the outcome of each at bat. No first lady in our history has ever loved the national pastime as passionately and authentically as she did.

In fact, in almost every conceivable way, Grace Coolidge was the opposite of her husband. She liked people. She was energetic and outgoing. She liked social events. She was the first wife of a president to graduate from a four-year college or university. She studied deaf education, learned sign language, and taught at the Clarke School for the Deaf in Northampton, Massachusetts. In later years, she worked with the Red Cross. She loved animals and kept a pet raccoon in the White House.

Although she was an accomplished and vibrant woman, she accepted her public role in the White House as a supportive spouse. Her husband forbade her "to drive a car, bob her hair, smoke in public, grant an interview, or voice an opinion on national affairs."[8] He also forbade her from riding in airplanes. But he didn't put any restrictions on her love of baseball.

And it was baseball, especially after she moved with her husband to Washington in 1921, that became her passion. Bucky Harris, the manager of the Washington Nationals, called her "the most rabid baseball fan I ever knew in the White House."

Grace Coolidge's enthusiasm peaked in 1924 when the Nationals clinched the American League pennant on the next-to-last day of the season, beating the Red Sox in Boston by a score of 4–2 to secure the first American League pennant for the franchise.

When the team returned home at the end of the season, the city responded with an exuberant celebration, starting at the train station. Police on horseback led the procession, followed by the United States Calvary Band. Convertibles carried the team members from Pennsylvania Avenue and then to the White House. Tens of thousands of loyal fans lined the noisy parade route. Horns honked and sirens shrieked. At the White House, a flag-draped viewing stand had been erected. President and Mrs. Coolidge waited there to greet the team.

President Coolidge offered words of congratulations and called Bucky Harris up to the platform to receive a silver loving cup. The director of the Board of Commissioners presented Harris with a plush blue box containing a golden key to the nation's capital.

Grace Coolidge clapped. The crowd cheered, then dispersed.

Game One of the 1924 World Series between the Giants and Nationals was set for Saturday, October 4, to be played at Griffith Stadium in Washington. John McGraw fielded one of the strongest teams he would manage in his career.[9] The roster included Frankie Frisch, Hack Wilson, George Kelly, Bill Terry, Billy Southworth, Ross Youngs—all future Hall of Famers—plus, Heine Groh and Irish Meusel. For the Nationals, Goose Goslin, Joe Judge, and Sam Rice had paced the offense throughout the season, but it was thirty-six-year-old Walter Johnson, in his eighteenth season with the team, who the fans loved the most.

A crowd of 35,760 filled the ballpark. Babe Ruth and Ty Cobb, putting aside their on-field animosities, took a taxi together to the game and watched from the press box while smoking cigars and trading baseball stories.[10]

President and Mrs. Coolidge had box seats, just behind the Nationals' dugout. Coolidge, only the second sitting president to attend a World Series game, was given the honor of throwing out the first ball. Coolidge's toss to umpire-in-chief Tommy Connelly was wild, but Connelly leapt and caught the ball barehanded. Then Coolidge sat down next to his wife and lit up a cigar.

In Game One, the Giants beat the Nationals and Walter Johnson in twelve innings, 4–3, to disappoint the home crowd. It was to be a tightly contested seven-game series with four of the games decided by one run. The Coolidges attended Game Seven as the Nationals beat John McGraw's New York Giants 4–3, thanks to a bad hop ground ball that let the winning run score in the bottom of the twelfth inning. Grace Coolidge, seated behind the Nationals' dugout, followed the action intently, pounding the knuckles of her right hand into the palm of her left hand during tense moments.

A year later, the Nationals were again American League champions and faced the Pittsburgh Pirates in the World Series. The seventh and deciding game of the 1925 series was played in Pittsburgh. At the White House, Grace Coolidge listened to Graham McNamee call the game for the radio audience. The game concluded in partial darkness and rain with the Pirates winning 9–7.

At the beginning of the 1926 season, baseball writers thought the chances were good that the Nationals could win a third straight AL title. Coming off back-to-back pennants and the World Series win in 1924, the 1926 Nationals—like their number-one fan, Grace Coolidge—had every reason to believe they would be contenders. Going into the season, they were the preseason favorite in the American League. The team had a solid starting lineup, featuring outfielders Sam Rice and Goose Goslin, first baseman Joe Judge, and player-manager Bucky Harris, the second baseman. They were not an old team. In fact, most of the starting lineup were in the prime years of their career. The average age of the starters was twenty-eight.

The pitching staff was anchored by a starting rotation of Walter Johnson, Stan Coveleski, and Dutch Ruether, a trio that had won fifty-eight games in 1925. In the off-season, the Nationals had traded Tom Zachery to the St. Louis Browns for veteran Joe Bush. Firpo Marberry and Alvin Crowder rounded out the pitching staff.

But following an early July game with the Yankees that ended after six innings in a 4–4 tie—stopped because of a heavy downpour that turned the field into a lake—the Nationals were thirteen games behind the first-place Yankees, residing in sixth place in the American League standings with an unimpressive record of 36–36.

So what went wrong? At midseason, Rice and Goslin were hitting an identical .347, and Judge was just a few points shy of .300. The Nationals could score runs. They would finish the season with the highest team batting average in the American League and the second most runs scored. The problem was the pitching staff. At midseason, Johnson and Coveleski were a combined 13–15, and Johnson would end the season with a record of 15–16. Joe Bush won only one game in his Senators career and was sold to the Pittsburgh Pirates on July 1.

For Grace Coolidge and other Nationals fans, 1926 was destined to be a long and disappointing season.

By midseason, the dominant team in the American League was the New York Yankees. A revitalized Babe Ruth, along with a strong supporting cast of younger players, had built a 10.5 game lead by the time they played the Athletics in Philadelphia on that rainy day when President Coolidge was in town to deliver his Sesquicentennial speech.

The first game of the doubleheader was played in a light rain. Lefty Grove dominated the Yankees, pitching a four-hitter and striking out twelve. The Athletics won 2–1. The losing pitcher was Bob Shawkey, who struck out ten. Both runs off Bob Shawkey were unearned, thanks to two errors by Mark Koenig.

Huggins benched the error-prone Koenig for the second game, commenting, "I have been losing too many ball games. If I have a better combination, I must find it out now."[11] Koenig had committed thirty-three errors by this point in the season and would lead the league in errors for the season with fifty-two. Koenig's errors were offset by his offensive production, but Koenig's errors would impact the outcome of two World Series games, one in 1926 and one in 1932.

The A's would win the second game, 6–3, to sweep the doubleheader. A little-known A's player named Jimmie Foxx made a brief appearance in this game as a pinch runner in the sixth inning. Foxx was just eighteen years old, the youngest player in the Major Leagues, and had been to bat just twenty-five times. He had not yet hit a home run. In the years to come, he would be one of the most feared power hitters in all of baseball.

By the end of the day, the 1926 baseball season had reached the halfway point.

Table 2. The American and National League standings after the July 5 doubleheaders

American League								National League							
Tm	*W*	*L*	W-L%	GB	RS	RA	*pythW-L%*	*Tm*	*W*	*L*	W-L%	GB	RS	RA	*pythW-L%*
NYY	50	26	.658	—	477	367	.618	CIN	46	31	.597	—	412	345	.580
PHA	42	35	.545	8.5	359	300	.581	PIT	38	32	.543	4.5	368	344	.531
CHW	43	36	.544	8.5	380	341	.549	STL	40	35	.533	5.0	376	357	.524
CLE	41	37	.526	10.0	380	337	.555	BRO	38	35	.521	6.0	333	332	.501
WSH	38	36	.514	11.0	370	374	.495	CHC	39	36	.520	6.0	382	365	.521
DET	38	39	.494	12.5	405	432	.471	NYG	37	39	.487	8.5	358	341	.522
SLB	33	44	.429	17.5	338	417	.405	PHI	30	44	.405	14.5	354	435	.407
BOS	21	53	.284	28.0	300	441		BSN	29	45	.392	15.5	328	392	.419

15

Judge Landis Takes Over

On September 9, 1926, Ban Johnson summoned representatives of the eight American League teams to a secret meeting in his Chicago offices. Seventeen days remained in the regular season. The New York Yankees had a seven-game lead in the pennant race, but Johnson didn't schedule the meeting to talk about the season or the upcoming World Series.

Johnson wanted to inform the owners about the allegations of game fixing that Dutch Leonard had brought to him four months earlier and discuss what the league should do about Ty Cobb and Tris Speaker—after the season, of course. On the day of the meeting, Cobb's Detroit Tigers were mired in sixth place with no realistic chance of finishing in the first division. Speaker's Cleveland Indians were in second place and still in contention, though they were seven games out of first and unlikely to overtake the first-place Yankees in the few weeks remaining.

Only a handful of people knew anything about the letters or Leonard's threat to go public with his accusations or the deal that had been struck in the spring between Johnson's office and Leonard. The American League attorney Henry Killilea and Detroit owner Frank Navin knew the details of the agreement. Bucky Harris, Edwin Eynon, and Harry Heilman had seen the letters, and of course, Cobb and Speaker were aware of the situation and how it had been handled.

Johnson assumed that rumors or knowledge about the letters would eventually leak out. Speaker had informed Smokey Joe Wood, now the varsity baseball coach at Yale University, that the letters were currently in the possession of the American League president. Johnson couldn't know for certain who else already knew or when the information would be discovered by others or the press—or when Judge Landis, Johnson's antagonist, might sniff out the particulars of the scandal. The meeting with the AL owners was proactive on Johnson's part, an attempt to get their blessing on how he had handled the situation and to stay in control of the situation.

Johnson laid out the facts and explained what he'd learned from the detectives who had investigated the betting habits of Cobb and Speaker. Johnson reported that Cobb wasn't much of a gambler, and that he had notable political connections. Earlier in his career, Cobb had socialized and sipped whiskey with President Warren Harding at the White House and played poker with him at a private club in Augusta, Georgia, but Harding was deceased, and that was several years ago, and the private poker games were not considered illegal or unethical.[1]

Speaker, however, bet and lost frequently, mostly on baseball and horseracing. None of these baseball men were shocked. Speaker's betting habits were well-known.

After Johnson presented his report, he allowed for discussion of the issues. Then Ernest Barnard, president of the Cleveland Indians, made a motion to send the matter, and all of Johnson's files and records, to baseball's commissioner, Judge Landis. The Yankees, represented by Jacob Ruppert, seconded the motion. The motion passed unanimously.

This was not what Johnson expected or wanted, but he had little choice but to comply. That same day, Johnson instructed Henry Killilea to send copies of the Wood and Cobb letters to Judge Landis. Other information or documentation in Johnson's files wasn't delivered to Landis until weeks later.

A few weeks after Johnson's meeting with the American League officials, he arranged to meet individually with Cobb and Speaker and inform them of the status of the situation. The two men were preparing to leave for a long-planned postseason hunting trip to Wyoming, where they intended to hunt bear and moose in the Grand Tetons.[2]

In addition to the news that Judge Landis was now involved and had copies of the Cobb and Wood letters, Johnson told each of the men that it had been decided that they should resign and retire from the game of baseball. Johnson told them that they could never again play in the American League, not because he had determined their guilt or because he believed Leonard's story, but because it would be best for the game and for their reputations. He told them they could submit their resignations after they got back from their hunting trip.

It was a gentleman's agreement, as Johnson explained it, and the real reason for the resignations—the alleged game-fixing scandal—would be covered up and kept from the public. That's what the hush-money deal with Leonard had been intended to do.

Cobb was frustrated and angry. He spoke with Johnson for two hours. A few months later, Johnson summed up Cobb's reaction, "He was heartbroken and maintained his innocence." Johnson didn't comment on how Speaker took the news, and Speaker never directly addressed how he reacted to Johnson's demands.

Whatever Johnson said, and however he explained his decision to force the two ballplayers into retirement, they appeared to accept it—at least at first. Both agreed to submit resignations when they returned from Wyoming.

Johnson thought he had the situation under control. He anticipated that Landis would accept his decision and the actions the American League intended to take.

But Johnson had badly misjudged how Landis would respond.

Ban Johnson and Judge Landis had a long-standing feud. The root causes of their conflict were both personal and professional.

Born three years apart, Johnson was thirty-four months older than Landis. The men were both native Midwesterners who loved baseball. Johnson had attended law school; Landis was a federal judge. Both were strong-willed and autocratic. But the similarities ended there.

At this point in his life, Johnson was not in good health. He was overweight and drank to excess. He had developed diabetes, the disease that would eventually take his life.

Landis was slightly built but stern, forceful, independently minded, vigorous, and charismatic. He had a distinctive look and demeanor. In Seymour and Seymour's *Baseball: the Golden Age*, Landis is described as a "scowling, white-haired, hawk-visaged curmudgeon who affected battered hats, used salty language, chewed tobacco, and poked listeners in the ribs with a stiff right finger."[3] In addition to a love of baseball, he had two hobbies: fishing and golf. Both offered him peace and solitude away from his office or courtroom.

In terms of professional baseball, Johnson had a three-decade head start over Landis. While Johnson was organizing and running the Western League, poaching players from other leagues, and building franchises to compete in a second major league with the established National League, Landis was busy in his courtroom, room 627 in the Chicago Federal Building.

The courtroom was two stories high, paneled in mahogany and decorated with marble and brass railings. As a judge, Landis had a reputation for theatrics, and this space became his stage.

A visitor would have noticed two paintings in the judge's courtroom. On a side wall was a mural of King John at Runnymede in 1215 signing the Magna Carta. On the opposite wall, a mural depicted Moses coming down from Mount Sinai with the Ten Commandments written on stone tablets.[4] One surmises the contrasting images of man's law and God's law appealed to the judge.

President Theodore Roosevelt had appointed Landis to the federal judiciary in 1905. His first significant case involved Standard Oil of New Jersey, the cartel headed by John D. Rockefeller, a powerful man reputed to be the wealthiest man in America. Standard Oil was accused of violating the Elkins Act (1903) and breaking the federal law regarding rebates on railroad freight lines.

The trial began on March 4, 1907, and lasted forty days. The jury returned a verdict in less than three hours, finding Standard Oil guilty on all 1903 counts. It was up to Landis to decide the penalty.

Landis wanted Rockefeller to testify in person as to the finances of the cartel. Rockefeller had not given testimony under oath since 1888 and had no desire to do so now. Landis subpoenaed Rockefeller who resisted being served by making his whereabouts unknown. When finally reached and informed of the subpoena, Rockefeller counteroffered: he would sit for a deposition instead of appearing in court.

Landis wouldn't compromise. He had issued the order and wanted Rockefeller to testify in person. In the end, Landis prevailed.

Rockefeller appeared in court on July 6, 1907. It was a brutally hot day in Chicago, and spectators filled the courtroom. Electric fans swirled overhead but did little to cool the room.

Landis questioned Rockefeller from the bench. Despite all the fanfare and build up, there was little drama in the testimony. Landis asked nineteen questions. Rockefeller asserted that, despite retaining the title of president, he had not been directly involved in the business for the past decade and didn't know even the most basic facts about the company's finances.

Four weeks passed as Landis decided how much Standard Oil would have to pay in fines. Finally, on August 3, he delivered his opinion in a fifty-five-minute monologue from the bench.

The verdict: Standard Oil was to be fined $29 million—the maximum allowed under the law.

The news was delivered to Rockefeller as he was playing a round of golf. His reaction was succinct and prescient: "Judge Landis will be dead a long time before this fine is paid."[5]

Rockefeller was right. Less than a year later, the United States Appeals Court for the Seventh Circuit overturned the verdict. After the Supreme Court declined to take the case, a new trial was ordered, and Standard Oil was acquitted.

As a judge in Chicago in the early part of the twentieth century, Landis didn't have to look too hard to find evidence of corruption. It was all around him.

Before Johnny Torrio and Al Capone, there was Diamond Jim Colosimo, a crime boss who controlled prostitution and gambling in Chicago in the first two decades of the twentieth century. After Colosimo's murder in the early days of Prohibition, Torrio and then Capone expanded the business to include bootlegging.[6]

A few years after the Standard Oil case, Landis turned his attention to organized crime in Chicago. He took a particular interest in Mont Tennes, the gambling czar of Chicago in the early twentieth century.

Tennes started as a bookie, but soon he was involved in both legal and illegal businesses that catered to gamblers. He developed a system for communicating horse racing information to bookmakers. He owned and operated pool halls and saloons. He received kickbacks from Chicago's downtown hotels that allowed gambling on their premises. In return, Tennes provided protection from police interference in their businesses.[7]

When Landis began his investigation, Tennes hired Clarence Darrow as his attorney. Darrow had been a labor lawyer but was now taking criminal cases. Darrow's advice to Tennes: invoke the Fifth Amendment whenever Landis questions you under oath. The advice seemed to work. Tennes was never indicted or convicted of a crime.

Landis had been a federal judge for fourteen years when a strongly favored Chicago White Sox team took on the Cincinnati Reds in the 1919 World Series. Even before the series commenced, however, rumors circulated that the series had been fixed by gamblers. After the Reds won the best-of-nine series, five games to three, there was more speculation.

As a Chicagoan and a devoted baseball fan, Landis paid close attention to the games and the stories about potential corruption. A year later, speculation arose that a game between the Cubs and Phillies might also have been fixed. A grand jury was created in Chicago to investigate baseball gambling.

A Philadelphia gambler named Billy Maharg came forward and gave an interview to a reporter for the *Philadelphia North American* in which he implicated players and gamblers who colluded to fix the 1919 series. He named Abe Attell, a former boxing champion, and Sleepy Bill Burns, a former Major League player, as two of the conspirators. As the story unfolded, it became apparent that there were at least two separate plots to fix the series and that White Sox players had been discussing a plan to fix the World Series with several gamblers, including Sport Sullivan, a well-known Boston gambler who often bet on baseball games.

The possibility that the games might be fixed was also known to Mont Tennes, who warned both Charles Weegham, the owner of the Cubs, and Charles Comiskey, owner of the White Sox. Neither of the owners took the threat seriously.

In October 1920, eight members of the Chicago White Sox and five gamblers were indicted and charged with various counts of conspiracy to defraud. Four members of the White Sox were questioned by the grand jury, admitted their role in the scheme, and signed confessions.

Arnold Rothstein, rumored to be the individual who funded the scheme, testified in front of the grand jury and acknowledged that he had been approached to finance the fixing of the series, but he had declined to participate in the plot. Rothstein was not charged.[8]

At the time, baseball governance was in the hands of a three-person National Commission. The members of the commission were Ban Johnson, president of the American League; John Heydler, president of the National League; and Garry Herrmann, owner of the Cincinnati Reds. Baseball's owners from both leagues were worried that fans would turn away from the game, if, indeed, it was proven that games were fixed. Ensuring the fair competitiveness of the games and the sport was essential to maintaining the value of their investments in their franchises.

Gambling on baseball games was nothing new. But fixing games—determining outcomes before the contests were played—could not be tolerated.

The owners had to act. They wanted a commissioner—a single czar—to oversee the game.

They waited until after the 1920 World Series—won by the Cleveland Indians—before hiring the man they wanted. That individual was Kenesaw Mountain Landis.

On November 12, 1920, Judge Landis signed a seven-year contract to become the first commissioner of Major League Baseball. He was given a wide range of powers and allowed to keep his position as a federal judge while overseeing baseball.

The trial of the eight members of the White Sox commenced eight months later, in the summer of 1921. All eight players pleaded not guilty. Conveniently for the defense, the four signed confessions had been lost or stolen. The case went to the jury on August 2, and after a brief time in the jury room, the jurors returned with their verdict.

The players and two gamblers were acquitted.[9] The verdict was loudly applauded by members of the public who attended the trial. A noisy party followed at a nearby Italian restaurant as jurors and ballplayers ate and drank and rejoiced and celebrated together.[10]

Judge Landis was not pleased with the jury's decision—or the public's acceptance of the verdict. Landis had been on the job for a short time, but he abhorred gambling and believed he had been hired to clean up the sport. He intended to do so.

Landis issued a fierce and definitive statement that left no doubt about how he intended to rule when game fixing was the issue:

> Regardless of the verdict of juries, no player that throws a game, no player that entertains proposals or promises to throw a game, no player that sits in a conference with a bunch of crooked gamblers where the ways and means of throwing games are discussed, and does not promptly tell his club about it, will ever play professional baseball.[11]

The Black Sox scandal and Landis's decision to ban the players involved shook up the world of baseball.

Landis's authority was to be tested again, just a few months after the Black Sox trial and acquittals, at the conclusion of the 1921 World Series, which featured John McGraw's Giants against Miller Huggins's Yankees. The Giants won five games to three. It was the last time the World Series had a best-of-nine format. Starting in 1922, the World Series would go to a best-of-seven format.

When the season ended, Babe Ruth and a few of his teammates planned to embark on a lucrative barnstorming tour.[12] Since 1911, though, players from the two teams that competed in the World Series opponents had been barred from postseason barnstorming. It was a clear rule but loosely applied or enforced. After an earlier barnstorming tour, Ruth had been fined one hundred dollars, a pittance considering the revenue he was able to generate from the tour.

In 1921 Ruth batted .378; broke his own home-run record, with fifty-nine; and drove in 177 runs. Ruth was the biggest star in the game and knew he would draw large, paying crowds wherever his team played. His salary was $20,000 in 1921, but he would earn more in ten weeks of barnstorming than he earned in a full season of baseball. His teammate and fellow barnstormer, Bob Meusel, had earned just $4,000 during that season; the money he earned through postseason barnstorming with Ruth would double his income for the year.

The Yankees gave Ruth permission to go on the tour, but Ed Barrow advised Ruth that he contact and get approval from Judge Landis before embarking on the tour. Ruth scoffed at this and avoided contacting Landis until the last minute. When he did communicate with the judge, Landis was not pleased and told Ruth he could not go—that he would be breaking a rule that he, Landis, intended to enforce. If Ruth did the tour anyway, he would face consequences.

Ruth's reaction: "That old man can jump in a lake."

Landis's reaction: "Who the hell does that big ape think he is?"

Ruth went on the tour. When he returned, Landis meted out the punishment: forfeiture of Ruth's World Series money ($3,300) and a sixty-day suspension without pay. Meusel received the same penalty.

Whether or not Ruth learned anything from this lesson, Landis had made it clear that he was in charge and unafraid of disciplining even the game's biggest attraction.

Then there was the strange case of Shuffling Phil Douglas, a pitcher with an excellent fastball, an even better spitball, and a serious drinking problem. He was well-liked by his teammates, though he had a reputation for having poor judgment and not always understanding the consequences of his actions. In 1922 he was the best pitcher on John McGraw's Giants pitching staff, but he clashed constantly with McGraw. In early August, the Giants were in a tight pennant race with the St. Louis Cardinals. On August 7, the Giants had a half-game lead over the Cardinals. That day, Douglas—likely after a bout of drinking—wrote a letter to his friend Les Mann, an outfielder with the Cardinals. Douglas proposed that he would "go down to a fishing camp" for the rest of the summer and not pitch again for the Giants that season—if someone on the Cardinals would pay him off. The letter didn't specify the amount of money that Douglas wanted, but he gave Mann detailed instructions on how to get the money to him. Les Mann—aware that Judge Landis would ban for life any player who even knew about a plan to interfere with honest competition—immediately took the letter to his manager, Branch Rickey. Rickey informed Landis and McGraw, who then confronted Douglas in a Pittsburgh hotel room. Douglas admitted writing the letter. McGraw placed him on the ineligible list, which effectively banned him forever from professional baseball. Landis concurred. Douglas seemed stunned by the decision. When he realized his career had just abruptly ended, he burst into tears.[13]

Two years later, Landis dealt with the somewhat less complicated but still bizarre story of Jimmy O'Connell and Cozy Dolan. Dolan, a coach with the New York Giants, induced O'Connell, a young infielder, to offer a $500 bribe to Heinie Sand, the Philadelphia Phillies shortstop, to not play his hardest in a game between the two teams at the end of the season. Sand rejected the bribe and reported the attempt to his manager, Art Fletcher. The accusation quickly reached Judge Landis. O'Connell claimed that other players—Ross Youngs, Frankie Frisch, George Kelly—were aware of the bribe offer. Under questioning from Landis, O'Connell admitted that he'd offered the bribe at the suggestion of Dolan. The three players that O'Connell claimed had talked to him about the bribe all denied any conversation with O'Connell.[14]

Landis decided quickly: Dolan and O'Connell were banned for life. No punishment was given to Youngs, Frisch, or Kelly.

The lifetime bans issued in the Douglas and O'Connell/Dolan cases were consistent with the application of rules that Landis had applied in the Black Sox case.

But one person was dissatisfied with Landis's ruling: American League president Ban Johnson. He was furious that he wasn't consulted about the O'Connell bribe attempt and demanded that the Giants be barred from the World Series. Johnson argued that the second-place Brooklyn Robins should represent the National League instead.

When Landis ignored Johnson's complaint, Johnson announced he was boycotting the World Series and would not attend any of the games. It would be the first time in American League history that Johnson had missed a World Series game.

Now, in the fall of 1926, Judge Landis turned his attention to Dutch Leonard and his allegations about a game played seven years earlier.

Landis read the Cobb and Wood letters. A few things stood out. Gambling had occurred, and three individuals—Leonard, Wood, and presumably Speaker—had collected on their bets. Speaker's name, however, did not appear in either of the letters. As for Cobb, he may have intended to bet on the game, but it did not seem that his funds had been used to place a bet.

The next thing for Landis to do, after the 1926 World Series concluded, was to speak directly to Dutch Leonard.

Landis intended to ask Leonard to come to Chicago to be interviewed.

16

The Golden Age of Sports

The biggest news story of 1926—even bigger than the tale of Aimee McPherson's disappearance and return—was the destructive hurricane that reached landfall in southern Florida in the early morning of September 18, imperiling the lives and property of more than a hundred thousand people. The storm tore the roofs off buildings, uprooted trees, destroyed cars, smashed boats and yachts, scattered lumber and building materials, and spread debris across its path. Massive flooding followed. Nearly four hundred people lost their lives; more than six thousand were injured. Fifty thousand people were left homeless. Property damage was estimated to be $105 million.[1]

For investors and property owners—many of whom had overpaid for their properties—the storm was a financial disaster. The boom times in Florida land speculation had come to an end in the spring and summer of 1926. The September hurricane simply accelerated the financial crisis.

Some savvy—or lucky—investors, like Miller Huggins, had sold their holdings earlier in the year. When the storm hit, Yankee owner Jacob Ruppert still owned property in St. Petersburg through the Ruppert Beach Development Company. How much money Ruppert may have lost on his investment isn't known.[2]

In 1925 John McGraw had also invested on the west coast of Florida. He had partnered with several other investors to form the McGraw-Pennant Park Corporation. Several Giants players went in on the deal: Jack Bentley, Irish Meusel, Freddie Lindstrom. The plan was to sell lots and build a community of homes, most of which faced the water. Residents would have access to a yacht club. The streets would be named after McGraw's favorite Giants players—Matthewson Park, Bresnahan Boulevard—and the development would be known as Pennant Park.[3] McGraw intended to build a retirement home for himself and his wife, Blanche, in the development. The corporation took out a mortgage of $307,431 to buy the land.[4]

After the deflation of land values in 1926 and the September hurricane, the value of McGraw's property significantly declined. The holders of the mortgage foreclosed on the property. McGraw's partially constructed retirement home was sold at a loss.[5]

Americans were increasingly transfixed in the 1920s by the achievements of athletes and the drama of athletic competition. The historian William Leuchtenburg joined other observers when he summed up the country's fascination with sports by declaring, in one clear and distinct observation, "It was the Golden Age of sports."[6]

The decade brought increased media attention to competitions and athletes. Newspaper articles reported the scores, and reporters created heroes out of their accomplishments. Radio broadcasts brought the excitement and drama of highly anticipated events directly into the homes of fans. Americans had more disposable cash and more leisure time. They bought radios to listen to sporting events and tickets to attend games and matches. Attendance soared, especially at featured events like heavyweight boxing matches, prestigious horse races, or World Series games. For those who were inclined to gamble—and many in the 1920s were willing to risk a few dollars on wagers to win big bets—there was ample opportunity to bet.

In addition to frequenting speakeasies and jazz clubs and motion picture theaters, men and women spent their money and leisure time on sports like golf and tennis. Fan bases for teams enlarged.

Boxing and horse racing had always been popular, in part because they offered opportunities for gamblers, large and small, to bet on the outcomes, but baseball remained the most popular team sport. Fans followed their favorite teams and the pennant races through the season and paid rapt attention to the year's World Series contests.

A new team sport—college football—was attracting thousands of fans. On one glorious afternoon in October, in the first quarter of a game between the University of Illinois and the University of Michigan, the college football star Red Grange scored four touchdowns in twelve minutes. In the second half of the game, he rushed for another touchdown, threw a touchdown pass, and intercepted two passes.[7]

Sportswriters transformed Grange into a celebrity. The Chicago sportswriter Warren Brown nicknamed Grange "the Galloping Ghost." Others called him "the Wheaton Ice Man."[8]

In an unprecedented move, Grange left college after this junior year to capitalize on his fame and pursue the riches offered by a professional career. The National Football League was in its infancy, but Grange negotiated a contract that paid him handsomely to participate in a series of exhibition games featuring the Chicago Bears, owned by George Halas. In the last two months of 1925, Grange earned $250,000 in appearance fees for participating in these games—more than the total annual salary of all the players on the roster of the New York Yankees, including Babe Ruth.[9]

In December, Grange and Halas were invited to the White House to meet President Calvin Coolidge. It's unclear how much the president knew, or cared, about the sport of football. When told that Halas and Grange were with the Bears, Coolidge quipped "Young men, I'm glad to know you. I always like animal acts."

In 1926 the amateur golfer Bobby Jones won both the British Open and U.S. Open in thrilling fashion, the first golfer to win those two events in the same year. The French dominated men's tennis. Rene Lacosta ended Bill Tilden's six-year reign as U.S. Open Tennis champion. The U.S. Open women's champ was Molla Bjurstedt Mallory, a Norwegian. A horse named Bubbling Over won the Kentucky Derby.

But the most astounding individual accomplishment of the summer belonged to Gertrude Ederle, a swimmer who had already earned accolades for her competitive achievements as an amateur in the 1924 Summer Olympics. Ederle was a shy nineteen-year-old when she turned professional after the Olympics and set her sights on achieving something no woman had ever done.

Ederle wanted to become the first woman to swim across the English Channel. Her father promised to buy her a red Buick Roadster if she achieved her goal.

On August 6, Ederle accomplished what others had told her was impossible. She completed a swim from Cape Gris-Nez in France to Kingsdown beach in England in fourteen hours and thirty-one minutes, becoming the first woman to swim across the English Channel. A boat carrying Ederle's father, sister, coach, and the journalist Julia Harpman accompanied her across the cold and choppy seas.[10] More than halfway to her goal as the currents swelled and the swim became more difficult, her coach urged her to abort the attempt. Ederle had a two-word response: "What for?"[11]

Only five men had accomplished the feat. Most remarkable was Ederle's time: two hours faster than any of the men who had successfully swum across the channel.

Ederle had swum her way into history and was hailed as a conquering hero. Crowds in Europe celebrated her accomplishment. In Stuttgart, Germany, thirty thousand people turned out to cheer her.[12]

On Friday, August 24, she was given a ticker-tape parade through New York City, the largest the city had ever seen. German American groups honored her, and New York Yankees owner Jacob Ruppert hailed her accomplishment as "a great American triumph."[13]

By late August, the Negro Leagues' regular season was just a few weeks from completion, and anticipation was building for the playing of what was billed as the 1926 Colored World Series, a best-of-nine series that would be played in various ballparks.

The goal of both the Negro National League (NNL) and the Eastern Colored League (ECL) had been to have all sixteen teams in the two leagues play a full schedule of at least fifty games. This was ambitious, and as it turned out, unrealistic. In the NNL, neither the Dayton Marcos nor the Cleveland Elites managed to play fifty games, and both teams dropped out of the league after the first half season with losing records. In the ECL, two teams failed to complete the season. The Newark Stars disbanded after playing just eleven games, winning only once. The Brooklyn Royal Giants concentrated on playing semipro teams and barnstorming, managing to complete just twenty-seven games in league play. Only two teams—the Bacharach Giants and the Hilldale Darby Daisies—played fifty games.

The first half winner in the NNL was the Kansas City Monarchs. The second half was still being contested, but the Chicago American Giants appeared to be the likely winners. A playoff between the Monarchs and American Giants would be needed to determine the league's representative in the World Series to take on the Bacharach Giants, the winners of the ECL.

Meanwhile, in the Black Minor Leagues, a star was emerging. He wouldn't appear in a Negro League game until the 1927 season, but admirers and sportswriters had already acknowledged his talent and, just as importantly, his charisma and fan appeal. The player's name, of course, was Satchel Paige. He had become famous enough in one short season that fans and journalists referred to him simply by his first name.[14]

In an early contest with the Chattanooga Black Lookouts, Satchel was the winning pitcher in a game against the Atlanta Black Crackers. In his next game, he struck out nine batters in six innings. In one inning, after allowing two baserunners, he struck out the next three batters on nine pitches.[15] He pitched with confidence and control. He didn't have a variety of pitches yet. His fastball alone was good enough to dominate Southern League hitters.

Satchel was the future of Black baseball. He would pitch for more than two decades in the Negro Leagues before the white Major Leagues tore down the wall of baseball apartheid. In the off-season, Satchel barnstormed and played against the best white Major Leaguers. Game by game, year by year, his reputation grew.

In late September, the sporting event of the summer was held in Philadelphia: a heavyweight championship fight between the reigning champion, Jack Dempsey, and his challenger, Gene Tunney. The fight was scheduled for September 23, just five days after the devastating Florida hurricane.

Dempsey had held the title for seven years, winning it on July 4, 1919, when he won by TKO over Jess Willard in the third round.[16] His last title defense had been on September 14, 1923, against the Argentinian fighter Luis Angel Firpo, a two-round bout at the Polo Grounds in New York City. In the action-packed first round of that fight, Dempsey floored Firpo seven times but couldn't knock him out. Before the round ended, Firpo was able to get off the canvas and knock Dempsey backward and out of the ring. The champion went sprawling through the ropes, where he landed on top of a reporter's typewriter. Dempsey climbed back into the ring and won the fight with a knockout in the second round.[17]

Since that dramatic contest—captured in a famous painting by American artist George Bellows—Dempsey had been content to earn a living through boxing exhibitions, product endorsements, and film work in Hollywood, where he met his wife, Ida Estelle Taylor, a stage and screen actress.[18]

Despite three years of inactivity in the ring, Dempsey was the heavy betting favorite. He was a proven quantity, nicknamed the Manassa Mauler.

Tunney was less well-known, an ex-Marine with an intellectual side. He liked to quote Shakespeare and relaxed by reading classic works of literature.[19] Physically, the two men were similar in height, weight, and reach, but they employed contrasting styles. Dempsey was the hard-hitting brawler, with a devastating left hook; Tunney was a strategist, quick on his feet, and adept with a jab.

The prospect of the first heavyweight title bout in three years excited boxing fans and celebrities. A poll was published in which Major League Baseball figures—Cobb, McGraw, Lazzeri, Gehrig, Wilbert Robinson—were asked to predict the outcome of the fight.[20] All predicted that Dempsey would win. Babe Ruth was asked for his opinion, but he declined to speculate on the outcome.

In the days prior to the fight, fans arrived on special trains from East Coast cities—New York, Baltimore, Washington—as well as from Chicago and California.[21] An estimated 130,000 individuals were expected to attend the fight, the largest crowd ever assembled to see a sporting event. A radio broadcast of the fight would reach another ten million households. Graham McNamee would call the fight for the radio audience.

The crowd included dozens of sportswriters; six state governors; three members of President Coolidge's cabinet; Mayor Jimmy Walker of New York City; Mayor W. Freeland Kendrick of Philadelphia; publishers Conde Nast and William Randolph Hearst; celebrities Tom Mix, Charlie Chaplin, and Norma Talmadge; baseball icons John McGraw, Wilbert Robinson, Jacob Ruppert, Babe Ruth; and members of the Philadelphia Phillies and Cincinnati Reds who had played to a 6–6 tie that afternoon in a fifteen inning game at the Baker Bowl.[22] Vice President Dawes was also in attendance. It was rumored that President Coolidge planned to listen to the fight on the radio in the White House.

The referee for the bout was Tommy Reilly. An hour before the boxers were due to meet in the ring, Reilly visited Tunney in his dressing room to go over the rules. Reilly found Tunney asleep on a training table, napping before the fight. Reilly explained the rules and cautioned Tunney, "I want you to know this isn't going to be a pink tea. This fight is going to be an honest one, and I don't want any complaints or alibis from the loser."[23]

Perhaps Reilly was aware that Abe Attell, a friend of Tunney's, had been observed at Tunney's training camp and visited the challenger in his dressing room prior to the fight. Attell, a former featherweight boxing champion, was better known as a business associate of Arnold Rothstein.[24] It had been alleged that Rothstein and Attell, with others, had managed to fix the 1919 World Series.

Rothstein, not so coincidentally, was also in Philadelphia and had a ringside seat for the night's bout. He liked to place bets on prize fights, especially when he had a good idea as to who was going to win. For this fight, Rothstein had wagered $125,000 at 4–1 odds that the underdog, Tunney, would be the winner.

The boxers entered the ring a little before 10:00 p.m. After months of anticipation, the fight commenced. It had begun to rain, a light drizzle at first, then a steadier downpour. Many expected a quick end to the fight, that Dempsey would win by a knockout of Tunney in an early round, but that isn't what happened. Tunney established himself as the aggressor midway through the first round, landing a solid right hand to Dempsey's head. Tunney dominated the fight, winning all ten rounds on the scorecards of both judges.[25] Neither fighter scored a knockdown. When the bell sounded to end the fight, Dempsey put his arm around Tunney and said, "Great fight, Gene. You won."[26]

The day after Gene Tunney defeated Jack Dempsey for the heavyweight title, Tunney talked to reporters.

Tunney appeared in a blue serge suit, wearing a light brown felt hat. His lips were noticeably swollen, and there was a bandage over one eye, but otherwise, he looked perfectly healthy. Without a trace of irony or condescension, he asked the assembled members of the press: "How is Jack this morning?"

Then Tunney excused himself. He had a lunch date with James Cox, the former governor of Ohio.[27]

Dempsey spent the day in a darkened room. His left eye was swollen shut. Six stitches were required to close the cut above that eye. His face was battered. He had taken a beating. There was no question who had won the fight.

When Estelle Taylor saw her husband, she burst into tears. She asked him what had happened. Dempsey replied, "Honey, I forgot to duck."[28]

It was a very lucrative event for the two fighters and their entourages. Dempsey earned $717,000. Tunney would receive a check for $200,000.

The other big winner was Arnold Rothstein, who didn't have to throw a punch or absorb any blows. Rothstein collected $500,000 for picking the underdog to win the fight.

The end of the fight in Philadelphia was not the end of the story.

Dempsey and Tunney would fight again. Tunney agreed to fight the winner of a bout between Dempsey and Jack Sharkey. Dempsey and Sharkey fought on July 21, 1927. It was a brutal match, with Sharkey stalking and aggressively attacking Dempsey while the former champion battled toe-to-toe with the challenger. Throughout the fight, Sharkey complained that Dempsey was hitting him with low blows.

To many observers, Sharkey was winning the fight through the first six rounds, but in the seventh round, Sharkey dropped his hands and turned to the referee to object, once more, about the low blows. That temporary loss of focus cost Sharkey the fight. Dempsey hit Sharkey with a vicious left hook and knocked him out.[29]

Asked later why he hit Sharkey when his opponent's head was turned and his hands were at his side, Dempsey replied, "What was I supposed to do? Write him a letter?"[30]

Dempsey's victory over Sharkey earned him a rematch with Tunney. The second meeting of Dempsey and Tunney—at Soldier Field in Chicago on September 22, 1927—is well-known to even casual boxing fans as "the long count" fight, one of the most controversial fights in the history of the sport. Once again, Tunney was the winner.

One wonders what Judge Kenesaw Mountain Landis must have thought about the heavyweight title fight in Philadelphia in late September of 1926. There's no indication that he attended the bout. That week, he was in his office in downtown Chicago, and he had a lot on his mind.

Two weeks before the fight, he had received the news about the alleged game-fixing scandal involving Speaker and Cobb. He planned to talk to Dutch Leonard in a few weeks, after the World Series, to hear his side of the story. He knew something about crooked deals and had more experience than anyone in getting to the truth about sporting events that might have been fixed.

As Landis read the news reports of the fight in Philadelphia, he might have been curious about the presence of Arnold Rothstein and Abe Attell at the fight, and the fact that Attell had visited Tunney's training camp just a week or so before the fight, and the fact that Rothstein had personal connections to Maxie "Boo Boo" Hoff, a sinister crime figure in Philadelphia, where the fight had been held.

Landis might have wondered what gave Rothstein so much confidence that Tunney, a big underdog, would win the fight against a boxer with the power and background of Dempsey.

In the previous year, F. Scott Fitzgerald had published a book titled *The Great Gatsby*, and in the book, a character named Meyer Wolfsheim was alleged to have fixed the 1919 World Series. Only a few sentences in the novel have to do with the Black Sox scandal, but the Wolfsheim character was clearly based on Arnold Rothstein. When told that Wolfsheim had fixed the World Series, the narrator, Nick Carraway, wondered how he could have gotten away with that—to fix a series of games played by teams of athletes.

It was so much easier to fix a horse race or, say, a boxing match, where one or two conspirators could influence the result. To fix a baseball game, several players would have to be involved and acting in concert.

We don't know if Landis was suspicious of Rothstein and his involvement in the heavyweight fight or his bet on Tunney. We know Landis hated gambling, but potentially crooked boxing matches weren't an issue for Landis to deal with.

Landis was focused on a baseball game that had been played in 1919 between the Tigers and the Indians, just a week before the start of that year's tainted World Series—and Landis needed to determine whether that regular-season game might have had a fixed outcome.

17

Final Days

In Philadelphia, less than eighteen hours after Gene Tunney battered Jack Dempsey through ten brutal rounds to win the heavyweight title, the Cincinnati Reds, still embracing faint hopes that they might win the National League pennant, were back at the Baker Bowl for a Friday doubleheader with the last-place Phillies. The field was wet, but the rains of the previous evening had subsided.

The good weather failed to revive the fortunes of the Reds. Red Lucas lasted less than two innings in the first game as the Phillies triumphed 9–2. In the second game, Dolf Luque struggled but pitched well enough to help the Reds break their six-game losing streak. The Reds won 8–4, sparked by catcher Bubbles Hargrave's three-run homer. Wally Pipp contributed three of the twelve hits registered by the Reds.

It made no difference. The St. Louis Cardinals clinched the National League pennant that day at the Polo Grounds in New York, beating the Giants 6–4. Cardinals starter Flint Rhem gave up six hits and a three-run homer to Bill Terry in the bottom of the first inning, but the Cardinals bounced back with five runs of their own in the top of the second. Les Bell led off with a double. Then Bob O'Farrell singled, and Tommy Thevenow doubled. George Toporcer followed with another double to tie the score at 3–3.

Billy Southworth, traded away by McGraw and the Giants in midseason, came to the plate. From the bench, Hornsby shouted, "Have your cut, Bill. Have your cut."[1] On the next pitch, Southworth homered deep to right field. It was a bit of sweet revenge. Later Southworth reflected on his pennant-winning hit. "That was the timeliest home run I ever hit, and to have hit it against the Giants, with McGraw snarling his defiance from the bench, made it double thrilling and satisfying."[2]

The Cardinals had battled back from a slow beginning to the season, peaking in August and September. In early August, they won six in a row on the road against Brooklyn. Sherdel won two of the games; Alexander pitched a four-hit shutout to win another. Back home after the road trip, the Cardinals won ten out of eleven, with Alexander winning three of the games.

As of September 2, the Cardinals had a slender one-game lead over the Pirates and Reds but faced the formidable task of playing their last twenty-four games on the road. To complicate matters, Hornsby had an increasingly acrimonious conflict with Branch Rickey and Cardinals owner Sam Breadon. Rickey and Breadon wanted to squeeze in a couple of exhibition games during the September road trip—to generate income and publicity. Hornsby was adamantly opposed to extra games during a tight pennant race. After a difficult loss to the Pirates, Hornsby confronted Breadon, shouting obscenities at the owner, telling him, "Now get the hell out of my clubhouse."[3]

To Hornsby's credit, he kept his team focused and competitive. In a key series in late September against the Phillies—six games in four days—the Cardinals won five of the games to hold on to their slender lead.

Six days later, Southworth's home run clinched the pennant for the Cardinals.

As the Cardinals celebrated, the Reds returned to their losing ways on the road in Philadelphia, playing a meaningless game and dropping a 5–1 decision to the Phillies. The Reds would finish three games out of first in the National League race. For this final game of the regular season, the stands were virtually empty—a strange sight after the enormous crowd that had attended the heavyweight fight just two days earlier. The official home attendance figure for the last Phillies game of the 1926 season was one thousand, the third-smallest crowd of the year at the Baker Bowl.[4]

For the Reds, what had once been a promising season was now over.

The Reds had spent seventy-two straight days in first place, from May 14 to July 25. Their lead was never more than five games, but they were the leaders in the National League for more than half the season.

Going into September and facing a long road trip, the Reds were half a game out of first place. They briefly regained the lead on September 14, during an eight-game winning streak, but when the winning streak ended, the Reds lost six games in a row, during which the Reds were shut out twice and lost three games by one run.

On paper—and statistically speaking—the Reds had a remarkably good season. Four players—Edd Roush, Bubbles Hargrave, Curt Walker, and

Cuckoo Christianson—hit over .300, and Wally Pipp wasn't far behind at .291. Eppa Rixey and Dolf Luque were standout starting pitchers. They had a good balance between hitting and pitching, finishing first in team batting average, third in runs scored, and second in team earned run average. If there was a statistical weakness, it was in the category of home runs. The Reds hit thirty-five home runs, second worst in the league. Only the weak-hitting Boston Braves had fewer, hitting just sixteen homers all season.

At the end of the season, though, the Reds offense sputtered and came to a stop. In their last ten games with pennant hopes still alive, the Reds averaged less than three runs a game.

For Grace Coolidge and fans of the Washington Nationals, it had been a frustrating and difficult American League season. With the roster intact after back-to-back American League championship seasons, expectations were high, and the team got off to a good start. A month into the season, the Yankees had taken over first place, posting a record of 18–9, but the Nationals were just a game behind with a record of 19–12.

Four weeks later, things had changed dramatically. The Nationals had slumped, winning just 7 of 20 games, and by June 10, the Nationals were in fifth place, 11.5 games behind the first-place Yankees. For most of the summer, the Nationals played .500 ball, never able to put together a winning streak that would propel them back into contention.

Grace Coolidge followed the progress of the team throughout the season, listening to games on radio station WRC, either in the White House or on the presidential yacht, *Mayflower*, as it cruised the Potomac. A late-season surge allowed the Nationals to close the gap somewhat and move up from fifth to fourth, but they were never serious contenders.

So what went wrong with the Nationals season? The Nationals finished first in the American League in batting average, posting a hefty .292 team average, and they were second to the Yankees in runs scored, 847–802. Goose Goslin, with 17 home runs, 108 RBIs, and a batting average of .354, was among the league leaders in every offensive category. Sam Rice led the league in hits. Four other regulars—Joe Judge, Buddy Myer, Earl McNeely, and Muddy Ruel—hit .291 or better.

The pitching staff's composite earned run average rose from 3.67 in 1925 to 4.34 in 1926, just slightly better than the earned run averages of the league's three worst teams: the Browns, the Red Sox, and the Tigers. The key starters for the Nationals were beginning to show their age. Walter Johnson, now thirty-eight years old and nearing the end of his playing career, went from a 20–7 record in 1925 to 15–16 in 1926. Stan Coveleski, just sixteen months younger than Johnson, posted a record of 20–5 in 1925 and led the league in ERA at 2.84. In 1926 Coveleski was a less stellar 14–11.

Once the season ended for the Nationals, manager Bucky Harris turned his attention to personal matters. On October 1, Harris married Mary Elizabeth Sutherland, a Washington socialite and the daughter of former West Virginia senator Howard Sutherland. The bride was described in the *New York Times* as a woman who was "widely known as a sportswoman and talented musician."[5] The wedding was attended by the owner of the Nationals, Clark Griffith; pitcher Walter Johnson; and by President and Mrs. Coolidge; as well as Secretary of State Frank Kellogg and Secretary of War Dwight Davis.

Before embarking on a six-week honeymoon in Europe, Bucky Harris and his wife planned to spend the first two days of their married life at Yankee Stadium, watching Games One and Two of the 1926 World Series.

The Yankees dominated the American League and had been in first place continuously since May 14, with a lead as large as ten games, but entering September they were still being chased by Tris Speaker's Cleveland Indians. The lead had shrunk to six games. Like the Cardinals and Reds in the National League, the Yankees faced a difficult final stretch of games: twenty games on the road in September, just six games at home.

At the start of their longest road trip of the season, the Yankees bats went cold, and they lost a doubleheader to Ty Cobb's Tigers. In the first game of the series on September 13, Urban Shocker, going for his twentieth win, lost 4–3. Earl Whitehill earned the win with relief help from Hooks Dauss. The second game featured Sam Gibson of the Tigers holding the Yankees to three hits and beating Waite Hoyt 4–1. Cobb didn't play in either of the games. Ruth contributed just two singles in seven at bats.

The Yankees moved on to face second-place Cleveland in a crucial six-game series. The Yankees came from behind with a seventh-inning rally to take the first game of the series 6–4. Bob Shawkey got the win with 4.1 innings of excellent relief. Earle Combs had four hits. Bob Meusel knocked in three runs. The Yankees lead was back to a more comfortable 6.5 games, but then the Indians won the next four games: 2–1, 5–0, 5–1, and 3–1. The Yankees scored just three runs in thirty-six innings. Ruth collected two singles and four walks in sixteen plate appearances but was a nonfactor.

Suddenly, the Yankees couldn't score, and the Indians were just 2.5 games out of first place. Babe Ruth hadn't gotten an extra base hit in over a week. The final game of the series was played on Sunday, September 19, and fortunately for the Yankees, the offense woke up. In the seventh inning, Ruth smashed a two-run homer, his forty-third of the season, but the main offense was provided by Lou Gehrig, who hammered a homer of his own as well as three doubles. The lead was back to 3.5 games. The Yankees had eight games left to play, the Indians had seven.

Neither team finished strong. Both teams were exhausted by the stress and rigors of the closing weeks of the season. The Yankees won three of their final eight games against the White Sox and Browns. The Indians won three of their final seven, dropping three in a row to the Athletics.

The season had ended. The New York Yankees would play the St. Louis Cardinals in the 1926 World Series. The two pennant winners had five days to prepare.

Game One was scheduled for Saturday, October 2, in Yankee Stadium.

Table 3. Final standings for the 1926 Major League Baseball season

American League								National League							
Tm	*W*	*L*	W-L%	GB	RS	RA	*pythW-L%*	*Tm*	*W*	*L*	W-L%	GB	RS	RA	*pythW-L%*
NYY	91	63	.591	—	847	713	.578	STL	89	65	.578	—	817	678	.585
CLE	88	66	.571	3.0	738	612	.585	CIN	87	67	.565	2.0	747	651	.563
PHA	83	67	.553	6.0	677	570	.578	PIT	84	69	.549	4.5	769	689	.550
WSH	81	69	.540	8.0	802	761	.524	CHC	82	72	.532	7.0	682	602	.557
CHW	81	72	.529	9.5	730	665	.543	NYG	74	77	.490	13.5	663	668	.497
DET	79	75	.513	12.0	793	830	.479	BRO	71	82	.464	17.5	623	705	.444
SLB	62	92	.403	29.0	682	845	.403	BSN	64	86	.427	23.0	615	712	.433
BOS	46	107	.301	44.5	562	835	.	PHI	58	91	.389	28.5	680	891	.379

3

The Postseason

18

World Series Games One and Two

For the Yankees, it was their fourth trip to the World Series in six years, though they had captured the world championship only once, in 1923. After the disaster of the 1925 season, no one expected the 1926 team to be in this position. As for the Cardinals, this would be their first World Series appearance.

The series would showcase a clash between two of baseball's biggest stars and most dominant hitters: Babe Ruth of the Yankees and Rogers Hornsby of the Cardinals. The games would also feature opposing managers who had a long history between them. Huggins had been the St. Louis manager during Hornsby's first three years in the Major Leagues.

Ruth and Hornsby would compete against each other on the playing field; Hornsby and Huggins would strategize against each other, game by game, inning by inning, in their respective roles.

Fan interest was high. The *New York Times* hired Wilbert Robinson, manager of the Brooklyn Robins, and assigned him the task of writing a daily column assessing the strengths and weaknesses of each team and offering his baseball insights and predictions. Robinson had some expertise. He had seen the Yankees up close in the spring as they barnstormed north from Florida, with Brooklyn losing twelve straight games to New York, and he had managed his team to a fifth-place finish in the National League pennant race that the Cardinals eventually won.

Robinson was one of the most popular and well-liked baseball personalities. Known affectionately as "Uncle Robbie," he was cheerful, outgoing, and garrulous with a wry sense of humor. A writer once compared him to the legendary and hefty Shakespearean character Sir John Falstaff. He had managed the Robins for thirteen seasons, guiding them to National League pennants in 1916 and 1920.[1]

Prior to his tenure as manager, Robinson had been a catcher for seventeen years. Short and solidly built—5 feet 8 inches and 215 pounds—he was a skilled tactician and a keen observer of the game who had a talent for sizing up and coaching pitchers. In a profile, the sports journalist John Kiernan wrote, "He knew baseball as the spotted setter knows the secrets of quail hunting, by instinct and experience."[2]

Robinson was also the central figure in one of baseball's strangest and most comic moments. It's no coincidence that one of Robinson's players—the legendary prankster Casey Stengel—played a part in the escapade, which attempted to replicate a stunt made famous by Gabby Street several years earlier.

In 1908 Street, then a twenty-five-year-old catcher for the Washington Nationals, was challenged by two fans to catch a baseball thrown from the top of the Washington Monument. On the fifteenth try, Street caught the ball after it had traveled 555 feet from the top of the monument. The ball hitting Street's glove sounded like a gunshot and the force of the ball—accelerating through the air for four-and-a-half seconds—nearly knocked Street to the ground.[3]

The incident involving Stengel and Robinson took place seven years later, in 1915, during spring training in Daytona Beach, Florida. At that time, Robinson was fifty-two years old and beginning his second full season as manager of the team. He was overweight, well past his prime as an athlete.

Like so many of the most bizarre and intriguing baseball stories and anecdotes of the eras before video cameras and cell phones captured everything happening on a ballfield, there are multiple versions of the story and varying interpretations. The basic story is mostly true.

Stengel, an outfielder at that point in his career, was involved, perhaps as the organizer of the stunt or perhaps as a direct participant. In later years, Stengel told the story of his involvement, sometimes embellishing the tale to appeal to his audiences.[4]

To duplicate Gabby Street's feat, Stengel, or an accomplice, recruited a young woman named Ruth Law to fly a plane over Brooklyn's training facility so that a passenger could drop a baseball from a height comparable to the height of the Washington Monument. Ruth Law was a skilled aviator and stunt pilot who had been hired by real estate developers to fly over a golf course in Daytona Beach and drop golf balls as advertising for the business.

Law agreed to participate. On the morning of March 13, 1915, Law and Stengel took off and reached a height of more than five hundred feet. But there was a glitch. No one had remembered to bring a baseball. A ball-like replacement was needed. A grapefruit was aboard the plane, so it was substituted for the ball.

The grapefruit was about the size of a softball but had a softer and less dense core than a baseball. The plane circled; Robinson waited below for the object to be dropped. The grapefruit—what Robinson thought was a baseball—was tossed from the plane.

When the grapefruit hit Robinson's glove, it exploded, drenching the manager in a sticky liquid and knocking him to the ground. He shouted, "Jesus, I'm killed. I'm killed," thinking that he had been mortally wounded by the bursting projectile and that the fluid was his own blood.[5]

Robinson recovered. Stengel escaped blame and went on to a colorful and successful career as a player, manager, and raconteur of baseball tales.

Wilbert Robinson's first column on the World Series appeared on October 2, 1926, the day of the opening game of the series. He picked the Cardinals to win in either six or seven games, favoring St. Louis because he reasoned that they had the better pitching staff and a stronger defense.

Robinson expected Willie Sherdel of the Cardinals and Herb Pennock of the Yankees to be the starting pitchers for the crucial first game. "The only game more worth winning," Robinson wrote, "is the last."[6]

Both teams, Robinson argued, had strong offenses led by the competing superstars, Babe Ruth and Rogers Hornsby. He doubted that speed on the basepaths or stolen bases would figure prominently in the outcome of games because neither team would want to "risk losing scoring opportunities by gambling on steals and taking extra bases on hits."[7]

In the column, Robinson praised the work and importance of Cardinals catcher Bob O'Farrell: "O'Farrell is the player most essential to the Cardinals' success."[8] Robinson described O'Farrell as "a great catcher who can throw, hit, and think."

Robinson's comments about base running and O'Farrell would turn out to be prophetic at a key moment in the deciding game of the series.

The day before the start of the series, Judge Landis arrived in New York and spent the morning checking out Yankee Stadium. The ballpark had been refreshed in anticipation of the large crowds that would be attending the games. A new coat of green paint had been applied to the seats and front of the grandstand. That morning the grounds crew had been busy picking up loose paper and hosing down the bleachers and reserved seats. Landis toured the facility, sat in various sections of the ballpark, and announced his satisfaction. "Everyone will have a good seat," he said.[9]

A crowd of more than sixty thousand fans, potentially the largest crowd to ever see a baseball game, was expected. Many baseball fans who had traveled to Philadelphia for the Tunney and Dempsey fight had stayed on the East Coast and relocated to New York City hotels. Special trains were bringing more fans to New York from St. Louis and other western cities.

Baseball writers and prominent executives and fans began checking in at the Commodore Hotel, a two-thousand room facility located at Grand Central Station on Forty-Second Street in midtown. To accommodate the writers, the hotel set up more than fifty typewriters on a line of tables for use by the sports journalists.

Baseball executives like Connie Mack of the Philadelphia Athletics and Garry Herrmann, president of the Cincinnati Reds, were spotted in the lobby of the hotel. Babe Ruth appeared as well, accompanied by his new dog, a Great Dane named Bambino. The Babe joked, "I don't know what to do about this mutt to keep him from following me."[10]

Nobody was more excited about the series than professional gamblers. It was estimated that over $1 million would be bet on Game One of the series and perhaps as much as $5 million would be wagered on the series if it went to six or seven games, as Wilbert Robinson had predicted.

The most highly regarded odds maker was a man named Jack Doyle, known as the "Sage of Broadway" or the "Commissioner of Broadway." Doyle owned the Doyle Billard Academy on Broadway and had been in business for more than two decades. Doyle claimed he did not gamble or bet for himself; he simply provided the odds for various sporting events.

Before Game One, Doyle quoted the following odds:

6 to 5 against the Cards to win the first game
7 to 10 against the Yankees to win the first game
16 to 5 the Cards do not win the first two games
12 to 5 the Yankees do not win the first two games
14 to 1 the Cards do not win four straight
12 to 1 the Yankees do not win four straight[11]

Fans began lining up at 10:00 p.m. on Friday night so they could buy tickets when the box office opened twelve hours later. The Yankees had reserved twenty thousand bleacher seats and eighteen thousand grandstand seats for sale.

First in line was Albert Aitken, a stagehand who worked in the city's theater district. Two young men from Passaic, New Jersey, who had never seen a World Series, were next in line.

The fourth individual in line was John Green, a dedicated baseball fan who claimed he had seen every World Series game ever played. He was fifty-two years of age and worked at the Bureau of Engraving at the United States Mint. For more than two decades, he had taken his vacation time in the fall to coincide with the dates the World Series was to be played. He already had plans to travel to St. Louis when the series continued.

By 1:00 a.m., twenty-one fans had gathered, standing in line or sitting on wooden boxes, enduring the chilly temperatures and threats of rainfall, trying to get a little sleep before daylight. More than forty members of the New York City Police Department patrolled the area to make sure the overnight vigil was calm and peaceful.

At dawn, when more fans arrived, the skies were a drab gray and threatening, as if a storm were approaching. During warm-ups, a mild drizzle moistened the field and dampened the heads of spectators, but by game time, the precipitation had ceased.

The official attendance was determined to be 61,658, the third largest crowd in World Series history.[12] John McGraw and Wilbert Robinson, managers of the two New York City teams that did not make it to the World Series, watched the game from the press box.

The 132 field-level box seats were occupied by various baseball executives, politicians, and other well-connected individuals. Philadelphia As manager Connie Mack was in attendance. The entertainer Will Rogers had a box seat. Judge Landis occupied a box with Jack Dempsey and his wife, Estelle Taylor. Yankee owner Jacob Ruppert shared a box with New York City mayor Jimmy Walker and state Supreme Court Justice Robert Wagner, the Democratic candidate for senator from New York.[13] From his seat, Justice Wagner was given the honor of tossing out the first ball to officially commemorate the proceedings.

In New York City, a carnival atmosphere existed. More than ten thousand fans gathered in City Hall Park and along Park Row to monitor the progress of the game on giant scoreboards. Broadway office workers with a view of the scoreboards leaned out of windows to follow the game. Vendors strolled through the park selling peanuts and ice cream.

In addition to those at the ballpark and those clustered around scoreboards in lower Manhattan, pitch-by-pitch accounts of the action would be heard by fifteen million radio listeners. Graham McNamee, a failed opera singer with an appealing baritone voice, announced the game for radio station WEAF of New York City. McNamee had been broadcasting World Series games since 1923. In a distinguished broadcasting career that lasted a quarter of a century, McNamee narrated many important sporting events—football and boxing contests, as well as World Series games. He was also on the scene to provide live coverage of political speeches and conventions and such newsworthy events as Lindbergh's return from Paris in 1927. But he is best known as the first prominent baseball radio announcer.

Before the first pitch of the series, McNamee supplied his audience with this vivid description of the scene in Yankee Stadium.

"The umpire is behind the plate now putting on his mask and adjusting his chest protector. The diamond and the ground and everything look beautiful. The dark brown chocolate color of the baseline and the beautiful ground is wonderful. Around the edges is a running track and still around that is an embankment of green."[14]

The pitching matchups for Game One were just as Wilbert Robinson expected. Miller Huggins named the veteran left-hander Herb Pennock as his starter. Pennock had posted a record of 23–11 during the season and was noted as a reliable and crafty pitcher with an excellent curveball. Over the past eight seasons—four with the Red Sox, four with the Yankees—Pennock averaged sixteen wins per year.

Rogers Hornsby countered with his ace lefty, Willie Sherdel. It was widely acknowledged that the power hitters in the Yankee lineup liked to hit fastballs. Sherdel didn't have a fastball. It was frequently quipped that Sherdel relied on two pitches: a slow ball and a slower ball. It worked. Sherdel finished the season with a record of 16–12. He gave up slightly more than a hit an inning and only struck out two or three batters a game, but he had a respectable earned run average of 3.49.

Both pitchers were shaky in the first inning. The Cardinals lead-off hitter, Taylor Douthit, doubled to right field and advanced to third on Billy Southworth's groundout. Hornsby, with a chance to drive in the first run of the series, hit a weak roller right back to Pennock who threw him out at first. Then Jim Bottomly hit a two-out single to left to score Douthit.

With a lead of 1–0 to protect, Sherdel experienced some uncharacteristic wildness in the bottom of the first inning, walking Combs, retiring Koenig on a fly ball, then walking Ruth and Meusel. Gehrig's groundout scored Combs to tie the score.

After the first inning, Sherdel settled down. He did not issue another walk and allowed just one more run. In the sixth inning, Ruth singled and Meusel sacrificed him to second. A slight delay occurred because Ruth, as he slid into second, ripped open a seam on the back of his pants. The Yankees trainer Doc Woods was summoned and dashed out of the dugout with a needle and thread. As the Babe stood near second base facing home plate, the trainer used eighteen stiches to repair Ruth's uniform.

The game resumed. Gehrig slugged one of Sherdel's slow balls into right field, and Ruth scored what would be the eventual winning run.

As good as Sherdel was, Pennock was better. After the first inning, Pennock allowed only one more hit—another single by Bottomly in the ninth inning. The Yankees had taken the first game of the series by a final score of 2–1.

Jack Doyle and the oddsmakers were quick to post new odds on the outcome of the series. The Yankees were now favored to win the series by odds of 5–3.

For Game Two of the series, Miller Huggins picked the thirty-six-year-old Urban Shocker, an experienced veteran noted for his spitball and competitiveness.[15] He had won nineteen games and lost eleven during the regular season.

Because Hornsby had used right-hander Jesse Haines in relief at the end of Game One, he chose the well-rested Grover Cleveland Alexander, who had not pitched in twelve days, to start Game Two. Hornsby intended for Haines to be the starter in Game Three back in St. Louis, and for young Flint Rhem to be available for Game Four.

The weather was cool, but the sun broke through the clouds right before game time, and there was a nice wind from the southwest. The crowd for Sunday's Game Two was a little bigger than the previous day's. The official count was 63,600, a sellout that set a record for attendance at a World Series game. Approximately four thousand frustrated fans made it to the ballpark but couldn't get tickets.

Alexander had his own way of preparing for a starting assignment. The ritual would begin twenty minutes before game time, and Alex would stay in the clubhouse as long as possible. He would take a bottle of Sloan's Liniment out of his locker, pour some on his right shoulder and right arm, and rub it in until his arm felt loose and warm. Then he would get up and wash his hands and come back and sit on a stool in front of his locker and slowly smoke a Camel cigarette. About ten minutes before game time, he'd get dressed in his uniform, put on his cap, pick up his glove, saunter out to the field and toss a few warm-up pitches at half speed. He never appeared to be in a hurry and didn't need to throw many pitches to feel ready.[16]

In the top of the first, Hornsby got a double off Shocker for his first hit of the series, but the Cardinals couldn't get him home. The game remained scoreless until the bottom of the second when Meusel singled off Alexander, advanced to second on a groundout, and scored on Tony Lazzeri's base hit. After Hank Severeid struck out, Joe Dugan singled to put runners on first and second. Dugan and Lazzeri attempted but failed to complete a double steal, thanks to some alert defense by catcher Bob O'Farrell. During the rundown, Alexander threw the ball away, allowing Lazzeri to score. It was an unearned run, but it put the Yankees ahead 2–0. The Cardinals came right back and tied the score in the top of the third with two singles, Hornsby's sacrifice bunt, and a two-run scoring single by Jim Bottomly.

Then it became a pitcher's duel. Alexander allowed a single by Earle Combs to lead off the bottom of the third then retired Koenig, Ruth, and Meusel, in that order. Combs would be the last Yankee batter to reach base.

Alexander retired the last twenty-one Yankee hitters in order. He faced Babe Ruth four times, striking him out once. Alexander recorded ten strikeouts in the game—and didn't allow Ruth to hit a ball out of the infield.

Shocker matched Alexander, shutout inning after shutout inning, until the top of the seventh, when O'Farrell led off with a double and light-hitting Tommy Thevenow followed with a single, putting runners on first and third. Shocker retired Alexander on a pop up and Douthit on a short flyball to left. But with two outs, Billy Southworth stepped in and crushed a homer deep to right field—a three-run blast that put the Cardinals securely in the lead. An insurance run was added in the ninth, but it was hardly needed, considering how well Alexander was pitching.

The heroes of the day—Alexander and Southworth—were the midseason acquisitions that paid off with a pennant and a critical World Series win. No one was more pleased with the outcome than Hornsby. After the game, he told reporters, "You will have to give the credit to Alexander. He pitched a wonderful game."[17]

Despite the loss, Huggins exuded confidence after the game. Sitting in his office, he smoked a corncob pipe and answered questions from reporters. Like his managerial counterpart, Huggins praised the pitching of Alexander. "We couldn't hit," Huggins said. "Alexander pitched an almost perfect game."[18]

Talking to reporters, Alexander said he felt good and mused contentedly, "May win another for Hornsby. You know, I sure like that young fellow. He don't tell me nothing, except to go in there and throw 'em the way I see fit."[19]

The series was tied, one game apiece. Now it was westward to St. Louis for the next three games.

Jack Doyle and bettors large and small would have to refigure the odds.

19

World Series Games Three, Four, and Five

After the two games in New York, the Cardinals returned home to St. Louis. They had been on the road for thirty-three days, and the city was ready for a celebration.

More than one hundred thousand joyous and noisy fans lined the streets to enjoy the parade of cars that carried the Cardinals' players and dignitaries through the city. Mayor Victor Miller ordered all city offices closed at 3:00 p.m. so city workers could participate in the festivities. The sounds of sirens, cowbells, and horns emanated from the crowd. Confetti drifted downward like snowflakes from the windows and roofs of office buildings. Two marching bands and police mounted on horseback accompanied the caravan of cars. Fans waved flags and banners.

Mayor Miller rode in the first car. The second car held Cardinals owner Sam Breadon, Branch Rickey, and Judge Landis. The players followed in groups of three. Rogers Hornsby was in the last car. When the parade ended, Hornsby was presented with the gift of a new car. Players received engraved watches.

At Sportsman's Park, the infield was covered with tarps to protect it from the early morning rain. Drains in the outfield collected the runoff from the downpour. Groundskeepers promised the field would be in good shape for Game Three.

Sportsman's Park had a seating capacity of 38,585, and interest in the games was high. Ticket sales were brisk. Scalpers were getting three times the face value of tickets they had managed to acquire. A small number of tickets for unreserved seats would go on sale in the morning.

A special guideline was in effect for vendors selling drinks at the game. Because St. Louis fans were known for throwing bottles on the field during games, vendors were now required to provide paper cups for any beverages they sold during the game.

Wilbert Robinson's pregame column boldly predicted that the Cardinals would win the series and that Billy Southworth would outhit Babe Ruth. Except for Pennock—who Robinson asserted was the Yankees' best pitcher—the Brooklyn manager seemed confident that the Cardinals' pitchers were superior to the Yankees' hurlers. He also expressed that the Cardinals were the more balanced team on defense. The Cardinals, Robinson wrote, "have a sharper edge because their pitchers look better now, their infield covers more ground, their hitting is normal, and they have lost the tightness of strain they showed in the first game."[1]

Oddsmakers weren't so sure. Betting was brisk in St. Louis, though not as much money was wagered on Game Three as had been bet on Games One and Two. Odds were placed at 4–5 with the bettor choosing which team would win the series. Odds of 5–1 were offered for anyone betting that one team or the other would sweep the three games in St. Louis. A few creative gamblers were making "freak bets"—for example, on who would get the first hit in Game Three or whether Babe Ruth would hit one or more home runs in St. Louis.[2]

At noon, as the teams came on the field for batting practice, a light rain fell. When the sun came out, a band played, optimistically, "It Ain't Gonna Rain No More."

By game time, the field was dry. The temperature was in the high fifties. Rain remained in the forecast, but the game started on time before a near-capacity crowd of 37,709. St. Louis mayor Victor Miller was on hand to throw out the first ball.

As Wilbert Robinson had anticipated, Miller Huggins gave the starting assignment to Dutch Ruether, a left-hander whose pitching style and approach was like Herb Pennock's. Ruether had started the season with Washington, posting a record for the Nationals of 12–6 before being acquired by the Yankees in late August. He had won two and lost three in his limited time with the Yankees.

Hornsby selected Jesse Haines as his starting pitcher. Haines had gotten off to a slow start in 1926 due to an injury but had been a steady and dependable hurler in the second half of the season, finishing the regular season with a record of 13–4.

The game was scoreless going to the top of the fourth. The skies had darkened. Ruth led off with a single and moved to second on Meusel's weak ground ball back to Haines. Then the rain resumed. The players retreated to their respective dugouts. The grounds crew rushed into action, pulling tarps over the infield.

As the players waited for the rain to stop, two policemen visited the dugouts and asked the players to sign a baseball for Johnnie Sylvester, a sick child in Essex Falls, New Jersey. Rogers Hornsby and fourteen of his Cardinals teammates signed one ball. Five Yankees, including Babe Ruth, signed the other ball. On one side of the ball, Ruth added a personal message and prediction for the young boy: "I'll knock a homer for you in Wednesday's game."[3]

When the rain stopped, the game resumed. It was still scoreless in the bottom of the fourth when Les Bell led off with a single and was sacrificed to second. Bob O'Farrell walked. Tommy Thevenow hit a ground ball to Lazzeri at second who flipped the ball to Koenig for a forced out. But Koenig threw wildly to first, trying for the double play. The ball skipped past Gehrig's ankles and rolled away. Bell scored, Thevenow advanced to second. Haines, the next batter and a decent hitting pitcher, drove a ball to deep right field, over the head of Babe Ruth, and over the fence. Suddenly the Cardinals led 3–0.

Haines had supplied all the runs he needed as he pitched a five-hit shutout. St. Louis had won two games in a row to take the lead in the series. The Yankees had managed just fifteen hits and four runs in three games. Referring to the Yankees nickname of "Murderers Row," a reporter wrote, "If the Yanks are 'murderers' they are keeping it a secret."[4]

Before Game Four, Ban Johnson visited the Yankees' locker room and launched into an inspired speech. He said the Yankees needed to "act like champions" and that "it is time to wake up and play ball." Apparently, what he said made an impression, especially on Babe Ruth.[5]

Flint Rhem and Waite Hoyt were named as starters for Game Four. Both were young pitchers—Rhem was twenty-five; Hoyt was twenty-seven. Rhem had posted a record of 20–7 during the regular season but had no postseason experience. Hoyt's record for the year was 16–12, but he had already pitched in six World Series games as a Yankee, five times as a starter.

Rhem was a confident—some would say headstrong or reckless—young ballplayer, a successful pitcher for his college team at Clemson, who once struck out sixteen batters in a game with a lively fastball and sharp curve. His Major League career was promising, though, like his teammate Alexander, he struggled with alcohol. St. Louis sportswriter Bob Broeg later lamented that Rhem "boozed away the greatness expected of him."[6]

In the top of the first, Rhem got the better of Earle Combs and Mark Koenig, striking out both batters. Then he faced Babe Ruth.

Although the Yankees and Ruth were known to like fastballs, Rhem figured he could throw his fastball past Ruth. That was a miscalculation. The Babe hit Rhem's first pitch to the upper deck in right field, just barely fair, fulfilling his promise to Johnnie Sylvester.

Two innings later, Ruth came up again, and this time Rhem tried a changeup. Again, Ruth swung at the first pitch; he drove this one over the bleachers in right center, out of the park, and across Grand Avenue, where the ball shattered a window of the Chevrolet dealership.[7]

The Cardinals rallied against Hoyt in the fourth inning. Hafey singled, O'Farrell reached on Koenig's error, Thevenow doubled, and after Toporcer's sacrifice fly, Douthit doubled. The Cards had taken the lead 4–3 and had Douthit in scoring position with two outs when Southworth singled to left. But Douthit was out trying to score from second, thanks to a superb throw from Ruth to the plate.

Rhem was out of the game when Ruth batted in the sixth against reliever Herman Bell, but Ruth wasn't finished. He homered again off Bell. The last two of his three home runs were estimated to have traveled 515 and 530 feet, respectively.[8] James Harrison, reporting for the *New York Times*, wrote that pitching to Ruth was like "tampering with a stick of dynamite."[9]

Ruth's three home runs paced the Yankees as he and his teammates broke out of their hitting slump against five Cardinals pitchers. In addition to the home runs, Ruth walked twice, drove in four runs, and scored four times.

No one had ever hit three home runs in a World Series game. Ruth was pleased with himself, contributing with both his bat and his fielding. In the locker room, he said, "I guess I had a pretty fair day today, didn't I?"

The final score was 10–5. Hoyt struck out eight batters and pitched a complete game. He was adequate, not brilliant, giving up fourteen hits and five runs, though only two runs were earned.

Hornsby was frustrated and disgusted after the game and placed blame for the debacle directly on his pitchers. "We lost because of poor pitching. It was more than poor. It was miserable pitching. . . . Rhem was a disappointment, but the greatest kick I have with his work was his pitching to Ruth. He just grooved the ball for Ruth every time. The relief pitching was a joke, too. There's no other way to describe it."[10]

The critical fifth game of the series featured Pennock and Sherdel in a rematch of the lefties who had faced each other in Game One. It would be a battle of Pennock's curve balls against Sherdel's slow balls.

Wilbert Robinson thought it would be another low-scoring game and that the Cardinals would win because Sherdel was the younger and stronger pitcher. Robinson also predicted that Alexander would win Game Six back in New York to give the Redbirds the world title.

A crowd of an estimated 41,000 fans managed to squeeze into a ballpark whose capacity was officially 38,585. As expected, it was a pitcher's duel. The Cardinals scored the first run in the bottom of the fourth. Bottomly lined a ball to left field and Ruth tried to make a shoe-top catch, but the ball fell safely to the turf and skipped past Ruth. Bottomly made it to second and was credited with a double. Bottomly scored on an RBI single by Les Bell. The Yankees came back with a rally in the sixth. Pennock reached second base on a wind-blown pop fly that fell in shallow left field. Combs walked. Then Koenig singled to score Pennock and tie the score. After Ruth struck out and Meusel flied out, the rally continued with a walk to Gehrig that loaded the bases with two out for Tony Lazzeri.

With the game and possibly the series on the line, the rookie Lazzeri, who had finished second in the American League in runs batted in, stepped in to face Willie Sherdel. Hornsby came in from second base to have a conversation with Sherdel about how to pitch to Lazzeri.

Lazzeri took the first pitch for a strike, then swung and missed on Sherdel's second offering. The next two pitches were outside. On the fifth pitch with the count 2–2, Lazzeri swung and connected, sending a long fly ball to right field. It looked at first that the ball would reach the bleachers for a grand slam, but the stiff wind held the ball up, and Southworth, with his shoulders pressed against the concrete wall, made the catch to end the inning.

In the bottom of the seventh, O'Farrell doubled and Bell singled him home as the Cardinals regained the lead. The Yankees tied it in the ninth on a double by Gehrig and an RBI single by the pinch hitter Ben Paschal, batting for Joe Dugan.

In the tenth, Koenig led off with a single, bringing Ruth to the plate just twenty-four hours after his three-homer outburst the day before. Huggins ordered Ruth to bunt. He bunted foul, took a pitch for a ball, and attempted to bunt again. Once more, he bunted foul. Working carefully, Sherdel walked Ruth. Meusel—also ordered to bunt—sacrificed the runners to second and third. Gehrig was walked intentionally, bringing Lazzeri, once again, to the plate with the bases loaded. This time Lazzeri hit a deep fly ball to left. Koenig scored on the sacrifice fly. The Cardinals failed to score against Pennock in the bottom of the inning. The final score was 3–2.

The Yankees—in a well-played and dramatic Game Five—had taken control of the series and were now one win away from a second world championship.

The teams packed up their gear and headed to the train station. One thing was certain: the series would end in Yankee Stadium.

20

World Series Games Six and Seven

On the train ride back to New York, the Yankees had reason to feel pleased and confident, if not quite satisfied. They had won two out of three in St. Louis and needed just one more win to claim their second world championship. They would play the remaining game, or games, of the series in their home park before large and friendly crowds.

Judge Landis was on the train with the team, and even he seemed relaxed and happy with the way the series was going. The revenue from the series was guaranteed to be the richest in baseball history. Players on the winning team would get shares worth more than $5,000 a person, and the losers would get slightly more than $3,000 each—both record amounts. For many players on the winning team the winner's share was a bonus of more than half their annual salary.[1]

Landis, dressed in men's golf knickers, walked up and down the aisle of the train, cheerfully talking about baseball and his other favorite sport: golf.

In New York, plans were brewing for a celebratory gathering of fans, including a band, to meet the players at Grand Central Station, as they debarked from the train. When Huggins heard about the arrangement, he made it clear that he didn't want the celebration or any distractions. "Let's wait until the title is clinched before we begin celebrating the victory," Huggins said. "You can never tell what will happen in a big game," he added prophetically.[2]

There was no rain in the forecast for Game Six, but the weather was colder than expected. Hopes for a sellout crowd of more than sixty-five thousand were overly optimistic. The paid attendance was a disappointing 48,615.

Alexander would pitch for the Cardinals and try to duplicate his dominant performance from Game Two.

Jack Doyle posted new odds on the Yankees chances to win the series, the odds now strongly favoring the Yankees by as much as 3–1. Gamblers, especially the big money bettors, waited until after noon of game day to place their bets, figuring the worse the weather, the better the Yankees' chances against Alexander, a thirty-nine-year-old with an aged arm. It was estimated that more than $1 million would change hands at the conclusion of Game Six.

If ordinary fans were worried that any of the games or the outcome of the series might be fixed, like the 1919 World Series had been, it wasn't evident in the enthusiasm shown by bettors putting money down on their best guesses.

Huggins finally decided on a starting pitcher for Game Six. He picked Bob Shawkey, who had turned in good relief performances early in the series. If Shawkey got in trouble, Urban Shocker would be ready to provide relief. If a Game Seven would need to be played, Huggins had Waite Hoyt rested and ready.

The Cardinals jumped on Shawkey in the first inning, scoring three times. Wattie Holm, leading off and playing centerfield in place of Taylor Douthit, singled. After Southworth forced Holm at second, Hornsby walked, and Bottomly doubled, scoring Southworth. Les Bell lined a single to left over Joe Dugan, and the Cardinals had three quick runs.

Despite the chilly temperature, Alexander was in fine form. He would later say it was so cold he didn't even break a sweat.

The Yankees, once again, failed to generate much offense against Alexander. Meusel doubled in the second but didn't score. Ruth came up with two on and two out in the third but was retired on a weak ground ball. The Yankees scored a run in the fourth, when Meusel tripled and came home on a ground out by Gehrig.

With the Yankees trailing 4–1 in the sixth and needing a rally, Ruth drew a lead-off walk, and when Gehrig went down swinging, Ruth stole second base, sliding in under the tag by Thevenow. Gordon McNamee told his listeners that Ruth had caught Alexander and the Cardinals by surprise. But Lazzeri flied out to Holm, and the inning ended.

The Cardinals, meanwhile, scored ten runs, including five in the top of the seventh, battering both Shawkey and his replacements.

Alexander was not as dominant as he had been in Game Two, but he gave up just eight hits and two runs. He struck out six and got a dozen outs on infield groundouts. Ruth batted four times, walking once and grounding out three times. Only Meusel presented a problem, collecting two extra base hits.

Alexander had done his part with a complete game victory on a cool Saturday in front of a large and hopeful Yankee Stadium crowd. Now it was up to his Cardinals teammates to come through with one more win.

Wilbert Robinson, in his next-to-last World Series column, continued to predict that the Cardinals would triumph, trusting that Jesse Haines would again be able to hold the Yankees in check.

Jack Doyle reported the odds for Game Seven were set at 10–9, slightly favoring the Cardinals and that $2 million was expected to be wagered on the final game, a new record in the history of sports betting.[3] Total wagering on the seven-game series was expected to exceed $20 million, also a record amount.[4]

On Sunday morning, dark-gray clouds hung ominously over the city and the ballpark. The air was cold. A steady rain fell. The Cardinals players gathered in the lobby of the Alamac Hotel at Seventy-First Street and Broadway, waiting for the official word that the game would be called off. A little before noon, though, Judge Landis made a different decision: the game would be played, if possible. Players collected their gear, climbed into taxicabs, and headed to Yankee Stadium.[5]

The inclement weather and the possibility that the game might be postponed suppressed the turnout, discouraging fans who might have traveled to the ballpark. As it was, only 38,093 fans paid for tickets, making the attendance the second lowest of the series. Nearly half the seats in Yankee Stadium were empty.

American League president Ban Johnson was an early arrival at Yankee Stadium. Before the game started, Johnson noticed Sport Sullivan, the well-known Boston gambler and indicted Black Sox fixer, sitting in a field-level box seat near the Cardinals' dugout. Johnson ordered Sullivan removed from the Stadium. Sullivan was escorted out.[6]

The hearty fans who showed up witnessed one of the best and most dramatic final games ever played. For baseball fans, it was well worth being drenched to watch this historic game in person.

Hoyt pitched well for the first three innings, allowing just a single by Hornsby in the first, and a single by Thevenow in the third. Haines shut the Yankees out in the first and second innings, but in the bottom of the third, he surrendered a long home run to Babe Ruth—Ruth's fourth homer of the series.

With the Yankees leading 1–0 in the top of the fourth, the Cardinals staged a comeback. After Hornsby grounded out, Bottomly looped a single to short left field. Bell grounded to Koenig, a tailor-made double play ball that Koenig fumbled and dropped. Everyone was safe. The inning should have been over right then, but instead a frustrated Hoyt now had to deal with two runners on base with just one out.

The next batter was Chick Hafey, and Hoyt got him to hit a weak fly ball to left that fell between Koenig, running out, and Meusel, charging in. Now the bases were loaded for O'Farrell. Fortunately for Hoyt and the Yankees, no runs had been scored at this point.

O'Farrell lifted a fly ball to the outfield. Meusel had plenty of time to settle under it. The ball dropped into his glove and bounced out, "like a rabbit from the magician's hat," as one reporter wryly commented.[7] O'Farrell was safe at first; Bottomly scored to tie the score.

Tommy Thevenow was up next. The supposedly weak-hitting shortstop blooped a single right over Lazzeri's outstretched glove, and two more runs were scored.

The pitching of both teams continued to dominate. The Yankees added a run in the sixth to cut the lead to 3–2. Pennock relieved Hoyt, who had not allowed an earned run in his six innings of work.

The game moved to the bottom of the seventh inning.

Few half innings in baseball history have been as much discussed and analyzed as the Yankee half of the seventh inning in Game Seven of the 1926 World Series.

Combs led off and lined a single to left field. Koenig sacrificed Combs to second. Ruth was walked intentionally, the third time he'd been walked in the game. Meusel grounded to Lester Bell at third who threw to Hornsby to force Ruth at second. Meusel was safe at first. Gehrig came to the plate and walked. The bases were loaded. The tying run was at third, the potential World Series winning runs were at second and first. Tony Lazzeri would be the next batter.

Hornsby realized that Jesse Haines was struggling. He called a meeting at the mound. Bell, Bottomly, Thevenow, and O'Farrell joined Hornsby and Haines.

Haines showed Hornsby his right index finger. It was bleeding. The skin was scraped off. "Can you throw it anymore?" Hornsby asked. Haines had two main pitches: a fastball and a knuckleball. "No," Haines said. "I can throw the fastball, but not the knuckler." "Well," Hornsby replied, "we don't want any fast balls to this guy."[8]

Hornsby made his decision quickly. Haines had pitched brilliantly and bravely, but Hornsby didn't want a subpar Haines pitching to the dangerous Lazzeri. No one had been warming up in the Cardinals' bullpen, but Hornsby knew that he had Flint Rhem and Alexander available to relieve. He wanted Alexander.

The skies had darkened. A gray mist hung over the field. Alexander, wearing a red sweater, ambled in from the left-field bullpen to the mound.

Tony Lazzeri waited at the plate, restless and impatient, knocking the dirt off his spikes with his bat.

Decades later, Les Bell, the Cardinals' third baseman, remembered the scene.

"I can see him yet, walking in from the leftfield [*sic*] bullpen. . . . The Yankee fans recognized him right off, and you didn't hear a sound from anywhere in Yankee Stadium as they sat still and watched him. And he took his time. Grover Cleveland Alexander was never in a hurry, and especially not this day. It was the seventh inning of the seventh game of the 1926 World Series, and we were leading 3–2. Alex had won two games for us already and he was coming in now to face a tough young hitter with two out and the bases loaded. I can still see him walking that long distance. He just came straggling along, a lean old Nebraskan, his face wrinkled, wearing a Cardinal sweater, his cap sitting on the top of his head and tilted to one side."[9]

James Harrison of the *New York Times* provided a similar description of Alexander in an account that was published the day after the game.

"His cap rode rakishly on the corner of his head. He walked like a man who was going nowhere in particular and was in no hurry to get there. He was a trifle knock-kneed and his gait was not a model of grace and rhythm."[10]

Hornsby handed the ball to Alexander and returned to his position at second base. Alexander took off the red sweater, threw three medium-speed warm-up pitches, nodded to the home-plate umpire, George Hildebrand, and indicated that he was ready to pitch.

Lazzeri had been waiting a long time. Twice in Game Five, he had come to bat with the bases loaded, and in both those previous at bats, he had made solid contact and hit long fly balls to the outfield. The crowd, sensing the drama and importance of the moment, was virtually silent.[11]

Lazzeri may have been nervous. Alexander was not. He had pitched more than 4,500 innings in the Major Leagues and lived by his motto: "I am a better pitcher than you are a hitter."[12]

The first pitch to Lazzeri was a ball. The second was a called strike. On the third pitch, Lazzeri swung and hit a long drive to left—it landed in foul territory.

From his perspective at second base, Hornsby thought it was foul "by about ten inches"; Bell, who watched the flight of the ball from third base, later said "it was foul all the way." No completely verifiable account resolves the debate. It might have been foul by inches or perhaps by as much as twenty feet.[13]

The count was now one ball and two strikes, and Alexander's next pitch was a curve that broke low and outside. Lazzeri chased it, swinging and missing. The historic half inning—and Lazzeri's most-remembered at bat—was over.

It was still a one-run game, and more drama would follow. The Cardinals did not score in the eighth or ninth innings. Alexander easily retired the Yankees—Dugan, Collins, and Pennock—in order, in the bottom of the eighth.

In the bottom of the ninth, with the Yankees trailing 3–2, Alexander retired Combs and Koenig on ground balls to Bell at third. With the Yankees down to their last out, Babe Ruth stepped into the batter's box.

Alexander pitched carefully to Ruth. The count went to 3–2, then Ruth walked.[14] It was the fourth time in the game and the eleventh time in the series that Ruth had been walked. The eleven walks set a new World Series record that would last for seventy-six years.[15]

Bob Meusel was the next hitter. Lou Gehrig was on deck. Meusel was an imposing figure at the plate, standing six foot three and weighing nearly two hundred pounds. He had a reputation as a power hitter and had doubled and tripled off Alexander the previous day.

Alexander had not surrendered a hit since coming into the game in the seventh inning. If his arm was weary or if he lacked concentration, it was not evident. He needed to get one more out.

Meusel was a right-handed hitter, so when the catcher Bob O'Farrell went into his crouch behind home plate, he had an unobstructed view of Ruth taking a short lead off first base. Bottomly was holding Ruth on. Hornsby had shifted to his right, near second base, on the edge of the outfield grass.

Ruth was focused on the back of Alexander's head as the pitcher stared at Meusel in the batter's box. When Alexander delivered the first pitch to Meusel, Ruth took off for second base. Meusel took the pitch for a strike. O'Farrell made a perfect throw to Hornsby at second base; Hornsby tagged Ruth; umpire Bill Dineen called Ruth out.

Suddenly, the game, and the series, was over, and the Cardinals were world champions. Ruth rose from the dirt, shook Hornsby's hand, and jogged off the field.[16]

Fans listening to the game on the radio heard Graham McNamee's deep and excited voice dramatically describing the ending play of the series.

> One strike on Bob Meusel. Going down to second—the game is over. Ruth tried to steal second and is put out, catcher to second.
>
> The World Series of 1926—we will never say it again—is over! It has come to a close, and the championship goes west, southwest, down to the sovereign state of Missouri.[17]

The scene in the Cardinals locker room was one of extreme jubilation. Players whooped and hollered, tossing gloves and bats in the air, embracing and congratulating each other, dancing on the concrete floor in their steel-cleated shoes.

Then they gathered in celebration around the usually taciturn Alexander at his locker. A reporter captured the scene:

> Alec got by far the greatest praise. The veteran was in imminent danger of having his skull dashed against the open door of his locker on several occasions as groups of players grabbed him on either side and started pulling simultaneously and in different directions, making him the centre line in a human tug-of-war. He was rocked from

side to side by the demonstrative squad; he was rolled backward and forward under the impetus of the demonstration, and he was almost knocked down several times as he sought to stand erect under this good-natured, loving, heart-felt expression of his comrades' reverence.

Through it all, Alec just grinned and grinned. He said nothing. He could say nothing. For he was choked with his own emotions at this demonstration for him because he did his bit on behalf of his team.[18]

The scene in downtown St. Louis was just as raucous. Radio loudspeakers had been set up around the city so fans could listen to Graham McNamee call the game, pitch by pitch, batter by batter. When Ruth was tagged out by Hornsby at second base to end the game, the assembled crowds went wild. Sidewalks overflowed with humanity. The sound of bells, sirens, and whistles filled the air. Automobiles and trucks raced in the streets, "engine exhausts exploding like machine guns."[19]

Cardinals fans celebrated as if the victory was a historic event. Indeed, it was: the first World Series win for a team west of the Mississippi River.

For ninety-nine years, baseball fans have contemplated the wisdom of the decision by Ruth to try to steal second base at that crucial moment in Game Seven. The Yankees and Cardinals involved in the series also debated what Ruth's thinking must have been.

Bell was puzzled: "Ruth got to first and then, for some reason I've never been able to figure out, tried to steal second."[20]

Hornsby remarked, "It was the only mistake I ever heard of him making in about twenty-five years of baseball."[21]

Alexander recounted his surprise at Babe's attempt: "I'll never know why the guy did it. . . . He probably figured it would catch us by surprise. I caught the blur of Ruth starting for second as I pitched and then came the whistle of the ball as O'Farrell rifled it to second. I wheeled around and there was one of the grandest sights of my life."[22]

O'Farrell, sometime later, asked Ruth about the play: "Ruth said he thought Alex had forgotten he was there. Also that the way Alex was pitching, they'd never get two hits in a row off him, so he'd better get in position to score if they got one."[23]

Ed Barrow called Ruth's decision "a dumb play," but Miller Huggins defended his player: "We needed an unexpected move. . . . Had Ruth made the steal, it would have been declared the smartest piece of baseball in the history of World Series play."[24]

The Yankees were not a team built to manufacture runs with speed on the base paths. They had finished first in the American League in home runs and runs scored and fifth in stolen bases. That said, at this stage of his career, Ruth was a decent baserunner and had the third most stolen bases for the Yankees during the 1926 season.[25] And Ruth had successfully stolen a base off Alexander in the previous day's game—the only stolen base recorded by the Yankees in the series.

How did the result of the play affect Ruth?

Robert Creamer, one of Ruth's biographers, wrote: "Despite his four home runs, a new World Series record, Babe was considered a bit of a goat. He didn't seem to mind. It was a hell of a try, he thought. Strikeouts never embarrassed him, and neither did this."[26]

21

The Colored World Series of 1926

On May 26, 1925, in a rooming house in Indianapolis, Rube Foster had been incapacitated by a gas leak and passed out on the floor of his bathroom. When he didn't show up at work, several of the Chicago American Giant's players went to check on him. The players forced open the door to his room and found their manager unconscious, leaning against a gas heater. An ambulance was called, and Foster was rushed to a local hospital. He regained consciousness that afternoon, but in the year that followed, his friends and family noticed increasing mental deterioration and irregularities in his behavior.[1] He reported that he heard voices. He locked himself in his office bathroom and refused to come out. He had a car accident, injuring a pedestrian. Sometimes he couldn't recognize family members.[2]

As Foster's condition worsened, he began to experience hallucinations. A newspaper reported on one incident: "Foster labors under a delusion that a world series is underway and that he is scheduled to pitch for one of the contesting teams."[3]

At times, Foster turned violent, breaking furniture in his home and threatening a friend with an ice pick. In the latter part of August 1926, his wife, Sarah, was forced to call the police to come and restrain him. He was arrested and ordered to appear in court. Shortly thereafter, a judge evaluated Foster and sentenced him to the Kankakee State Hospital, a mental health facility near Chicago.[4]

Dave Malarcher, the American Giant's third baseman and captain, replaced Rube Foster as manager midway through the 1926 season, when it became evident that Foster was incapable of performing his duties. Malarcher was the logical choice to take over the managerial duties in Foster's absence.

After six years on the roster of the American Giants, he had absorbed the philosophy and studied the strategies of Foster.

A slender 5 foot-7 inch, 150-pound athlete, Malarcher was thirty-one and a well-respected veteran ballplayer with a keen baseball intelligence. He had grown up as the youngest of eleven children in Union Parish, Louisiana, where his father worked on a sugar plantation. His mother, born into slavery, had taught herself to read and write, and she encouraged her children to pursue an education. Malarcher's older brothers introduced him to baseball. An older sister homeschooled him before he entered New Orleans University, where he played college baseball before signing a professional contract in 1916.

After military service during World War I, he returned to play three seasons with the Indianapolis ABCs and one season with the Detroit Stars before joining the American Giants in 1920, the first full year of the newly formed Negro National League. A .264 career hitter, Malarcher's best season at the plate was 1925, when he hit .324.

As the manager of the American Giants in 1926, his challenge was to win the second half pennant of the NNL and get his team into a playoff with the Kansas City Monarchs, the first-half winners.

Although Rube Foster was absent from the team, his much younger half brother, Willie Foster, joined the American Giants early in the summer after pitching that spring for Alcorn Agricultural and Mechanical College. The younger Foster was twenty-two years of age and in just his third year of professional baseball, but he was already on the verge of greatness. During the regular season in 1926, Willie Foster won twenty-six straight games for the American Giants, against both league and nonleague opponents.[5] In the postseason, his pitching would be even more impressive.

The Kansas City Monarchs were a strong team in 1926. Bullet Rogan, one of the best pitchers in the league, was having another excellent year. The Monarchs won the first-half pennant easily, with a record of 35–12, but like the American Giants, they were coping with a tragic situation involving their most valuable everyday player—Dobie Moore.

Moore had been the Monarchs' best hitter and a superb shortstop. For his fielding prowess, he was called "The Black Cat." On May 18, 1926, Moore went to visit Elsie Brown, a twenty-two-year-old female friend—a woman who was not his wife. What happened next is unclear. Maybe Brown thought Moore was a prowler, or perhaps in a different version of the story, Brown and Moore engaged in a domestic argument that became heated and then violent. The encounter ended when Brown picked up a gun and shot Moore six times in the leg. He survived the shooting, but it ended his career in the Negro Leagues.[6]

To determine which team would represent the NNL in the Colored World Series, the American Giants and Monarchs played a best-of-nine series for the NNL Championship. At home in Kansas City, the Monarchs won the first three games of the series. The American Giants finally got a win in Game Four. The series moved to Chicago, and the Monarchs also took Game Five, to lead four games to one in the series, needing just one more win. Once again, the American Giants came back, winning the next two games.

The teams agreed to settle the series with one game, or two, if necessary, on September 29. The climax of the series featured a historic pitching duel between Bullet Rogan, the Monarchs' player-manager, and Willie Foster, the American Giants' young left-hander.

It was a cold, almost wintery day, cold enough that a few snowflakes drifted in the air above the infield.[7]

Fans who braved the weather witnessed a classic baseball game. Rogan and Foster pitched shutouts through eight innings of Game Eight, and the Monarchs failed to score in the top of the ninth. In the bottom of the ninth, Sanford Jackson reached first on an infield single. Willie Foster sacrificed him to second, and Sandy Thompson drove in the game-winning run with a single to center. The series was now tied four games apiece; a final game would decide who would represent the NNL in the Colored World Series.

It was late in the afternoon and darkness approached. The teams agreed to play a final five-inning game to determine the league championship. Malarcher asked his team to decide who should pitch the nightcap. They wanted Willie Foster, if possible, to go back on the mound and try to win the series. When Rogan saw Foster warming up to pitch the final game, he decided that he, too, would pitch the deciding game.

The game was one-sided, and the American Giants prevailed, scoring five runs off Bullet Rogan. Willie Foster, relying on a fastball and a sharp curveball, held the Monarchs scoreless, pitching a second straight shutout—fourteen consecutive shutout innings against the best team in the NNL. The final score was 5–0.

It was settled. Without Rube Foster, but with his half brother pitching brilliantly, the American Giants had earned the right to face the Atlantic City Bacharach Giants in the Colored World Series of 1926.

The Bacharach Giants took their team's name from former Atlantic City mayor Harry Bacharach.[8] The city itself was a playground for East Coast tourists. During the summer months, and especially over the Fourth of July holiday, hundreds of thousands of visitors crowded into the city to enjoy the boardwalk and the beaches. A beauty pageant in September crowned a young woman "Miss America."[9]

Prohibition was the law of the land, but it wasn't strictly enforced on the boardwalk. A reporter called Atlantic City "the wettest town in the United States," noting that liquor was sold openly in "saloons, cafes, and cabarets." New York City bootleggers controlled the flow of alcohol to the city. Operators of motorboats transported the illegal cargo and cases of alcohol to shore for distribution to local businesses.[10]

The season for the Bacharach Giants had started with controversy and some disruption. Their player-manager John Henry "Pop" Lloyd was unhappy with his contract and the team's management. After two years with the Bacharach Giants, he left the team to take a position with the New York Lincoln Giants. Dick Lundy, the team's superb shortstop, was installed as the new manager. Except for Lloyd, most of the team's players from 1925 returned, including a strong pitching staff headed by Claude Grier and Rats Henderson.

Atlantic City got off to a slow start. At the end of June, their record stood at 9–12, good for sixth place in the eight-team league. Then came July, and the Giants went on a thirteen-game winning streak to move into second place. During the second half of the league season, Atlantic City battled the defending champion Hilldale Darby Daisies and Oscar Charleston's Harrisburg Giants for the ECL title. Another winning streak—this time nine victories in a row at the end of August and beginning of September—provided Atlantic City with a slim winning margin.

The teams were set for the Colored World Series of 1926. To accommodate fan interest across the league, the series would be played in various locations, with Game One scheduled for October 1 at Bacharach Park in Atlantic City.

A small fire broke out under the grandstand prior to Game One, but it was extinguished before it did significant damage. The Knights of Pythias band performed to entertain the crowd. Atlantic City mayor Edward Bader attended and threw out the ceremonial first ball to officially start the series.

Both starting pitchers, Rats Henderson and Rube Curry, were effective, and the score was tied at 3–3 when Atlantic City loaded the bases in the bottom of the eighth inning with two outs. Luther Farrell, who had homered in his previous at bat, came to the plate. Malarcher responded by replacing Curry on the mound with Willie Foster, relieving on two day's rest after pitching fourteen innings in the final game in the NNL championship series. Foster was up to the challenge, striking out Farrell to end the rally. Neither team scored in the ninth. At that point, it was too dark to continue. The game ended as a tie.

Game Two was held the next day at the same ballpark. Atlantic City's Claude Grier was knocked out of the box in the second inning as the American Giants scored seven runs. Atlantic City battled back, but Chicago held on for a 7–6 win.

The series moved to Baltimore for Game Three at Maryland Park. Manager Dick Lundy decided to give Claude Grier another chance, and on this day, less than twenty-four hours after the previous day's debacle, Grier was wild but unhittable. He pitched the first no-hitter in professional baseball's postseason play, shutting out Chicago 10–0. He "got his vengeance and rubbed it in," as one reporter wrote.[11] Grier walked six, and two batters reached base on errors, but no one got a hit, and no one scored.

The teams moved on. Games Four and Five were played at the Baker Bowl in Philadelphia. In Game Four, Willie Foster got his first start in the series, opposing Rats Henderson. That game ended in a 4–4 tie. Once again, after nine innings, it was deemed too dark to continue. Fay Young, the sports reporter for the *Chicago Defender*, proposed that games should begin at 2:30 p.m. instead of 3:00 p.m., so that the contests could be completed in daylight. But no other games in the series had to end early because of darkness.

Game Five was played the next day, with Atlantic City scoring a 7–5 win, thanks to a six-run fifth inning.

Game Six was back in Atlantic City. Claude Grier got his third start in the series, and while he was shaky at times and allowed six hits, he hurled a complete game, and Atlantic City scored a 6–4 win.

The teams had now played six games in six days, and Atlantic City had taken a 3–1 lead in the series, needing two more victories to claim the title. The series shifted to Chicago for the final games.

Three days passed before Game Seven was played on October 9. It was a must-win game for Chicago in their return to Schorling Park. They won 5–4, scoring the winning run in the bottom of the ninth on a single by John Hines. Willie Foster pitched an eight-hitter, allowing all four runs.

On Sunday, October 10—the same day that the final game of the white Major League World Series was being played in Yankee Stadium—Game Eight of the Colored World Series was played in Chicago. The game attracted the largest crowd—3,620—that would see any of the games in the series.

A light mist moistened the field, and hometown fans didn't have much to cheer about on this damp and chilly day. Chicago's bats went cold as Rats Henderson tossed a solid three-hit shutout, and Atlantic City won 3–0, putting them just one win away from the championship.

In Game Nine, Rube Curry started for the third time in the series and Claude Grier for the fourth time. A sparse crowd of 905 fans showed up to see the contest. Grier's wildness—he walked six—put runners on base in the fourth and sixth innings; they eventually scored. Chicago took a 6–0 lead before Atlantic City staged a late rally. Curry pitched a complete game. The final score was 6–3.

Game Ten was played on a Wednesday before a small crowd of just 733 fans. Those who came out to the ballpark saw the only lopsided contest of the series, a 13–0 win for Chicago. Willie Powell pitched the shutout, allowing six hits, walking one, and striking out one.

Now the stage was set. After thirteen days, ten games, two ties, a no-hitter, a one-sided blowout, and contests in four different ballparks, the 1926 Colored World Series would be decided on Thursday afternoon, October 14, in Chicago's Schorling Park.

The series deserved a dramatic climax. Fans—2,089 for this game—would not be disappointed. Once again, Willie Foster got the start for Chicago in the deciding game—just as he had more than two weeks before against Bullet Rogan and the Kansas City Monarchs. Atlantic City pitched Hubert Lockhart.

Atlantic City threatened early and often. In the first inning, Atlantic City loaded the bases with two outs. Foster got out of the inning by striking out Chance Cummings. In the fourth, Atlantic City got two baserunners but couldn't score. Foster pitched out of another bases-loaded jam in the seventh. He gave up two singles and a walk but got Chaney White to fly out to centerfielder Jelly Gardner. Atlantic City did not score in the eighth or ninth. Through nine innings, Foster had allowed ten hits and given up three walks, but the game was still scoreless.

The game moved to the bottom of the ninth. Chicago had gotten only two hits off Lockhart and advanced only one runner to third base.

Jelly Gardner led off with a single. Malarcher sacrificed him to second. For just the second time in the game, Chicago had a runner in scoring position. Sandy Thompson came to the plate and lined a single to centerfield. The ball took a bad bounce away from Chaney White, and Gardner raced home with the winning run.

It was an abrupt ending, but the game was over, and the Chicago American Giants were the champions. A dramatic and historic season had come to an end.

22

Judge Landis Steps Up to the Plate

After the World Series ended, Landis focused on his investigation into the allegedly fixed game between the Indians and the Tigers in 1919—the one that Cobb and Speaker had been involved with.

To hear Dutch Leonard's side of the story, Landis invited Leonard to sit for an interview at his office in Chicago. Leonard refused to come to Chicago, saying, "They got guys in Chicago who bump people off for a price."[1]

Dutch had a point.

By 1926 Al Capone had established himself as the kingpin of bootlegging and other illegal activities in Chicago. His supremacy was not to be challenged. Capone and his competitors were involved in numerous bloody battles and targeted assassination attempts. On October 11, just as the World Series was ending in New York, Hymie Weiss, a rival of Capone's, was murdered in Chicago in broad daylight on State Street by assassins using machine guns and a shotgun.[2]

Since Dutch wouldn't come to Landis, the judge went to California. His trip was advertised to the press as a routine golf outing in Los Angles, but after playing just one round in a tournament, Landis took a train to Fresno. He told the press that the reason for his visit was because he wanted to see his good friend Dutch Leonard and "to rest and see a whole lot of scenery"[3]

Leonard picked Landis up at the Fresno train depot a little before noon and drove the judge to Leonard's farm, near the small town of Sanger. It was a hot day, temperatures in the mid-80s. Leonard offered the judge a tour of his land, and the two men set out on foot, walking between the rows of grapevines. It was painful for Landis. He was wearing ill-fitting golf shoes. His regular shoes had been stolen the night before the start of the tournament.[4]

After the tour, Landis interviewed Leonard and took a statement. Then Landis departed for Chicago.

On November 3, four days after Landis met Leonard in California, Ty Cobb resigned as manager of the Tigers and announced his retirement from the game.

The public was unprepared for Cobb's decision. True, Cobb was nearly forty years of age and had played in only seventy-nine games in 1926, but he had still hit .339. There had been questions about Cobb's lack of success as a manager. In six years as the manager of the Tigers, Cobb had not taken a team to the World Series. There were rumors that Frank Navin might replace him before the next season. As one of Cobb's biographers, Charles Alexander, wrote, "Cobb's departure was plausible enough."[5]

Twenty-six days later—after the baseball world had absorbed Cobb's news—fans and the media were shocked again, this time by the news that Tris Speaker was resigning as manager of the Cleveland Indians and also going into retirement. Speaker responded to questions by saying, "I am taking a vacation from baseball that I suspect will last the remainder of my life."[6]

The two resignations, so close together, raised suspicions.

Speaker and Cobb had plenty of time on their Wyoming hunting trip to get their stories straight and ponder what to do about Leonard's accusation and Ban Johnson's forceful request that they resign and step away from baseball. They may have had second thoughts about resigning, but they had taken that step, as they told Johnson they would.

Then they reconsidered. What they wanted was to confront their accuser face-to-face. They asked Landis to arrange a meeting with Leonard. Landis scheduled a meeting for late November and asked Leonard to attend.

Leonard declined the invitation to come to Chicago and be interrogated. Landis canceled the November meeting and scheduled a new one for December 20. Once again—predictably at this point—Leonard refused to leave California. Landis had no way to force him to comply.

By now, Cobb and Speaker had gone one step further. Since Cobb and Speaker couldn't get a face-to-face meeting with Leonard, they did the next best thing: they hired lawyers. Cobb retained James Murlin, a former Michigan circuit judge and a regent at the University of Michigan, and Edward Burke, an attorney who had done legal work for the Tigers. Speaker hired

William Boyd, a well-respected attorney from Cleveland.[7] If nothing else, the hiring of attorneys let Landis know that they intended to contest the accusations against them.

On December 20, Landis held the inquiry at his office in the People's Gas Building at 122 South Michigan Avenue. He was in a good mood. Two days earlier, baseball's owners had extended his contract for another seven years and raised his salary from $50,000 to $65,000. He was now the highest-salaried employee in baseball, outearning even Babe Ruth.[8]

The judge questioned Speaker and Cobb, as well as Smokey Joe Wood, now the baseball coach for Yale University, and Fred West, the Detroit Tigers' park attendant who had placed the bets for the ballplayers. Landis read the statement he'd obtained from his interview with Leonard in October about the meeting under the stands. Then Landis questioned the ballplayers.

Landis asked Cobb: "Was there any such conversation such as Leonard relates with Wood and Speaker and yourself?"

Cobb responded: "Positively not."

Landis asked: "Did you bet any money on the game?"

Cobb: "Positively did not."

Landis: "Did you intend to?"

Cobb: "I did not."[9]

Cobb's denial that he intended to bet on the game contradicts what Cobb wrote in his letter to Leonard in 1919, but Landis chose to ignore the discrepancy.

The day after the hearing concluded, Landis released one hundred pages of documents to the press and the public, including Leonard's letters and the transcript of the meeting in his office. Some parts of Leonard's story were confirmed. West had placed bets for Wood and Leonard and a third party—likely Speaker. The players, Cobb and Wood, testified that it was common practice for players to bet on games, ones they played in and ones they didn't play in. In 1919 there was nothing illegal or unethical about players betting on games.

Two major points of contention remained. Had the four players met under the grandstand and had a conversation about the next day's game, as Leonard alleged? Cobb, Wood, and Speaker all emphatically denied such a meeting had taken place. Even more important, had the outcome of the September 25 game been arranged or predetermined? Again, Cobb and Speaker, the managers of those two teams, vigorously denied the accusation.

That evening there was more baseball news—unexpected news. Ten weeks after guiding the St. Louis Cardinals to their first world championship—five days before Christmas—Rogers Hornsby was informed by the Cardinals' traveling secretary that Sam Breadon, the owner of the Cardinals, had traded Hornsby to the New York Giants for infielder Frankie Frisch and pitcher Jimmy Ring.

Hornsby had spent all twelve years of his Major League career with the Cardinals. He was appreciated by fans, had won six batting championships, and was widely regarded as the best right-handed hitter in baseball history. He was still relatively young, at age thirty.

The split between Hornsby and Sam Breadon mostly had to do with money. Hornsby wanted a three-year contract at $50,000 per year; Breadon refused to offer a contract for longer than one year. Breadon and Hornsby had tangled over one thing or another for a decade. It was reported that Breadon once said that "listening to Hornsby was like having the contents of a rock crusher emptied over [one's] head."[10] The relationship between owner and manager-player had finally reached an inevitable breaking point.

As for the Giants and manager John McGraw, they were delighted to acquire Hornsby as a "metropolitan rival" for Babe Ruth.[11]

Hornsby's reaction to the trade: "If they want to trade me, it's all right with me. But it doesn't seem right that I should be traded from a club that I just managed to a world championship."[12]

The day after the Hornsby story hit the front pages, the focus was back on Cobb and Speaker.

With the story out in the open, Ban Johnson's secret plan to hide the scandal from the public was exposed. Landis had gained the upper hand. Now everyone knew about Leonard's allegations and the letters.

Cobb and Speaker received immediate support from the world of baseball. Cobb's fans rallied in his hometown of Augusta, Georgia, under a banner that read "TY IS STILL OUR IDOL AND THE IDOL OF AMERICA."[13]

Billy Evans, a veteran American League umpire, said, "It is a crime that men of the stature of Ty and Tris should be blackened by a man of this caliber with charges that every baseballer knows to be utterly false."[14]

The former baseball player and evangelist Billy Sunday also expressed an opinion: "They are both my friends. It is impossible to imagine that two great stars would risk their fame and fortune for a few hundred dollars."[15]

Cobb and Speaker still weren't quite satisfied with the way things stood. They didn't feel fully exonerated, and they had thoughts of playing another season or two. The day after Christmas, they traveled to Washington DC to talk to some of Cobb's political connections, thinking that somehow the federal government might be able to intercede and restore their credibility. Nothing came of that trip.

Meanwhile, Landis believed things were settled, at least temporarily. Everyone had had their say. The evidence had been shown to the public. Cobb and Speaker had publicly denied Leonard's allegations. So long as Cobb and Speaker were retired, Landis didn't have to decide about punishing them in some way or banishing them or even exonerating them.

Then on New Year's Day—as if Landis needed another headache or scandal to deal with—Charles "Swede" Risberg, the banned-for-life shortstop of the 1919 Black Sox who was now managing a family dairy farm in Minnesota, showed up in Chicago with a new allegation: that in 1917 White Sox players had collected $1,100 to bribe the Detroit Tigers to lose a September doubleheader during that year's pennant race.[16]

Risberg provided Landis and local sportswriters with a statement. His banned-for-life Black Sox teammate Chick Gandil supported Risberg's allegation.

A frustrated Landis muttered to friends, "Won't these God damn things that happened before I came into baseball ever stop coming up?"[17]

Landis acted quickly and invited three dozen players from the 1917 Tigers and White Sox to defend or confirm Risberg's claim. As many as seventy people—witnesses, players, sportswriters—crowded into Landis's office in early January to hear the testimony. It was established that the money had been collected and given as a "bonus" or "gift" to the Tigers' pitchers and their catcher to reward them for beating the White Sox's rival, the Boston Red Sox, in a crucial end-of-season series. Everyone acknowledged that this was a common practice: players on one team gifting cash to players on another team for outstanding performances that benefited both teams. There was no confirmation or proof that any games had been fixed.

One of the witnesses was Ty Cobb. He had traveled from Georgia to attend the meeting and, once more, forcefully proclaimed his innocence. Cobb took the opportunity in front of the audience packed into Landis's office to say publicly, "There has never been a baseball game in my life that I played in, that I knew was fixed."[18]

Landis disposed of the Risberg-Gandil charges a week later, issuing a statement on January 12, 1927, that indicated disapproval of the gifting practice but acknowledgment that it didn't constitute a violation of baseball rules or ethics. The cash bonuses were, Landis said, an act of "impropriety, reprehensible, and censurable, but not corrupt."[19]

On January 27, Landis followed up by issuing a long statement summarizing the Cobb-Speaker case and pronouncing his judgment: "These players have not been, nor are they now, found guilty of fixing a ball game. By no decent system of justice could such finding be made. Therefore, they were not placed on the ineligible list."[20]

Based on the evidence—even considering the incriminating letters—Landis had decided that there was no conclusive proof that the four ballplayers had engaged in game fixing. That didn't mean that Landis, or others, might not have harbored some doubts about the stories told by Cobb, Speaker, and Wood. Landis may have decided in this case that baseball needed a break from a scandal that was seven years in the past and tied by circumstances to the Black Sox affair. Landis may also have considered that Cobb and Speaker were icons of the game and idolized by fans. They were at the end of their careers. Landis likely decided that a severe punishment was not in the best interest of baseball.[21]

In response to the Landis decision, Detroit and Cleveland gave Cobb and Speaker their unconditional releases. Landis specified that the two players could be signed by any American League team, but not by any National League club.

In the end, Landis had made Ban Johnson seem foolish and weak by exposing Johnson's secret plan and then reversing Johnson's decision on whether Cobb and Speaker could continue their careers in the American League. To the extent it mattered, the scandal was about something more than Cobb and Speaker and their gambling on a game in 1919; the affair was also about the feud and power struggle between Landis and Johnson.

But for Cobb and Speaker, it was more straight forward: the two players had been formally vindicated and were now free agents.

At last, the curtain had come down on the drama of the 1926 baseball season. The beginning of spring training was just three weeks away.

Judge Landis would soon be traveling to Florida to play golf and watch some exhibition games.

Epilogue

Greatest Baseball Team of All Time. If the greatest baseball team of all time was the 1927 New York Yankees, as many people would argue, then where does the 1926 Yankees team rank? The rosters were almost identical. All eight position players were the same. Pennock, Hoyt, and Shocker anchored the pitching staff in both years. The main statistical difference between the two teams is that the '27 Yankees scored more runs and had better power numbers than the '26 team. Ruth and Gehrig combined for 63 home runs in '26 and 107 in '27. The lineup deserved the nickname "Murderers Row."[1] The pitching staff was better in '27 too, giving up half a run less per game than the '26 team.

But were the 1927 Yankees the best baseball team ever assembled? An argument can be made for other teams: for example, the 1906 Cubs, who posted a record of 116–36. Or the powerhouse 1975 Big Red Machine.

The great Negro League teams of the 1930s should also be considered. Negro League historian Phil Dixon analyzed data from that era and concluded that the 1931 Homestead Grays should be in the conversation for greatest baseball team of all time.[2] Others argue that the best Negro League team of all time was the 1935 Pittsburgh Crawfords, a team that featured four future Hall of Famers: Oscar Charleston, Josh Gibson, Cool Papa Bell, and Judy Johnson, all of whom rank near the top of any list of players at their positions.

St. Louis Cardinals. In the years after the Cardinals' first National League pennant and World Series win in 1926, the franchise thrived, winning eight National League crowns and five World Series titles over the next twenty seasons.

New York Yankees. From 1927 through 1946, the Yankees dominated Major League Baseball, winning ten American League pennants and nine World

Series championships. Joe DiMaggio arrived in 1936, and in his first eight years, the Yankees won seven league titles.

Negro Leagues. Without Rube Foster's vision and leadership, a new generation of owners and players faced the future: the coming economic crisis of the Depression and then the disruption of American life during World War II.[3] The 1927 Colored World Series featured a rematch between the Chicago American Giants and the Atlantic City Bacharach Giants, but that was the last Colored World Series game for fifteen years as the Depression and the insolvency of various teams made it impossible for leagues to survive. The ECL dissolved in 1928. A new league—the American Negro League—replaced the ECL, but it only lasted one season. Teams formed and disappeared. Many of the most successful teams—the Homestead Grays; the Pittsburgh Crawfords—operated independently of the leagues and acquired many of the best players.

The annual East-West All-Star game, originating in 1933 and continuing until 1960, featured the best Negro League players. This immensely popular event—the creation of Gus Greenlee, owner of the Pittsburgh Crawfords—set attendance records.[4] In the 1930s and 1940s, Black barnstorming teams played before appreciative Black and white audiences across America.

World War II disrupted Black baseball. More than two hundred Negro League players served in the segregated United States military during the war, which officially ended on V-E Day, May 8, 1945.[5] Twenty-three months later, on April 15, 1947, Jackie Robinson played his first game for the Brooklyn Dodgers, and the desegregation of the white Major Leagues commenced.

Full integration of the white Major Leagues—Rube Foster's dream—was tortuously slow but completed in 1959 when Pumpsie Green was signed by the Boston Red Sox. Finally, every white Major League team employed at least one Black player on its roster.

Ty Cobb. After being reinstated in good standing by Judge Landis in January 1927, Cobb signed with the Philadelphia Athletics and played his last two seasons under Connie Mack. At age forty, Cobb could still hit. In 1927 he posted a batting average of .357 and stole twenty-two bases. He hit .323 in 1928, his final season in the Major Leagues.

Tris Speaker. In 1927 Speaker played 141 games with the Washington Nationals and batted .327. The next year, he joined Cobb on the A's, where his batting average fell to .267. Like Cobb, he retired after the 1928 season.

Dutch Leonard. Leonard enjoyed a quiet and prosperous retirement in California, living in an elegant house and overseeing 2,500 acres of productive farmland. For several years, he managed the farms of neighboring Japanese American farmers who had been forced off their land and relocated to internment camps. When the Japanese American farmers were released from the internment camps, Leonard returned the land to the farmers, with $20,000 in profits from the harvests that he oversaw on their properties. Leonard liked to barbecue, and he hosted parties where he told baseball stories. He was especially proud of his collection of phonograph records and claimed to own 150,000 albums. Leonard died of a cerebral hemorrhage in 1952 at the age of sixty. He left an estate valued at over $2 million dollars.

Grover Cleveland Alexander. After the 1926 World Series, Alexander pitched three more seasons for the Cardinals, winning forty-six games and losing twenty-seven. He then pitched nine games for the Phillies in 1930 before retiring at age forty-three with a career record of 373–208. He recorded ninety shutouts over twenty seasons, second most in Major League history. For four years, Alexander pitched for and managed a traveling House of David team. In 1934, with Alexander as manager and Satchel Paige as the team's starting pitcher, the House of David team won the Denver Post tournament. It was the first year the tournament was open to Black teams and Black players. In the last years of his life, Alexander made a meager living telling baseball stories in the basement of Hubert's Museum, a flea circus located in New York City's Time Square. Throughout his later years, in addition to epilepsy and alcoholism, he struggled with other health problems: cancer, which required amputation of his right ear; injuries from a bad fall; and a heart attack.

From a farm in Nebraska to the Major Leagues, from combat in Europe to heroics in the World Series, from battles with alcoholism and epilepsy to the Hall of Fame—this was the life journey of Grover Cleveland Alexander. Along the way, he married and was divorced by the same woman twice. At the end of his life, he was back in Nebraska.

If Alexander's life story sounds like a movie plot, in fact, it became one. A film titled *The Winning Team* was released in June 1952, eighteen months after Alexander died alone in a rooming house in St. Paul, Nebraska. The team in the title referred not just to the Cardinals but also to the relationship between Alexander and his wife, Aimee.

The trailer for the movie pitches the film as "the warmest, most wonderful, most human story ever told—the true story of Grover Cleveland Alexander and the woman who shared all the adventures of his fabulous career." The film ends with Alex's triumphant performance in the 1926 World Series. It does not portray the darkest days of his later life.

Doris Day received top billing and played the role of Aimee, Alexander's loyal and forgiving wife. Alexander was played by Ronald Reagan.

Rogers Hornsby. Hornsby had an excellent 1927 season with the Giants, batting .361 and playing in 155 games, but he clashed with players and management and was traded again after the season to the seventh-place Boston Braves, where he played just a single season. He joined the Chicago Cubs in 1929—his fourth team in four years. Plagued by injuries and controversy, he bounced from team to team, including three full seasons and two partial seasons with the lowly St. Louis Browns. He owed money to the IRS and to bookies. In 1944 he agreed to manage and play for the Vera Cruz Blues, a team in a six-team Mexican League. He lasted nine days, returned to St. Louis, and said, "I'd rather be a lamppost in America than a general down there."[6] He finished his Major League career with a lifetime batting average of .358 and always contended that the biggest thrill he had in baseball was tagging Ruth out for the final putout of the 1926 World Series.

Billy Southworth. Southworth had a long career in professional baseball as a player, a manager, and a scout. The 1926 season was his best as a player. As a manager, he led four teams to the World Series. In 1952, as a scout for the Boston Braves, he evaluated a skinny shortstop who had not attended high school and was playing sandlot ball. He graded the prospect as "good" in the categories of fielding, hitting, and attitude but only "fair" as a power hitter. Southworth recommended signing the prospect but estimated it would take four or five years in the Minors before he was ready for the Majors. The prospect's name was Henry Aaron. Two years later, Aaron was the starting right fielder for the Milwaukee Braves. He would go on to hit 755 Major League home runs.

Frankie Frisch. The trade of Hornsby for Frisch worked out to the advantage of the Cardinals. As Hornsby struggled to stay healthy, Frisch put together a Hall of Fame career with the Cardinals, batting .316 for his playing career and leading the Cardinals to four National League pennants.

Miller Huggins. By the end of the 1926 World Series, Huggins was exhausted, worn out physically and emotionally. He had lost nearly twenty pounds during the season and was on the verge of a nervous breakdown. He considered retirement.[7] In the off-season, he recuperated at Bill Brown's Health Farm, a resort in Garrison, New York. Huggins returned to manage the Yankees for three more seasons, winning American League pennants in 1927 and 1928, sweeping the Pittsburgh Pirates four games to none in the '27 World Series, then sweeping the St. Louis Cardinals four games to none in the '28 series. In 1929, another stressful year for Huggins, the Yankees finished second to the Philadelphia Athletics, but Huggins didn't live to see the end of the season. In September, he developed a carbuncle on his cheek that became infected and led to a condition known as erysipelas, or blood poisoning. Huggins resisted going to see a doctor, but he finally relented and entered St. Vincent's hospital in Greenwich Village on September 20. He died five days later at the age of fifty-one.

Babe Ruth. Ruth's 1926 baseball season ended when he was thrown out at second base in the ninth inning of Game Seven, but Ruth was a busy man in the off-season. Shortly after the end of the World Series, he embarked on a vaudeville tour for which he was paid $8,333 a week. After the vaudeville tour, he went to Hollywood to prepare for his role in a film titled *The Babe Comes Home*. Meanwhile, Ruth's agent, Christy Walsh, arranged for the Babe to earn some additional cash by endorsing "Chevrolets, Cadillacs, Packards, Studebakers, and Chryslers, as well as home appliances, boarding kennels, and housing developments."[8] His demanding off-season schedule didn't impair his preparation for the 1927 season. Ruth returned to the Yankee lineup and hit sixty home runs, another new single-season record.

Tony Lazzeri. After a stellar fourteen-year career with many highlights and six trips to the World Series, Lazzeri retired to California, where he owned and operated a tavern in San Francisco. Despite his long and illustrious career with the Yankees, his strikeout against Alexander in the 1926 World Series was never to be forgotten. Baseball fans talked about it for years. Lazzeri was always reminded of it.

In 1945, a year before his death at age of forty-two, Lazzeri was interviewed in his San Francisco tavern by Bob Considine, a syndicated sports columnist.[9]

"Funny thing, but nobody seems to remember much about my ball playing, except that strikeout," Lazzeri told Considine. "There isn't a night goes by but what some guy leans across the bar, or comes up behind me at a table in this joint, and brings up the old question. Never a night."

After Lazzeri's death, sports columnist Red Smith wrote, "It was Lazzeri's misfortune that although he was as great a ball player as ever lived the most vivid memory he left in most minds concerned the day he failed."[10]

Urban Shocker. Despite a serious heart condition, Shocker won eighteen and lost six as a key pitcher on the Yankees' exceptional 1927 championship team. After that season, he considered retirement but decided to continue his career. In July 1928 he collapsed while pitching batting practice in Chicago; he was released by the Yankees for medical reasons shortly thereafter. He moved to Denver, sought medical attention, and was hospitalized in mid-August. He died of heart disease a few weeks later. He was thirty-eight.

Rube Foster. Rube Foster, the brilliant architect of the Negro Leagues, spent the last four years of his life as a patient at the Kankakee State Hospital. He never saw or participated in another baseball game. He died from a heart attack on December 9, 1930, at the age of fifty-one. Foster's importance to the history of professional baseball, and especially to Black baseball, cannot be overstated. His passing from the scene marked the end of an era in Black baseball.

Satchel Paige. In his prime, Paige was the best right-handed pitcher, Black or white, in all of baseball. Red Sox legend Johnny Pesky said Paige had "the best control of anybody I ever saw" and estimated that his fastball was "at least a hundred miles an hour."[11] Joe DiMaggio concurred, stating unequivocally that Paige was the best pitcher he ever batted against and praised his breaking ball: "Satch has a curve with so many bends it looks like a wiggle in a cyclone."[12] Paige was not just a stellar pitcher. He was also a brilliant showman, a box office draw, and a masterful promoter. He was as famous as any ballplayer in America.

Paige barnstormed with Dizzy Dean in the 1930s and with Bob Feller in the 1940s.[13] He pitched for more than a half dozen different Negro League teams, including the Pittsburgh Crawfords and the Kansas City Monarchs. In 1933 and 1935, he pitched for a team in Bismarck, North Dakota, posting a record of 35–2. He pitched nine seasons in the California Winter League, compiling a record of 56–7. He pitched in Mexico and the Dominican Republic; he pitched in Puerto Rico for the Guayama Witches and in Cuba for the Santa Clara Leopards. In the 1934 Denver Post tournament, Paige pitched for a House of David team, managed by Grover Cleveland Alexander. In his three starts and one relief appearance, Paige struck out forty-four batters in twenty-eight innings, and the House of David team won the tournament.[14]

In 1948, at age forty-two and well past his prime, Paige was signed to pitch for the Cleveland Indians in the white Major Leagues. That season the Indians won the pennant and the World Series and Paige became the first Negro League pitcher to pitch in a World Series game. He pitched five more years in the Majors, two seasons with Cleveland and three seasons with a very bad St. Louis Browns team.[15] He was elected to the National Baseball Hall of Fame in 1971, the first electee of the Committee on Negro Baseball Leagues.

Judge Landis. Judge Landis served as baseball's powerful commissioner from November 12, 1920, until November 25, 1944, when he died in office. He was seventy-eight years old. Two weeks after his death, he was voted into the Hall of Fame. He guided Major League Baseball through the scandals of the 1920s, the Depression of the 1930s, and the first years of World War II. Judge Landis was a man with a distinctive look and a huge ego who loved baseball and hated all forms of gambling. Throughout his tenure, he relished and used his power to enhance the integrity and appeal of the white Major Leagues. What role he played in supporting baseball's years of segregation is a debate that persists. No one questions that he was a monumental and influential figure in the history of the sport.

Ban Johnson. Ban Johnson was one of the most powerful executives in baseball for more than three decades. He oversaw the American League from its inception in the early 1900s until he resigned as president of the league in 1927. He was a talented organizer and visionary. In his last years, he argued that Major League Baseball needed to expand coast to coast. He had serious health problems in his later years and succumbed to diabetes in 1931 at the age of sixty-seven.

Aimee Semple McPherson. Aimee McPherson remained a controversial figure throughout her life. Shortly after her reappearance in June 1926, Los Angeles district attorney Asa Keyes called for an investigation into her alleged kidnapping. Two weeks later, McPherson testified before a grand jury and told her story. Titillating rumors and gossip filled the papers, insinuating that she had not been kidnapped but had run off with a lover. A California judge determined there was sufficient evidence to bring charges of "conspiracy and obstruction of justice." A trial was scheduled for January 1927; at the last minute, the case was dismissed. McPherson wrote an autobiography titled *In the Service of the King*, then went on a nationwide tour, presenting a monologue she called "Story of My Life." She continued to preach and draw new followers to her church. In 1944 she died, at age fifty-three, of an overdose of sleeping pills. Her death was ruled accidental. The Foursquare Church that McPherson founded has continued to flourish. As of 2024, the church proudly claimed to have 67,500 congregations and 8.8 million followers in 150 countries.[16]

Calvin Coolidge. In 1928 President Calvin Coolidge announced he would not run for another term. He left the White House on March 4, 1929, and died in Northampton, Massachusetts, on January 5, 1933, at the age of sixty. The cause of death was determined to be coronary thrombosis.

Grace Coolidge. If there was a Baseball Fans Hall of Fame, Grace Coolidge would be the first inductee. After Calvin Coolidge left the White House in 1929, the Coolidges moved back to Northampton, Massachusetts, and Grace switched her allegiance to the Boston Red Sox. "I am an American League fan," she declared, and the American League office provided her a season pass to all games she wanted to attend. She was a student of the game and its history and had strong opinions about the way the game was played.

In particular, she abhorred the intentional walk and, once expressing her views on the subject to a group of baseball writers, argued that it should be abolished.

She told friends, "You may not give a hoot for baseball, but to me, it is my life."[17]

Notes

Introduction

1. One of the most famous of the wing walkers was Lillian Boyer, a former waitress, who performed in hundreds of shows. Boyer survived (some didn't) and died peacefully and quietly in 1989 at the age of eighty-eight.

1. A Dynasty Is Born

1. Appel, *Pinstripe Empire*, 11–12.
2. Appel, *Pinstripe Empire*, 11.
3. Bill Lamb, "Bill Devery."
4. Farrell had a close relationship with Big Tim Sullivan, a key player in Tammany Hall and a former U.S. congressman. Sullivan was a man of influence and wealth.
5. In March 1903, as Farrell was being considered for ownership of a new Major League franchise, he was being sued for losses an individual suffered at one of his gambling establishments. Farrell testified that he was innocent of any wrongdoing or even knowledge of such activities going on. He was acquitted. Appel, *Pinstripe Empire*, 10.
6. Appel, *Pinstripe Empire*, 10.
7. Appel, *Pinstripe Empire*, 70.
8. Huston was primarily a businessman and a civil engineer. He had served in the Spanish-American War with a company of volunteer engineers; in World War I, he rejoined the military and rose to the rank of colonel. Ruppert was a colonel in a National Guard unit.
9. Who actually introduced Ruppert and Huston is debatable. It may have been McGraw, but it might also have been Billy Fleischmann, a friend of Ruppert's. Either way, McGraw, along with Ban Johnson, was involved in arranging the sale of the Yankees to new owners.
10. Steinberg and Spatz, *The Colonel and Hug*, 49, 62–63.

2. Miller Huggins

1. The baseball "Wild" Bill Donovan should not be confused with the "Wild" Bill Donovan who was a World War I hero and Medal of Honor recipient. The baseball Bill Donovan died tragically in a train accident in December 1923.
2. Appel, *Pinstripe Empire*, 86–87.
3. Details about the interior of Ruppert's office come from the Waite Hoyt interview in Murdock, *Baseball Between the Wars*, 41.
4. "Shoot Our Traitors at Home, Root Warns at Welcome Here From His Mission to Russia," *New York Times*, August 16, 1917.
5. Murdock, *Baseball between the Wars*, 42.
6. For details of Ruppert's lifestyle and interests, see Steinberg "Jacob Ruppert." See also Steinberg and Spatz, "The Colonel and Hug: The Odd Couple . . . Not Really."
7. Myrtle Huggins, as told to John B. Kennedy, "Mighty Midget," *Collier's*, May 24, 1930.
8. Finkel, "Eddie Plank."
9. Eig, *Luckiest Man*, 62.
10. Montville, *The Big Bam*, 206–7.
11. Flaspohler, *St. Louis Baseball History* 84.
12. Montville, *The Big Bam*, 207–8.
13. Montville, *The Big Bam*, 208.
14. Monville, *The Big Bam*, 208.

3. The Cardinals and Hornsby

1. Golenbock, *Spirit*, 12–19.
2. Golenbock, *Spirit*, 12–19.
3. Golenbock, *Spirit*, 16. What Von der Ahe had created was essentially an amusement park first, and a ballpark second.
4. Golenbock, *Spirit*, 16–19.
5. Golenbock, *Spirit*, 51–55.
6. Stangl, "St. Louis Cardinals Team Ownership History." Stanley Robison's will provided that three-quarters of the shares would be Helene Britton's and one-quarter would be her mother's.
7. Suitors included Charles Weegham, a Chicago restauranter, and James McGill, president of the Denver baseball team in the Western League.
8. Lowenfish, *Branch Rickey*, 42–43.
9. Lowenfish, *Branch Rickey*, 42.
10. Alexander, *Rogers Hornsby*, 101.

11. Alexander, *Rogers Hornsby*, 158–59. Hornsby claimed that he lost more in the stock market than from bets on horse races.
12. Wolf, *The Called Shot*, 47–48.
13. Alexander, *Rogers Hornsby*, 107.
14. Alexander, *Rogers Hornsby*, 109.
15. "Hornsby on Stand Denies Debt to Moore, Who Alleges He Bet $327,995 in Year," *New York Times*, December 21, 1927.
16. Goldman, "Goldman's Baseball Quotables #7."

4. Terrell Woods

1. Golenbock, *Spirit*, 100.
2. Michael Bamberger quoting Andy Seminick in "Hail to the Rajah."
3. Golenbock, *Spirit*, 105.
4. In fairness to Hornsby, he managed the St. Louis Browns for five years, during which time the Browns had a very weak roster. Despite his lack of success as a manager, Hornsby kept getting chances to manage. In addition to the Cardinals and the Browns, he spent time as the manager of the Cubs, the Braves, and the Reds.
5. Alexander, *Rogers Hornsby*, 129.
6. Golenbock, *Spirit*, 106.
7. White Major League catchers who played during O'Farrell's career include Gabby Hartnett, Mickey Cochrane, Bill Dickey, Ray Schalk, Rick Ferrell, and Ernie Lombardi—all of whom are in the Hall of Fame. Negro League catchers of the same era include Josh Gibson, Biz Mackey, and Louis Santop. Gibson, Mackey, and Santop are also in the National Baseball Hall of Fame.
8. No box score of the game exists to verify that Keen pitched against Johnson and Santop, but both were members of the Darby Daisies that summer. In future years, such Negro League stars as Oscar Charleston and Biz Mackey played for the Hilldale team, which won three consecutive Eastern Colored League championships between 1921 and 1923.
9. Griffin, "Flint Rhem."
10. Everyone knew that Rhem had a serious drinking problem. In 1930 he disappeared and later claimed he had been kidnapped and forced to drink large quantities of alcohol. For the full story, see Wolf, *The Called Shot*, 81–82 and Nancy Snell Griffin's SABR biography of Rhem.
11. Greg H. Wolf, "Bill Sherdel."
12. How "Wee" was Wee Willie Sherdel? The *Baseball Encyclopedia* lists him as 5 feet 10 inches and 160 pounds, but his draft card puts his height at 5 feet 8 inches, and it's likely his playing weight was around 150 pounds or less.
13. Greg H. Wolf, "Bill Sherdel."

14. Greg H. Wolf, "Bill Sherdel."
15. Bob Gibson had 251 career wins; Jesse Haines had 210 wins. Willie Sherdel is the winningest left-hander in Cardinals history, with 153 wins.

5. St. Petersburg

1. Montville, *The Big Bam*, 216–25.
2. GrizzleX, "Babe Ruth Boxing," May 14, 2007, YouTube video, 0:22, https://youtu.be/7BjR1mSir58.
3. Richard Vidmer, "Yankee Vanguard Starts for Camp," *New York Times*, February 20, 1926.
4. "Miller Huggins, Sells Out His Real Estate Holding to Give Yanks Undivided Attention," *The Evening Independent*, February 18, 1926. The article described Huggins as the "midget pilot" of the Yankees.
5. Scott Deitche, "Capone, Torrio, and the Sunshine City, St. Petersburg, Florida," The Mob Museum, August 27, 2020, https://themobmuseum.org/blog/capone-torrio-and-the-sunshine-city-st-petersburg-florida/.
6. Eig, *Luckiest Man*, 69.
7. Cal Ripken broke Lou Gehrig's consecutive-game streak on September 6, 1995. Gehrig had appeared in 2,130 consecutive games. Ripken's streak ended on September 20, 1998, after he had appeared in 2,632 consecutive games.
8. Steinberg and Spatz, *The Colonel and Hug*, 246.
9. Baker, *The New York Game*, 249.
10. Walker's life story was told in the 1957 film *Beau James*. In the film, Walker was played by Bob Hope, in a rare dramatic role. The film was based on the nonfiction book *Beau James*, written by Gene Fowler, a journalist and close friend of Walker's.
11. Baker, *The New York Game*, 249.
12. James Harrison, "Yanks Send Back Curtis Fullerton," *New York Times*, February 24, 1926.
13. The "swarthy Neapolitan" comment appears in "4 Yankee Homers Bury Robins, 10–2," under the byline Harry Cross, *New York Times*, March 30, 1926. The "famed spaghetti farmer" comment appears in "Lazzeri Hits 1.000 as Yanks Win Again," under the byline Harry Cross, *New York Times*, April 3, 1926.
14. Harry Cross, "Yanks and Robins Kept Idle by Rain," *New York Times*, March 31, 1926.

6. Opening Days

1. Every president from Taft until Carter—Taft, Wilson, Harding, Coolidge, Hoover, FDR, Truman, Eisenhower, Kennedy, Johnson, Nixon, and

Ford—had participated in the ceremony at least once during their administration. Carter threw out a first pitch after he left the presidency. Reagan, H. W. Bush, Clinton, George Bush, and Obama also participated in the ritual. Donald Trump and Joe Biden are the only sitting presidents since Taft to eschew the practice all together, although Biden threw out the first pitch as vice president in 2009.

2. There was only one new manager in the Majors at the start of 1926. Joe McCarthy of the Cubs was in his first season. McCarthy, however, had many years as a Minor League manager, so Hornsby was the least experienced manager.
3. "Babe Ruth Afoul of Bay State Rules," *New York Times*, April 14, 1926.
4. "Seize Radio Burglar at Baseball Game: He Admits Murder," *New York Times*, April 14, 1926.
5. "Seize Radio Burglar."
6. Hilton stole radios because he could sell them for cash at pawn shops. He was alleged to have stolen between fifty and one hundred radios. After one of his thefts, Hilton shot and killed policeman Arthur Kenny, who had chased him and tried to make an arrest. Hilton was convicted of murder and put to death in Sing Sing's electric chair on February 17, 1927, just ten months after his arrest. See "Radio Burglar Dies in Chair at Sing Sing," *New York Times*, February 18, 1927.

7. Babe Ruth and Ty Cobb

1. James Harrison, "Yanks and Red Sox Suspend for a Day," *New York Times*, April 16, 1926.
2. Harrison, "Yanks and Red Sox."
3. Koenig, the ex-Yankee, was playing in the Pacific Coast League in the summer of 1932 when the Chicago Cubs, having just fired player-manager Rogers Hornsby, needed another infielder. Koenig contributed with his bat, getting key hits in August and September that helped propel the Cubs to the World Series, where Koenig faced his former team. Prior to the World Series, Koenig was voted a half-share of World Series money, based on his limited time on the roster. That decision sparked a trash-talking confrontation between Ruth and the Cubs' bench that became part of the story of Ruth's called shot home run at Wrigley Field in Game Three of the 1932 World Series. See Thomas Wolf's book *The Called Shot* for the full story.
4. Leerhsen, *Ty Cobb*, 12.
5. Ruth's second wife was Claire Hodgson, an actress who had grown up in Georgia and knew Ty Cobb socially as a young girl.
6. Leerhsen, *Ty Cobb*, 25.

7. Leerhsen, *Ty Cobb*, 281.
8. Montville, *The Big Bam*, 190–91.
9. In his short Major League career, Johns would win just six games. On the other hand, Shawkey had already won 184 games.
10. The relatively unheralded Hooks Dauss won 223 Major League games, just one fewer than Hall of Fame pitchers Jim Bunning and Catfish Hunter.

8. Early Season Blues

1. Alexander was 2–1 at the start of the 1918 season before he was drafted into the army, but he returned from military service in time to play in the 1919 season, when he recorded sixteen wins against eleven losses.
2. Coulson, *Wee Willie Sherdel*, 182.
3. Coulson, *Wee Willie Sherdel*, 182.
4. Golenbock, *Spirit*, 87. A slightly different quote can be found in Lowenfish, *Branch Rickey*, 118.
5. Golenbock, *Spirit*, 100.

9. Grover Cleveland Alexander

1. Bichloride of gold is also known as auric chloride. It's not clear if this treatment worked or cured many people of their dependence on alcohol, but the Keeley Institute operated worldwide from 1879 to 1965 and claimed to have treated more than three hundred thousand patients.
2. William Wrigley bought Catalina Island in 1919 and built a ballpark there so the Cubs could use the facility for spring training. The Cubs held spring training on the island from 1921 to 1941 and from 1946 to 1951.
3. Skipper, *Wicked Curve*, 105.
4. Quoted in Levy, *Joe McCarthy*, 105.
5. Skipper, *Wicked Curve*, 103.
6. Skipper, *Wicked Curve*, 10.
7. Skipper, *Wicked Curve*, 12–13.
8. The historical record is unclear about exactly where Alexander was hit. Some reports say it was on the right temple; others say it was on the left temple or the middle of his forehead. Depending on the source, reports also vary as to whether he was hit running to first base or to second. Regardless, it was a severe and debilitating injury.
9. Skipper, *Wicked Curve*, 12–15.
10. Alexander faced Ruth ten times in their careers, all in World Series games. In those ten at bats, Ruth went 0–8 and walked twice.
11. Leeke, *The Best Team*, 10.
12. Leeke, *The Best Team*, 13.

13. Leeke, *The Best Team*, 14.
14. Skipper, *Wicked Curve*, 68–69; Leeke, *The Best Team*, 32–34.
15. Leeke, *The Best Team*, 34.
16. The holdout—Alex wanted a two-year contract and a signing bonus. He eventually got a $5,000 bonus and immediately invested it in Liberty Bonds.
17. Skipper, *Wicked Curve*, 71.
18. Skipper, *Wicked Curve*, 72.
19. For an in-depth and historical perspective of Alexander's military experience, see Jim Leeke's excellent book *The Best Team Over There: The Untold Story of Grover Clevland Alexander and the Great War.*
20. See Baseball Reference, "World War I," https://www.baseball-reference.com/bullpen/World_War_I. In addition to these players, more than fifty Minor League, semipro, and college players died in the war. See Baseball's Greatest Sacrifice, "World War I Deaths," https://www.baseballsgreatestsacrifice.com/world_war_i.html.
21. Skipper, *Wicked Curve*, 75.
22. Skipper, *Wicked Curve*, 76; Leeke, *The Best Team*, 161.
23. Levy, *Joe McCarthy*, 372; regarding McCarthy's drinking issues.
24. James Crusinberry, "Cubs Beaten by Cardinals, 3–2; Then Win, 5–0" *Chicago Tribune*, June 28, 1926.
25. Crusinberry, "Cubs Beaten."

10. Away from the Ballpark

1. Knickerbocker, "Billy Sunday."
2. Knickerbocker, "Billy Sunday."
3. Okrent, *Last Call*, 2.
4. Okrent, *Last Call*, 3.
5. Okrent, *Last Call*, 176.
6. Okrent, *Last Call*, 177.
7. Lerner, 96–110.
8. Some of that credit might go to one particular New York Yankee player named Babe Ruth as baseball experienced a transition from the Deadball Era to the Babe Ruth era.
9. Okrent, *Last Call*, 208.
10. It's not surprising that ballplayers were attracted to the theater. The movie industry was in its infancy, so theater offered the kinds of dramatic and comedic stories that would later attract movie goers. Many Major Leaguers also performed in vaudeville or on the stage in the off-season and had an affinity for live productions. The most famous example is Mike Donlin, who played for the New York Giants in the early

twentieth century. Donlin and his wife, Mabel Hite, a vaudeville actress, often performed together. Their story is well told in *Mike Donlin* by Steve Steinberg and Lyle Spatz.

11. The intriguing and complicated backstory of Frazee's sale of Ruth and the play Frazee produced using the money is highlighted in Montville's *The Big Bam*, 101–5.
12. Other Broadway shows that season include Eugene O'Neill's *The Emperor Jones* and Henrik Ibsen's *Hedda Gabler*.
13. *Sex* did not receive good reviews, but it was a hit with audiences and ticket sales were good. It was the only play that opened on Broadway in 1926 to last through the summer and into the next season. Its run ended in February 1927 when closed down by the New York City Police Department. See "The Time Mae West Spent Eight Days in Jail," American Masters, PBS, https://www.pbs.org/wnet/americanmasters/the-time-mae-west-spent-eight-days-in-jail/14642/. A vivid description of Mae West's time in jail and thoughts about her play also appear in Charlotte Chandler, *She Always Knew How: Mae West: A Personal Biography*, 99–115. Data on ticket sales and performances comes from Wikipedia "Sex (play)."
14. The "American Series" featured white Major League teams and Cuban teams. In 1908 the Brooklyn Royal Giants, a Negro Leage team, also participated and played one game against the white Cincinnati Reds team.
15. Shortly after Judge Landis became baseball's commissioner in 1921, he ordered McGraw and Stoneham to divest themselves from the ownership and operation of the racetrack and casino.
16. Ruth's salary in 1920, his first season with the Yankees, was $20,000. The next highest-paid Yankees were pitchers Carl Mays and Bob Shawkey who earned $8,000 each.
17. Fitzgerald, "Echoes of the Jazz Age," in *The Crack Up*, 14–15.
18. Baker, *The New York Game*, 213. The incident occurred during spring training in Shreveport, Louisiana. Kevin Baker refers to it when discussing Ruth's appeal to women.
19. Ruth didn't always travel with Helen, or his second wife, Claire, but when he was in the company of either of his wives, his behavior was less extreme. This was especially true in the latter years of his career.
20. Nowlin and Diaz, "Cigars, Horses, and a Couple of Homers."
21. Monagan, "The Cuban Star Who Outslugged the Babe." Torriente was nicknamed "The Black Babe Ruth" and "The Cuban Babe Ruth." His talent as a ballplayer in the Cuban leagues, and later in the Negro Leagues, is unquestioned by players who saw him and played against him. Documentation of his achievements is incomplete. See his SABR biography in Bjarkman, "Cristobal Torriente." As for the three home runs Torriente hit

in the game against Ruth and the Giants, it's likely that the homers were inside-the-park home runs rather than over-the-fence home runs, if that makes a difference in evaluating his performance on that day.

22. Nowlin and Diaz, "Cigars."
23. Montville, *The Big Bam*, 125.
24. Ruth's postseason barnstorming caused a clash with Judge Landis, who had decreed that players involved in the World Series could not go on the road and play more games. Ruth and Meusel went anyway; both were fined and suspended for the first part of the 1922 season.
25. Sources differ on how much Ruth was paid. I'm citing the figure $2,500 a week that appears in Leavy's *The Big Fella*. Ruth biographers Creamer and Wagenheim suggest the contract was for $3,000 a week.
26. Wagenheim, *Babe Ruth*, 97.
27. Wagenheim, *Babe Ruth*, 98.
28. Wagenheim, *Babe Ruth*, 97–98.
29. Wagenheim, *Babe Ruth*, 99–100.
30. Abbott, *Sin and the Second City*, 7. Ms. Hicks operated the premier brothel in Philadelphia.
31. Differing versions of the story appear in Smelser, *The Life That Ruth Built*, 295; Wagenheim, *Babe Ruth*, 130–31; Reisler, *Babe Ruth*, 253–54; Montville, *The Big Bam*, 191.
32. My best guess, based on the stories and clues in Ruth's biographies, is that this game was played on Monday, April 28, 1924.
33. Leavy, *The Big Fella*, 248.
34. Leavy, *The Big Fella*, 256.
35. Leavy, *The Big Fella*, 256.
36. Baker, *The New York Game*, 132.

11. Leonard Has a Story to Tell

1. Ginsburg, *The Fix Is In*, 201; Gay, *Tris Speaker*, 227; Leerhsen, *Ty Cobb*, 341.
2. The size of the proposed bets is worth noting. For each man, the amount of the bet was close to 10 percent of the player's annual salary. They must have been very confident that Speaker was right that his team would lose.
3. It was reported that during most at bats, players swung at the first pitch. There seemed little evidence that players on either team cared who won. For the Indians, they had an additional incentive for the game to end quickly: they wanted to catch the last train back to Cleveland that evening so that they didn't have to spend another night in Detroit or travel by boat from Detroit to Cleveland.
4. Pomrenke, "Gambling in the Deadball Era."
5. Gay, *Tris Speaker*, 226.

6. Pomrenke, "Gambling." The most notorious game fixer of the early twentieth century was Hal Chase, a talented first baseman for the New York Giants, who was expelled from Major League Baseball after multiple incidents of alleged game fixing.
7. "Launch Drive on Baseball Gamblers," *New York Times*, May 25, 1920.
8. Tannenbaum, "The Ever Watchful Eye."
9. Reiss, *Touching Base*, 87.
10. Pomrenke, "Call the Game!" Note: Sport Sullivan is rumored to be the individual who tried to bribe Cy Young to throw a game in the 1903 World Series. Sullivan was later implicated in the attempt to fix the 1919 series.
11. Pomrenke, "Call the Game!"
12. Some accounts indicate that Leonard's trip was in May or "late spring," but the Nationals were in town to play the White Sox on June 12–15; since Leonard met with Nationals manager Bucky Harris on this trip, it had to be when the Nationals were staying in Chicago.
13. Pietrusza, *Judge and Jury*, 287; Leerhsen, *Ty Cobb*, 348.

12. Yankee Pitchers and Lazzeri

1. In 2020, *Time* named a "Woman of the Year" for every year from 1920 to 2020. *Time*'s selection for 1926 was Aimee Semple McPherson.
2. Gilbert King, "The Incredible Disappearing Evangelist," *Smithsonian Magazine*, June 17, 2013. See also Epstein, *Sister Aimee*.
3. Epstein, *Sister Aimee*, 294.
4. Hoyt is listed on the Wikipedia page of Erasmus Hall as a prominent alum, but he did not graduate from high school. Famous graduates of Erasmus Hall do include Neil Diamond, Roger Khan, Bernard Malamud, Mickey Spillane, and Barbra Streisand, among others.
5. Hoyt, Dugan, and Pennock had all been teammates when they played for Boston. Meusel was Pennock's roommate on Yankee road trips.
6. Hoyt, *Schoolboy*, 151.
7. Hoyt, *Schoolboy*, 151.
8. Eig, *Get Capone*, 166–67.
9. Hoyt, *Schoolboy*, 152.
10. Dean Balsamini, "Al Capone Played Semi-Pro Baseball in Brooklyn before Turning to Crime," *New York Post*, May 17, 2020, https://nypost.com/2020/05/17/al-capone-played-semi-pro-baseball-before-turning-to-crime/. Capone's cousin, Charlie Fischetti, also moved to Chicago, worked as a bodyguard for the Capones, and acquired the nickname "Trigger Happy."
11. Deirdre Maria Capone's book is titled *Uncle Al: The Untold Story from Inside His Family*. It is based largely on conversations she had with

her grandfather, Ralph Capone. According to the stories in the book, Al Capone intended to make William Wrigley "an offer he couldn't refuse"—using the exact language later used in the *Godfather* movie. Capone also planned to hire Babe Ruth to manage the Cubs and to sign Negro League players for the Cubs' roster.

12. Vaccaro, "Herb Pennock."
13. Vaccaro, "Herb Pennock."
14. Vaccaro, "Herb Pennock."
15. Wancho, "Urban Shocker."
16. Steinberg, *Urban Shocker*, 154–55.
17. Steinberg, *Urban Shocker*, 155–56.
18. Baldassaro, *Tony Lazzeri*, 1–7.
19. Baldassaro, *Tony Lazzeri*, 12–13.
20. Glueckstein, "Tony Lazzeri." Lazzeri played in 192 games for Salt Lake City during the 1925 season. His complete stats for that season: .355 batting average, 60 home runs, 202 runs scored, 222 runs batted in, 52 doubles, 14 triples, 39 stolen bases.
21. Baldassaro, *Tony Lazzeri*, 34–35.
22. "The History and Stigma of Epilepsy," 12–14 . As late as 1956, seventeen states still had laws on the books prohibiting epileptics from marrying. Employment opportunities were also limited for people with epilepsy. The first law to protect the employment rights of people with epilepsy was passed in 1973.
23. Baldassaro, *Beyond DiMaggio*, 48.
24. Richard Gambino, "Twenty Million Italian-Americans," *New York Times*, April 30, 1972.
25. Baldassaro, *Tony Lazzeri*, 47.
26. Although Barrow's official title with the Yankees was "business manager," he functioned as the team's general manager and would hold that position from 1921 to 1939. In 1939 Barrow was promoted to team president. He remained in that position until 1945.
27. Baldassaro, *Tony Lazzeri*, 34–35.
28. Baldassaro, *Tony Lazzeri*, 35.
29. Levitt, *Ed Barrow*, 21–24.
30. The Atlantic League existed for five seasons from 1896 through 1900 before it disbanded. Barrow was president for three of those years. The league featured teams located on the East Coast, from Connecticut to Virginia. Seventeen different teams participated, during one season or another.
31. Levitt, *Ed Barrow*, 33–36. Lizzie Stroud, who played under the name Lizzie Arlington, was a short, stocky woman who knew how to pitch and had an

agent who negotiated one hundred dollars a week for her to pitch in exhibition games against Atlantic League teams.

32. Baldassaro, *Tony Lazzeri*, 36.

13. Rube Foster and Black Baseball

1. As his career progressed, Paige named his pitches, to the delight of fans. See Tye, *Satchel*, 262–63, for a list of nearly two dozen names that Paige used to describe his pitches. In addition to Long Tom, there was Little Tom. Other pitch names: the Trouble Ball, the Wobbly Ball, the Step-n-Pitch-It, the Midnight Creeper, the Bow Tie, the Hesitation, and the Whipsy-dipsy-do, to name a few.
2. Information about the California Winter League, the first integrated league, comes from McNeil's *The California Winter League*.
3. Peterson, *Only the Ball Was White*, 104.
4. Cottrell, *The Best Pitcher in Baseball*, 19. The date when Rube Foster pitched against Rube Waddell can't be clearly identified. Ken Burns asserts it was in 1902; see page 157 in *The Best Pitcher in Baseball*. Robert Peterson in *Only the Ball Was White* gives the score as 5–2 but doesn't mention a date.
5. Smokey Joe Williams was inducted into the National Baseball Hall of Fame in 1999, Pete Hill in 2006, and John Henry "Pops" Lloyd in 1977.
6. Bill James rates Oscar Charleston as the fourth best baseball player of all time, just behind Babe Ruth, Honus Wagner, and Willie Mays. Charleston was elected to the National Baseball Hall of Fame in 1976. Torriente, known as "The Cuban Babe Ruth," was elected to the National Baseball Hall of Fame in 2006.
7. Quote is from John Holway and appears in McNeil, *The California Winter League*, 38.
8. Cottrell, *The Best Pitcher in Baseball*, 45–46. Crowds greeted the team when they arrived at rail stations and packed ballparks to see the games. The games were often sold out.
9. Cottrell, *The Best Pitcher in Baseball*, 45.
10. At the time of Foster's injury, he had won eleven straight games, including four shutouts. He was at his peak as a pitcher in this season.
11. Cottrell, *The Best Pitcher in Baseball*, 47. Cub players Johnny Evers and Frank Chance apparently refused to play—suggesting the resistance among some white players to compete in games against Black players.
12. Schorling was a coal dealer, a tavern owner, a booking agent, and later in his life, a real estate investor. He was a loyal supporter of Foster and Black baseball in Chicago, eventually taking control of the Chicago American Giants after Foster's death.

13. Quoted in Cottrell, *The Best Pitcher in Baseball*, 79. The original source is an interview in the *Seattle Post-Intelligencer*, April 5, 1914.
14. Cottrell, *The Best Pitcher in Baseball*, 67.
15. Peterson, *Only the Ball Was White*, 83–91.
16. The Hilldale team was also known as the Hilldale Athletic Club.
17. Torriente pitched some and was a strong hitter for a half dozen seasons, but his career power stats don't rival Ruth's. According to Seamheads .com, Torriente had 83 documented home runs in 4,435 at bats. Ruth hit 714 home runs in 8,399 at bats.

14. Sesquicentennial Games

1. Leuchtenburg, *The American President*, 126.
2. Leuchtenburg, *The American President*, 126.
3. Leuchtenburg, *The American President*, 126.
4. Ferrell, *Grace Coolidge*, 34–35; Leuchtenburg, *The American President*, 127.
5. Richard V. Oulahan, "Coolidge, Tired Out, Will Drop Politics for Vacation Rest," *New York Times*, July 5, 1926.
6. *Variety*, August 25, 1926.
7. The speech has been reprinted (online) and frequently commented on. It is considered a significant historical speech that focused on the values and principles of the country being based more so on Judeo-Christian beliefs than on the philosophy of Rousseau and Jefferson.
8. Leuchtenburg, *The American President*, 128.
9. McGraw would manage for thirty-three years, win 2,840 regular-season games, and take nine teams to the World Series.
10. Henry Thomas, *Walter Johnson*, 221–22.
11. James Harrison, "Yankees Are Felled Twice by Athletics," *New York Times*, July 6, 1926.

15. Judge Landis Takes Over

1. Gay, *Tris Speaker*, 332. Alexander, *Ty Cobb*, 166.
2. Gay, *Tris Speaker*, 335.
3. Seymour and Mills, *Golden Age*, 367.
4. Pietrusza, *Judge and Jury*, 40–41.
5. Pietrusza, *Judge and Jury*, 67; *Chicago Tribune*, August 4, 1907; *New York Times*, August 4, 1907.
6. Colosimo was shot in the head on May 11, 1920, at one of his own businesses: the Colosimo Café.
7. Pietrusza, *Judge and Jury*, 102–6.

8. Rothstein testified in front of the grand jury and named Abe Attell, a former boxing champion and one of Rothstein's associates, as one of the principal conspirators. Rothstein admitted he was approached about funding the criminal enterprise but said he had refused to do so.
9. Of the five gamblers charged, only Carl Zork and David Zelcer appeared at the trail; they were both acquitted. Sport Sullivan and Abe Attell resisted extradition to Chicago and didn't face the charges in court. Nat Evans, also known as "Rachael Brown," was indicted but did not go to trial with the others.
10. Wolf, *The Called Shot*, 39; Asinof, *Eight Men Out*, 273.
11. Wolf, *The Called Shot*, 39; Asinof, *Eight Men Out*, 273.
12. Barnstorming benefited the players financially—especially the most well-known stars—as they traveled from town to town to play exhibitions and supplement their annual salaries with the gate receipts. For the audiences in smaller towns and cities, barnstorming teams provided baseball fans a chance to see Major Leaguers in person.
13. Pietrusza, *Judge and Jury*, 241–53.
14. Blaisdell, "Mystery and Tragedy."

16. The Golden Age of Sports

1. Allen, *Only Yesterday*, 234–46. See also: "Hurricane of September 20th, 1926," National Weather Service, last updated September 2022, https://www.weather.gov/mob/1926hurricane.
2. Steinberg and Spatz, *The Colonel and Hug*, 239–41; Huggins was a vice president of Ruppert's corporation, so he may have had some financial liability from his involvement in the project.
3. Alexander, *John McGraw*, 266–72.
4. Alexander, *John McGraw*, 270.
5. Alexander, *John McGraw*, 272–73.
6. Leuchtenburg, *The Perils of Prosperity*, 195.
7. The famous Illinois versus Michigan game was played on October 18, 1924. Grange played both offense and defense in the contest.
8. The nickname "The Wheaton Ice Man" refers to Grange growing up in Wheaton, Illinois, and as a youth, earning money for his family—$37.50 a week—delivering ice to customers.
9. Information in this paragraph comes from Allen, *Only Yesterday*, 178–81, and from Eisenberg, *The League*, 40–41.
10. Harpman, a crime reporter for *The New York Daily News*, was married to the journalist Westbrook Pegler. Pegler was with Harpman and Ederle during the days leading up to the channel attempt, but he returned to the United States to report on the baseball pennant races and the upcoming

Dempsey-Tunney heavyweight fight, so he wasn't on the boat when Ederle attempted and completed the channel swim. See pages 224–30 in Glenn Stout's *Young Woman and the Sea.*

11. Stout, *Young Woman and the Sea*, 264–65.
12. Stout, *Young Woman and the Sea*, 292.
13. Stout, *Young Woman and the Sea*, 285; Steinberg and Spatz, *The Colonel and Hug*, 249–50. Steinberg and Spatz note that the United States was in a "fierce nativist and anti-immigration mood, as reflected in the restrictive immigration laws that Congress had been passing in the 1920s." Ruppert identified with Ederle since he, too, was the child of German immigrants. Though he may have been proud of Ederle's heritage, Ruppert's praise of her achievement focused on her as an American.
14. Tye, *Satchell*, 41.
15. Tye, *Satchell*, 41.
16. Dempsey knocked down Willard, who outweighed him by sixty pounds, seven times in the first round. Willard suffered a broken jaw, a broken cheekbone, and several broken ribs. He also lost several teeth. He lasted until the third round, when the fight was mercifully stopped. Observers were awestruck by Dempsey's punching power.
17. The first round of the Dempsey-Firpo fight is often described as the most dramatic opening round in prizefighting history.
18. The George Bellows painting titled *Dempsey and Firpo* hangs in the Whitney Museum of American Art in New York City. In the bottom left corner of the painting, Bellows has painted himself at ringside as an older balding man.
19. In addition to Shakespeare, Tunney enjoyed the work of Samuel Butler and Somerset Maugham.
20. Kahn, *A Flame of Pure Fire*, 396.
21. Elmer Davis, "Dempsey to Defend Title Tonight; 130,000 to See Bout," *New York Times*, September 23, 1926.
22. Sportswriters at the fight included Grantland Rice, Ring Lardner, W. O. McGeehan, Paul Gallico, Damon Runyon, Westbrook Pegler, and Heywood Broun.
23. Cavanaugh, *Tunney*, 373. *Merriam-Webster Unabridged Dictionary* defines a *pink tea* as "a decorous or namby-pamby affair or proceeding."
24. Rothstein had many business associates, including Charles Stoneham, owner of the New York Giants, and Billy Gibson, who happened to be the manager of Gene Tunney. In addition to legitimate business interests and contacts, Rothstein had connections to leading crime figures on the East Coast, such as Maxie "Boo Boo" Hoff, described as a "Philadelphia gang lord and sometime fight promoter." See Pietrusza, *Rothstein*, 236. Anyone

who spotted Rothstein at ringside might have wondered if the fight had been fixed. See *Rothstein.*

25. In 1926 in Pennsylvania, prize fights were scored by two judges and a referee, but the referee's scorecard was consulted only if the judges disagreed on the fight's winner. Tunney won all ten rounds on the scorecards of both judges.
26. Kahn, *A Flame of Pure Fire*, 400.
27. Tunney had friends and acquaintances in the world of politics. Cox was not just the former governor of Ohio. He had been the Democratic candidate for president in 1920, on a ticket with his running mate Franklin Delano Roosevelt, the vice-presidential candidate.
28. Kahn, *A Flame of Pure Fire*, 400. Ronald Reagan said these same words to his wife, Nancy, after he was shot by John Hinckley on March 31, 1981.
29. Kahn, *A Flame of Pure Fire*, 408–10.
30. Kahn, *A Flame of Pure Fire*, 410.

17. Final Days

1. Golenbock, *Spirit*, 107.
2. Golenbock, *Spirit*, 107.
3. Lowenfish, *Branch Rickey*, 162; Wolf, *The Called Shot*, 22–23; See also Alexander, *Rogers Hornsby*, 114.
4. Attendance figures are not complete for games at the Baker Bowl in 1926, but two games drew only five hundred fans, including the season-ending doubleheader. The Phillies home attendance ranked last in the National League in 1926. That season, only 240,600 fans paid to see the Phillies play baseball.
5. "Coolidges Attend Harris Wedding," *New York Times*, October 2, 1926.

18. Games One and Two

1. Semchuck, "Wilbert Robinson." The team's nickname reflected the admiration the Brooklyn fans and players had for him.
2. Quoted in Semchuck, "Wilbert Robinson."
3. Wancho, "Gabby Street." See also "1908 Baseball Dropped from Top of Washington Monument Caught by Gabby Street," Heritage Auctions, April 24, 2009, https://sports.ha.com/itm/baseball-collectibles/balls/1908-baseball-dropped-from-top-of-washington-monument-caught-by-gabby-street/a/714-81847.s.
4. There are many versions of this story, none of which can be completely trusted. In one story, Stengel was sitting in a chair on the wing of the plane. Stengel in other retellings was a passenger in the plane, but a trainer named Kelly dropped the grapefruit. In another version, Stengel

wasn't even in the plane. For entertaining reflections on the incident, see Appel, *Casey Stengel*, 44–47.

5. Semchuck, "Wilbert Robinson."
6. Wilbert Robinson, "Robinson Expects Drawn-Out Series," *New York Times*, October 2, 1926.
7. Robinson, "Robinson Expects."
8. Robinson, "Robinson Expects."
9. Ike Shuman, "Series Rivals Hold Their Drills," *New York Times*, October 2, 1926.
10. Seabury Lawrence, "Hotels Absorbing Series Fans Easily," *New York Times*, October 2, 1926.
11. "$1,000,000 Wagered on the First Game," *New York Times*, October 2, 1926.
12. Previously, the two largest crowds at a World Series game had been 62,817 for Game Five of the 1923 World Series and 62,430 for Game Three of that series.
13. Robert Wagner was a justice on the New York State Supreme Court. In November of 1926, he was elected as a senator of New York State and served twenty-two years in that office.
14. "Yankees Win, 2 to 1, While 63,000 Watch, 15,000,000 Listen In," *New York Times*, October 3, 1926.
15. When the spitball was outlawed, Shocker was one of the pitchers grandfathered in and allowed to continue using the pitch.
16. Ed Froelich, the Cubs' clubhouse attendant, observed Alexander's pregame routine many times and describes it in Golenbock, *Wrigleyville*, 186.
17. "Hornsby is Pleased by Change in Team," *New York Times*, October 4, 1926.
18. "Hornsby is Pleased."
19. Golenbock, *Spirit*, 109.

19. Games Three, Four, and Five

1. Wilbert Robinson, "Robinson Expects Drawn-Out Series," *New York Times*, October 2, 1926.
2. Freak bets are similar to what are called prop bets today—betting not on the outcome of a game or series but a wager on a specific occurrence or result from a player or team.
3. Wolf, *The Called Shot*, 23–24. The Johnnie Sylvester story is well told in Charlie Poekel's *Babe and the Kid*. In the summer of 1926, Sylvester had been thrown from a horse and kicked in the head. A series of medical complications followed, and he was hospitalized. His parents requested a signed ball from the World Series as a way to cheer him up. Sylvester's father, a bank vice president, used his professional connections to get word to the Yankees and Cardinals about his son's request, and that

resulted in the balls being taken to the opposing dugouts during the rain delay in Game Three.

4. James Harrison, "Cards Lead Series; St. Louis in Ecstasy as Yanks lose 4–0," *New York Times*, October 6, 1926.
5. "Ban Johnson Gives Yankees a Lecture," *New York Times*, October 7, 1926.
6. Quoted in Griffin, "Flint Rhem."
7. Appel, *Pinstripe Empire*, 147.
8. Appel, *Pinstripe Empire*, 147.
9. James Harrison, "Ruth Hits 3 Homers and Yanks Win, 10–5; Series Even Again," *New York Times*, October 7, 1926.
10. "'I Told You So!' Huggins Chortles," *New York Times*, October 7, 1926.

20. Games Six and Seven

1. James Harrison, "Yanks and St. Louis Resume Here Today," *New York Times*, October 9, 1926.
2. Harrison, "Yanks and St. Louis."
3. "Wild Series Bets Looked for Today," *New York Times*, October 10, 1926.
4. "$20,000,000 Shifts on World's Series," *New York Times*, October 11, 1926.
5. Golenbock, *Spirit*, 112.
6. Stout, *Yankees Century*, 119–20. The incident had been reported by sportswriter Joe Vila.
7. James Harrison, "Cards Win World Series, Taking Final Game, 3–2; $1,207,864 Is Record Gate," *New York Times*, October 11, 1926.
8. Golenbock, *Spirit*, 112–13.
9. Quoted in Golenbock, *Spirit*, 114.
10. Harrison, "Cards Win."
11. James Harrison observed: "Throughout the park there came a silence. The fans slid forward to the edge of their seats."
12. Golenbock, *Spirit*, 114.
13. Golenbock, *Spirit*, 115–16.
14. Alexander thought Ruth should have been called out on strikes when he took ball four. Alexander questioned George Hildebrand as to why he called the pitch a ball, and the umpire indicated the pitch was a few inches outside. Alexander told him, "For that much, you might have given an old sonofagun [*sic*] like me a break." Golenbock, *Spirit*, 116.
15. Gene Tenace tied Ruth's record when he was walked eleven times in the 1973 World Series. The record was broken by Barry Bonds in the 2002 World Series when Bonds was walked thirteen times.
16. Ruth shook hands with Hornsby. See Golenbock, *Spirit*, 116.
17. Halberstam, *Sports on New York Radio*, 144.
18. "Joyful Cardinals Praise Alexander," *New York Times*, October 11, 1926.

19. "St. Louis in Frenzy as Cardinals Win," *New York Times*, October 11, 1926.
20. Golenbock, *Spirit*, 116.
21. Golenbock, *Spirit*, 116.
22. Golenbock, *Spirit*, 117.
23. Golenbock, *Spirit*, 117.
24. Montville, *The Big Bam*, 236.
25. Lazzeri and Meusel tied for the team lead in stolen bases in 1926 with sixteen each; Ruth had eleven. For his career, Ruth had 123 stolen bases.
26. Creamer, *Babe*, 306–7.

21. Colored World Series of 1926

1. Cottrell, *The Best Pitcher in Baseball*, 168–71.
2. Cottrell, *The Best Pitcher in Baseball*, 168–69.
3. *Logansport Pharos-Tribune*, September 3, 1926.
4. Cottrell, *The Best Pitcher in Baseball*, 169.
5. Quoted in Kern, "Bill Foster."
6. Adam Darowski, "Dobie Moore." There are multiple and conflicting stories about this incident. Elsie Brown may have been working at a brothel when the shooting occurred. Some of the damage to Moore's leg might have been the result of him jumping off a second-floor balcony to escape the gun shots. He was a large man, big for a shortstop, perhaps weighing as much as 230 pounds. He was an excellent hitter, with power. According to Seamheads.com, Moore hit .359 in his career and led the league in 1924 with a .453 batting average. Bill James rates Dobie Moore as the fourth best Negro League shortstop, behind John Henry "Pop" Lloyd, Willie Wells, and Dick Lundy.
7. Hogan, *Shades of Glory*, 191.
8. The Bacharach Giants were formerly the Duval Giants of Jacksonville, Florida. They moved from Jacksonville to Atlantic City in 1916.
9. Overmeyer, *Black Ball and the Boardwalk*, 141.
10. Overmeyer, *Black Ball and the Boardwalk*, 141–42.
11. Quoted in the *Afro-American*, October 9, 1926.

22. Judge Landis Steps Up

1. Pietrusza, *Judge and Jury*, 288.
2. Weiss had taken over a rival gang previously led by Dean O'Banion, who was himself murdered in his flower shop in 1924. Capone maintained his power and supremacy in the gang wars of Chicago of the 1920s by eliminating his competition through targeted assassinations.
3. "Judge Landis Is Visitor at Fresno," *Modesto News Herald*, October 31, 1926.
4. Taylor, *Baseball at the Abyss*, 1–2.

5. Alexander, *Ty Cobb*, 185.
6. Gay, *Tris Speaker*, 231.
7. Alexander, *Ty Cobb*, 191.
8. James Harrison, "Pay Raise to Landis Was Spontaneous," *New York Times*, December 19, 1926.
9. Pietrusza, *Judge and Jury*, 290–91; "Baseball Scandal Up Again, Cobb and Speaker Named," *New York Times*, December 21, 1926.
10. C. Paul Rogers III, "Rogers Hornsby."
11. James Harrison, "Giants Get Hornsby; Trade Big Surprise," *New York Times*, December 21, 1926.
12. Golenbock, *Spirit*, 120.
13. Leerhsen, *Ty Cobb*, 348.
14. Alexander, *Ty Cobb*, 189.
15. "'Impossible to Believe' Billy Sunday Avers in Defense of Cobb and Speaker," *The Minneapolis Star*, December 23, 1926.
16. Alexander, *Ty Cobb*, 191–92.
17. Leerhsen, *Ty Cobb*, 349.
18. Gay, *Tris Speaker*, 237.
19. Alexander, *Ty Cobb*, 193.
20. Pietrusza, *Judge and Jury*, 310.
21. Not all commentators or historians agreed with the Landis decision. Landis seemed to be saying let others dredge up and piece together the facts of the case—as Lowell Blaisdell did later in "The Cobb-Speaker Scandal."

Epilogue

1. Appel, *Pinstripe Empire*, 153–54. The term "Murderer's Row" was coined to describe the row of cells on the second floor of the Tombs prison in New York City, where prisoners charged with murder were incarcerated.
2. See Charles Fouche's article, "The 1931 Homestead Grays."
3. Notable Negro League owners in the 1930s and 1940s include Cum Posey, Abe and Effa Manley, and Gus Greenlee. Posey, who attended Penn State to study chemistry, was first known as a skilled basketball player. He later managed and owned the Homestead Grays, which became an extremely successful independent Black baseball team. *Pittsburgh Courier* sportswriter Wendell Smith called Posey "the smartest man in Negro baseball and certainly the most successful." The Manleys owned the Newark Eagles (originally the Brooklyn Eagles), a successful franchise. Greenlee, a successful businessman, owned the Pittsburgh Crawfords, one of the powerhouse Black teams of the 1930s. He is also credited with the idea of the East-West Classic, an end-of-the-year All-Star Game, featuring all the best players in the Negro Leagues.

4. Alan Cohen, “Negro League Baseball at Comiskey Park.” See also Hogan, *Shades of Glory*, 284–88. The games were often sellouts. In 1943 in the midst of World War II, 51,723 fans attended the game to see Satchel Paige pitch three innings for the West squad.
5. The U.S. military was officially desegregated by executive order of President Harry Truman on July 26, 1948.
6. Rogers, “Rogers Hornsby.”
7. Steinberg and Spatz, *The Colonel and Hug*, 253.
8. Eig, *Luckiest Man*, 81.
9. Baldassaro, *Tony Lazzeri*, 261–62. Lazzeri's body was found at the bottom of a flight of stairs. The cause of death was never definitely determined. It's possible the fall caused his death or perhaps a heart attack. An epileptic attack may have contributed, in one way or another.
10. Baldassaro, *Tony Lazzeri*, 268.
11. Tye, *Satchel*, 87.
12. Tye, *Satchel*, 97.
13. The tours with Dean and Feller drew large crowds: A November 1934 matchup in Los Angeles drew eighteen thousand fans, as Paige and Dean each pitched thirteen innings, with Paige's team eventually winning 1–0. A Paige and Feller game in Yankee Stadium in October 1946 attracted a crowd of 27,462. An estimated 250,000 baseball fans bought tickets to see at least one of the Paige-Feller games.
14. Gay, *Satchel*, 301–4.
15. In Paige's three seasons with the Browns, they finished next to last once and last twice. Rogers Hornsby was the manager of the 1952 team.
16. Data about the Foursquare Church comes from Wikipedia: “Foursquare Church,” Wikipedia, last updated July 28, 2024, https://en.wikipedia.org/wiki/Foursquare_Church.
17. “Grace Coolidge Overview,” Calvin Coolidge Presidential Foundation, https://coolidgefoundation.org/presidency/grace-coolidge-overview/.

Bibliography

Abbott, Karen. *Sin in the Second City: Madams, Ministers, Playboys, and the Battle for America's Soul.* New York: Random House, 2008.

Abrams, Roger I. *The Dark Side of the Diamond: Gambling, Violence, Drugs, and Alcoholism in the National Pastime.* Burlington MA: Rounder Books, 2007.

———. *Legal Bases: Baseball and the Law.* Philadelphia: Temple University Press, 1998.

Alexander, Charles C. *Breaking the Slump: Baseball in the Depression Era.* New York: Columbia University Press, 2002.

———. *John McGraw.* New York: Viking, 1998.

———. *Rogers Hornsby.* New York: Henry Holt, 1995.

———. *Ty Cobb.* New York: Oxford University Press, 1984.

Allen, Frederick Lewis. *Only Yesterday: An Informal History of the 1920s.* New York: Harper & Row, 1931.

Allsop, Kenneth. *The Bootleggers: The Story of Chicago's Prohibition Era.* New Rochelle NY: Arlington House, 1968.

Appel, Marty. *Casey Stengel: Baseball's Greatest Character.* New York: Doubleday, 2017.

———. *Pinstripe Empire: The New York Yankees from before the Babe to after the Boss.* New York: Bloomsbury, 2012.

Ardell, Jean Hastings. *Breaking Into Baseball: Women and the National Pastime.* Carbondale: Southern Illinois University Press, 2005.

Asinof, Eliot. *Eight Men Out: The Black Sox and the 1919 World Series.* New York: Owl Books, 1987.

Auker, Elden, with Tom Keegan. *Sleeper Cars and Flannel Uniforms: A Lifetime of Memories from Striking Out the Babe to Teeing It Up with the President.* Chicago: Triumph Books, 2001.

Baker, Kevin. *The New York Game: Baseball and the Rise of a New City.* New York: Alfred A. Knopf, 2024.

Baldassaro, Lawrence. *Beyond DiMaggio: Italian Americans in Baseball.* Lincoln: University of Nebraska Press, 2011.

———. *Tony Lazzeri: Yankees Legend and Baseball Pioneer.* Lincoln: University of Nebraska Press, 2021.

Bales, Jack. "Baseball's First Bill Veeck." *Baseball Research Journal.* (Fall 2013).

———. *Before They Were Cubs: The Early Years of Chicago's First Professional Baseball Team.* Jefferson NC: McFarland, 2019.

Bamberger, Michael. "Hail to the Rajah: Before Ted Williams, There Was Rogers Hornsby, the Forgotten Father of the Father of Hitting." *Vault.* June 24, 2002. https://vault.si.com/vault/2002/06/24/hail-to-the-rajah-before-ted-williams-there-was-rogers-hornsby-the-forgotten-father-of-the-father-of-hitting.

Barthel, Thomas. *Babe Ruth Is Coming to Your Town.* Independently published, 2018.

Beer, Jeremy. *Oscar Charleston: The Life and Legend of Baseball's Greatest Forgotten Player.* Lincoln: University of Nebraska Press, 2019.

Bergreen, Lawrence. *Capone: The Man and the Era.* New York: Simon & Schuster, 1996.

Bjarkman, Peter C. "Cristobal Torriente." SABR BioProject. sabr.org/bioproject.

Blaisdell, Lowell. "The Cobb-Speaker Scandal: Exonerated but Probably Guilty." *Nine: A Journal of History and Culture* 13, no. 2 (Spring 2005): 54–70.

———. "Mystery and Tragedy: The O'Connell-Dolan Scandal." *Baseball Research Journal* (May 1982).

Bryan, Patricia L., and Thomas Wolf. "On the Brink: Babe Ruth in Dennis Lehane's *The Given Day.*" In *The Cooperstown Symposium on Baseball and American Culture, 2009–2010*, edited by William M. Simons, 42–56. Jefferson NC: McFarland, 2011.

Bryson, Bill. *One Summer: America, 1927.* New York: Doubleday, 2013.

Carroll, Brian. "Beating the Klan: Baseball Coverage in Wichita before Integration, 1920–1930." *Baseball Research Journal* (2008).

Cavanaugh, Jack. *Tunney: Boxing's Brainiest Champ and His Upset of the Great Jack Dempsey.* New York: Ballantine Books, 2009. Kindle.

Chadwick, Bruce. *When the Game Was Black and White: The Illustrated History of Baseball's Negro Leagues.* New York: Abbeville Press, 1992.

Chiarello, Mark, and Jack Morelli. *Heroes of the Negro Leagues.* New York: Henry N. Abrams, 2007.

Cieradkowski, Gary Joseph. *The League of Outsider Baseball: An Illustrated History of Baseball's Forgotten Heroes.* New York: Touchstone, 2015.

Clark, Dick, and Larry Lester, eds. *The Negro Leagues Book.* Cleveland OH: The Society for American Baseball Research, 1994.

Cohen, Alan. "Negro League Baseball at Comiskey Park: The East-West Game, an All-Star Legacy." Society for American Baseball Research. https://sabr.org/research/article/negro-baseball-at-comiskey-park-the-east-west-game-an-all-star-legacy/.

Cohen, Jonathan D., and Schwartz, David G., eds. *All In: The Spread of Gambling in Twentieth-Century United States*. Reno: University of Nevada Press, 2018.

Cook, William A. *Waite Hoyt: A Biography of the Yankees' Schoolboy Wonder*. Jefferson NC: McFarland, 2004.

Cottrell, Robert Charles. *The Best Pitcher in Baseball: The Life of Rube Foster, Negro League Giant*. New York: New York University Press, 2001.

Coulson, John G., with John T. Sherdel. *Wee Willie Sherdel: The Cardinals' Winningest Left-hander*. Victoria BC: FriesenPress, 2018.

Creamer, Robert W. *Babe: The Legend Comes to Life*. New York: Simon & Schuster, 1974.

———. *Baseball in '41*. New York: Viking Penguin, 1991.

Darowski, Adam. "Dobie Moore." SABR BioProject, sabr.org/bioproject.

Dickson, Paul. *Bill Veeck: Baseball's Greatest Maverick*. New York: Walker Publishing Company, 2012.

Dixon, Phil S. *Andrew "Rube" Foster: A Harvest on Freedom's Fields*. Xlibris, 2010.

———. *Wilber "Bullet" Rogan and the Kansas City Monarchs*. Jefferson NC: McFarland, 2010.

Doutrich, Paul E. *The Cardinals and the Yankees, 1926*. Jefferson NC: McFarland, 2011.

Edelman, Rob. "The Winning Team: Fact and Fiction in Celluloid Biographies." *The National Pastime* 26 (2006).

Ehrgott, Roberts. *Mr. Wrigley's Ball Club: Chicago & The Cubs During the Jazz Age*. Lincoln: University of Nebraska Books, 2013.

Eig, Jonathan. *Get Capone: The Secret Plot That Captured America's Most Wanted Gangster*. New York: Simon & Schuster, 2010.

———. *Luckiest Man: The Life and Death of Lou Gehrig*. New York: Simon & Schuster, 2005.

Eisenberg, John. *The League: How Five Rivals Created the NFL and Launched a Sports Empire*. New York: Basic Books, 2018.

Epplin, Luke. *Our Team: The Epic Story of Four Men and the World Series That Changed Baseball*. New York: Flatiron Books, 2021.

Epstein, Daniel Mark. *Sister Aimee: The Life of Aimee Semple McPherson*. New York: Harcourt Brace, 1993.

Ferrell, Robert H. *Grace Coolidge: The People's Lady in Silent Cal's White House*. Lawrence: University Press of Kansas, 2008.

Fimrite, Ron. "The Raging Rajah Rogers Hornsby, One of This Century's Best Ballplayers, Was Also One of Its Biggest Boors." *Sports Illustrated*. October 1, 1995.

Finkel, Jan. "Eddie Plank." SABR BioProject. sabr.org/bioproject.

———. "Pete Alexander." SABR BioProject. sabr.org/bioproject.

Fitzgerald, F. Scott. "Echoes of the Jazz Age." In *The Crack Up*, edited by Edmund Wilson. New York: New Directions, 1945.

Flaspohler, Brian. *St. Louis Baseball History: A Guide*. Charleston SC: History Press, 2022.

Forman, Sean, and Cecilia Tan, eds. *The Negro Leagues Are Major Leagues: Essays and Research for Overdue Recognition*. Phoenix AZ: Sports Reference, 2021.

Fouche, Charles. "The 1931 Homestead Grays: The Greatest Baseball Team of All Time." Society for American Baseball Research. https://sabr.org/journal/article/the-1931-homestead-grays-the-greatest-baseball-team-of-all-time/.

Fowler, Gene. *Skyline: A Reporter's Reminiscence of the 1920s*. New York: Viking Press, 1961.

Gay, Timothy M. *Satch, Dizzy & Rapid Robert: The Wild Saga of Interracial Baseball Before Jackie Robinson*. New York: Simon & Schuster, 2010.

———. *Tris Speaker: The Rough-and-Tumble Life of a Baseball Legend*. Guilford CT: Lyons Press, 2007.

Gehrig, Eleanor, and Durso, Joseph. *My Luke and I*. New York: Thomas V. Crowell and Company, 1976.

Giamatti, A. Bartlett. *A Great and Glorious Game: Baseball Writings of A. Bartlett Giamatti*. Chapel Hill NC: Algonquin Books of Chapel Hill, 1998.

Ginsburg, Daniel E. *The Fix Is In: A History of Baseball Gambling and Game Fixing Scandals*. Jefferson NC: McFarland, 1995.

———. "Ty Cobb." SABR BioProject. sabr.org/bioproject.

Glueckstein, Fred. "Tony Lazzeri." SABR BioProject. sabr.org/bioproject.

Goldman, Steven. "Goldman's Baseball Quotables #7: Rogers Hornsby and Ray Rice." *SBNation*. September 11, 2014. https://www.sbnation.com/mlb/2014/9/11/6136425/baseball-quotes-rogers-hornsby-ray-rice-brutality.

Golenbock, Peter. *The Spirit of St. Louis: A History of the St. Louis Cardinals And Browns*. New York: William Morrow, 2000.

———. *Wrigleyville: A Magical Mystery Tour of the Chicago Cubs*. New York: St. Martin's Press, 1998.

Griffin, Nancy Snell. "Flint Rhem." SABR BioProject. sabr.org/bioproject.

Halberstam, David J. *Sports on New York Radio: A Play-by-Play History*. Chicago: Masters Press, 1999.

Hawkins, Joel, and Terry Bertolino. *The House of David Baseball Team*. Chicago: Arcadia, 2000.

Heidenry, John. *The Gashouse Gang: How Dizzy Dean, Leo Durocher, Branch Rickey, Pepper Martin, and Their Colorful, Come-from-Behind Ball Club Won the World Series—and America's Heart—During the Great Depression*. New York: Public Affairs, 2007.

"The History and Stigma of Epilepsy." *Epilepsia* 44, no. s6 (September 2003): 12–14, https://doi.org/10.1046/j.1528-1157.44.s.6.2.x.

Hogan, Lawrence D. *Shades of Glory: The Negro Leagues and the Story of African-American Baseball*. Washington DC: National Geographic, 2006.

Honig, Donald. *A Donald Honig Reader*. New York: Simon & Schuster, 1988.

Hornsby, Rogers. *My Kind of Baseball*. New York: David McKay, 1953.

Hornsby, Rogers, and Bill Surface. *My War with Baseball*. New York: Coward-McCann, 1962.

Hoyt, Waite, with Tim Manners. *Schoolboy: The Untold Journey of a Yankees Hero*. Lincoln: University of Nebraska Press, 2024.

Huggins, Myrtle, as told to John B. Kennedy. "Mighty Midget." *Collier's*. May 24, 1930.

James, Bill. *The New Bill James Historical Abstract*. New York: Free Press, 2003.

Jenkinson, Bill. *The Year Babe Ruth Hit 104 Home Runs: Recrowning Baseball's Greatest Slugger*. New York: Carroll & Graf, 2007.

Jones, David. "Dutch Leonard." SABR BioProject. sabr.org/bioproject.

Kahn, Roger. *A Flame of Pure Fire: Jack Dempsey and the Roaring '20s*. New York: Harcourt, 1999.

Kern, Thomas. "Bill Foster." SABR BioProject. sabr.org/bioproject.

———. "Leon Day." SABR BioProject. sabr.org/bioproject.

King, Gilbert. "The Incredible Disappearing Evangelist." *Smithsonian Magazine*. June 17, 2013.

Knickerbocker, Wendy. "Billy Sunday." SABR BioProject. sabr.org/bioproject.

Lamb, Bill. "Bill Devery." SABR BioProject. sabr.org/bioproject.

Lamb, Chris. *Conspiracy of Silence: Sportswriters and the Long Campaign to Desegregate Baseball*. Lincoln: University of Nebraska Press, 2012.

Leavy, Jane. *The Big Fella: Babe Ruth and the World He Created*. New York: HarperCollins, 2018.

Leeke, Jim. *The Best Team Over There: The Untold Story of Grover Cleveland Alexander and the Great War*. Lincoln: University of Nebraska Press, 2021.

Leerhsen, Charles. *Ty Cobb: A Terrible Beauty*. New York: Simon & Schuster, 2015.

Lerner, Michael A. *Dry Manhattan: Prohibition in New York City*. Cambridge MA: Harvard University Press, 2007.

Lester, Larry. *Baseball's First Colored World Series: The 1924 Meeting of the Hilldale Giants and the Kansas City Monarchs*. Jefferson NC: McFarland, 2006.

———. "Can You Read, Judge Landis?" Society for American Baseball Research. https://sabr.org/journal/article/can-you-read-judge-landis/.

Lester, Larry, and Wayne Stivers. *The Negro Leagues Book, Volume 2: The Players, 1862–1960*. Kansas City MO: NoirTech Research, 2020.

Lesy, Michael. *Murder City: The Bloody History of Chicago in the Twenties.* New York: W. W. Norton, 2007.

Leuchtenburg, William E. *The American Presidency: From Teddy Roosevelt to Bill Clinton.* New York: Oxford University Press, 2015.

———. *The Perils of Prosperity 1914–32.* Chicago: University of Chicago Press, 1958.

Levitt, Daniel R. *Ed Barrow: The Bulldog Who Built the Yankees' First Dynasty.* Lincoln: University of Nebraska Press, 2008.

Levy, Alan H. *Joe McCarthy: Architect of the Yankee Dynasty.* Jefferson NC: McFarland, 2005.

Lieb, Fred. *Baseball as I Have Known It.* New York: Grosset and Dunlap, 1977.

Lowenfish, Lee. *Branch Rickey: Baseball's Ferocious Gentleman.* Lincoln: University of Nebraska Press, 2009.

Lynch, Michael T. *Harry Frazee, Ban Johnson and the Feud That Nearly Destroyed the American League.* Jefferson NC: McFarland, 2008.

McKenna, Bernard. *The Baltimore Black Sox: A Negro Leagues History, 1913–1936.* Jefferson NC: McFarland, 2020.

McMurray, John. "Joe McCarthy." SABR BioProject. sabr.org/bioproject.

McNeil, William F. *The California Winter League: America's First Integrated Professional Baseball League.* Jefferson NC: McFarland, 2002.

Mead, William B., and Paul Dickson. *Baseball: The President's Game.* Washington DC: Farragut Publishing, 1993.

Menand, Louis. "The Big Heinie: How Babe Ruth and Lou Gehrig Brought Stardom to America's Pastime." *The New Yorker.* May 25, 2020.

Monagan, Matt. "The Cuban Star Who Outslugged the Babe." *MLB.* November 5, 2023. https://www.mlb.com/news/cristobal-torriente-beats-out-babe-ruth?msockid=2d7e40b13ef765e4060a50273fdb6469.

Montville, Leigh. *The Big Bam: The Life and Times of Babe Ruth.* New York: Doubleday, 2006.

Motley, Bob, with Byron Motley. *Ruling Over Monarchs, Giants, and Stars: Umpiring in the Negro Leagues and Beyond.* Champaign IL: Sports Publishing, 2007.

Murdock, Eugene. *Baseball between the Wars: Memories of the Game by the Men Who Played it.* Westport CT: Meckler Corporation, 1992.

———. *Baseball Players and Their Times: Oral Histories of the Game, 1920–1940.* Westport CT: Meckler Corporation, 1991.

Nowlin, Bill, and Reynaldo Cruz Diaz. "Cigars, Horses, and a Couple of Homers: Babe Ruth's Experience in Cuba." In *The Babe*, edited by Bill Nowlin and Glen Sparks. Society for American Baseball Research, 2019. https://sabr.org/journal/article/cigars-horses-and-a-couple-of-homers-babe-ruths-experience-in-cuba/.

Oates, Joyce Carol. *On Boxing*. New York: Ecco Press, 2002.

Okrent, Daniel. *Last Call: The Rise and Fall of Prohibition*. New York: Scribner, 2010.

O'Neil, Buck. *I Was Right on Time: My Journey from the Negro Leagues*. New York: Simon & Schuster, 1996.

Overmeyer, James E. *Black Ball and the Boardwalk: The Bacharach Giants and Atlantic City, 1916–1929*. Jefferson NC: McFarland, 2014.

Paige, Satchel. *Maybe I'll Pitch Forever*. Lincoln: University of Nebraska Press, 1993.

Peterson, Robert. *Only the Ball Was White: A History of Legendary Black Players and All-Black Professional Teams*. New York: Oxford University Press, 1970.

Pietrusza, David. *Gangsterland: A Tour Through the Dark Heart of Jazz-Age New York City*. New York: Diversion Books, 2023.

———. *Judge and Jury: The Life and Times of Judge Kenesaw Mountain Landis*. South Bend IN: Diamond Communications, 1998.

———. *Rothstein: The Life, Times, and Murder of the Criminal Genius Who Fixed the 1919 World Series*. New York: Carroll and Graf Publishers, 2003.

Poekel, Charlie. *Babe & the Kid: The Legendary Story of Babe Ruth and Johnny Sylvester*. Charleston SC: History Press, 2007.

Pomrenke, Jacob. "Call the Game! The 1917 Fenway Park Gamblers Riot." https://jacobpomrenke.com/black-sox/1917-fenway-park-gamblers-riot/.

———. "Gambling in the Deadball Era." Society for American Baseball Research. June 3, 2013. https://sabr.org/latest/pomrenke-gambling-in-the-deadball-era/.

Posnanski, Joe. *The Soul of Baseball: A Road Trip through Buck O'Neil's America*. New York: Harper Collins, 2007.

Reisler, Jim. *Babe Ruth: Launching the Legend*. New York: McGraw-Hill, 2004.

———. *Black Writers/Black Baseball: An Anthology of Articles from Black Sportswriters Who Covered the Negro Leagues*. Jefferson NC: McFarland, 2007.

Riess, Steven A. *Touching Base: Professional Baseball and American Culture in the Progressive Era*. Revised edition. Urbana: University of Illinois Press, 1999.

Ritter, Lawrence S. *The Glory of Their Times: The Story of the Early Days of Baseball Told by the Men Who Played It*. Enlarged edition. New York: HarperCollins, 2002.

Robinson, Arthur. "The Babe." *The New Yorker*. July 31, 1926.

———. "My Friend Babe Ruth." *Collier's*. September 20, 1924.

Roessner, Amber. *Inventing Baseball Heroes: Ty Cobb, Christy Mathewson, and the Sporting Press in America*. Baton Rouge: Louisiana State University Press, 2014.

Rogers III, C. Paul. "Rogers Hornsby." SABR BioProject. sabr.org/bioproject.

Ross, Ishbel. *Grace Coolidge and Her Era: The Story of a President's Wife*. New York: Dodd, Mead & Company, 1962.

Ruth, Babe. *Babe Ruth's Own Book of Baseball*. Lincoln: University of Nebraska Press, 1992.

Sarnoff, Gary. *Team of Destiny: Walter Johnson, Clark Griffith, Bucky Harris, and the 1924 Washington Senators*. Lanham MD: Rowman & Littlefield, 2024.

Semchuck, Alex. "Wilbert Robinson." SABR BioProject. sabr.org/bioproject.

Seymour, Harold, and Dorothy Seymour Mills. *Baseball: The Early Years*. New York: Oxford University Press, 1960.

———. *Baseball: The Golden Age*. New York: Oxford University Press, 1989.

———. *Baseball: The People's Game*. New York: Oxford University Press, 1990.

Shirley, Daniel. "Mark Koenig." SABR BioProject. sabr.org/bioproject.

Skipper, Doug. "Bill Donovan." SABR BioProject. sabr.org/bioproject.

———. "Connie Mack." SABR BioProject. sabr.org/bioproject.

Skipper, John C. *Wicked Curve: The Life and Troubled Times of Grover Cleveland Alexander*. Jefferson NC: McFarland, 2006.

Smelser, Marshall. *The Life That Ruth Built: A Biography*. Lincoln: University of Nebraska Press, 1975.

Smith, Averell "Ace." *The Pitcher and the Dictator: Satchel Paige's Unlikely Season in the Dominican Republic*. Lincoln: University of Nebraska Press, 2018.

Smith, Curt. *Voices of the Game: The Acclaimed Chronicle of Baseball Radio & Television Broadcasting—from 1921 to the Present*. Updated edition. New York: Simon & Schuster, 1992.

Spatz, Lyle, and Steve Steinberg. *1921: The Yankees, the Giants, and the Battle for Baseball Supremacy in New York*. Lincoln: University of Nebraska Press, 2010.

Spivey, Donald. *"If You Were Only White": The Life of Leroy "Satchel" Paige*. Columbia: University of Missouri Press, 2012.

Stangl, Mark. "St. Louis Team Ownership History." SABR Team Ownership History Project. Accessed August 10, 2024. https://sabr.org/bioproj/topic/st-louis-cardinals-team-ownership-history/#britton.

Stanton, Tom. *Ty and the Babe: Baseball's Fiercest Rivals: A Surprising Friendship and the 1941 Has-Beens Golf Championship*. New York: Thomas Dunne Books, 2007.

Steinberg, Steve. *Baseball in St. Louis 1900–1925*. Chicago: Arcadia, 2004.

———. "Jacob Ruppert" SABR BioProject. sabr.org/bioproject.

———. "Miller Huggins." SABR BioProject. sabr.org/bioproject.

———. *Urban Shocker: Silent Hero of Baseball's Golden Age*. Lincoln: University of Nebraska Press, 2017.

Steinberg, Steve, and Lyle Spatz. "The Colonel and Hug: The Odd Couple . . . Not Really." *Baseball Research Journal* (Fall 2015). https://sabr.org/journal/article/the-colonel-and-hug-the-odd-couple-not-really-4/.

———. *The Colonel and Hug: The Partnership That Transformed the New York Yankees*. Lincoln: University of Nebraska Press, 2015.

———. *Mike Donlin: A Rough and Rowdy Life from New York Baseball Idol to Stage and Screen*. Lincoln: University of Nebraska Press, 2024.

Stout, Glenn. *The Cubs: The Complete Story of Chicago Cubs Baseball*. Boston: Houghton Mifflin, 2007.

———. *Yankees Century: 100 Years of New York Yankees Baseball*. Boston: Houghton Mifflin, 2002.

———. *Young Woman and the Sea: How Trudy Ederle Conquered the English Channel and Inspired the World*. New York: Mariner Books, 2009.

Swanson, Ryan A. *When Baseball Went White: Reconstruction, Reconciliation, and Dreams of a National Pastime*. Lincoln: University of Nebraska Press, 2014.

Tannenbaum, Seth S. "The Ever Watchful Eye of the Magnate: Policing and Ballpark Gambling in the Twentieth Century." In *All In: The Spread of Gambling in Twentieth Century United States*, edited by Jonathan D. Cohen and David G. Schwartz, 44–69. Reno: University of Nevada Press, 2018.

Taylor, Dan. *Baseball at the Abyss: The Scandals of 1926, Babe Ruth, and the Unlikely Savior Who Rescued a Tarnished Game*. Lanham MD: Rowman & Littlefield, 2023.

Thomas, Henry W. *Walter Johnson: Baseball's Big Train*. Lincoln NE: Bison Books, 1998.

Thomas, Joan M. "Helene Britton." SABR Bio project. sabr.org/bioproject.

Thorn, John. *Baseball: Our Game*. New York: Penguin Books, 1995.

Tye, Larry. *Satchel: The Life and Times of an American Legend*. New York: Random House, 2009.

Vaccaro, Frank. "Herb Pennock." SABR BioProject. sabr.org/bioproject.

Vecsey, George. *Baseball: A History of America's Favorite Game*. New York: Modern Library, 2008.

Veeck, Bill, with Ed Linn. *The Hustler's Handbook*. Chicago: Ivan R. Dee, 1965.

———. *Veeck as in Wreck: The Autobiography of Bill Veeck*. Chicago: University of Chicago Press, 2001.

Vitti, Jim. *Chicago Cubs: Baseball on Catalina Island*. Charlestown SC: Arcadia, 2010.

Wagenheim, Kal. *Babe Ruth: His Life and Legend*. Chicago: Olmstead Press, 2001.

Walker, James. *Crack of the Bat: A History of Baseball on the Radio*. Lincoln: University of Nebraska Press, 2015.

Wancho, Joseph. "Bob O'Farrell." SABR BioProject. sabr.org/bioproject.

———. "Gabby Street." SABR BioProject. sabr.org/bioproject.

———. "Urban Shocker." SABR BioProject. sabr.org/bioproject.

Ward, Geoffrey C., and Ken Burns. *Baseball: An Illustrated History*. New York: Alfred A. Knopf, 1994.

Weintraub, Robert. *The House That Ruth Built: A New Stadium, the First Yankees Championship, and the Redemption of 1923*. New York: Little, Brown, and Company, 2011.

White, Sol. *Sol White's History of Colored Baseball, with Other Documents on the Early Black Game, 1886–1936*. Lincoln: University of Nebraska Press, 1995.

Wolf, Greg H. "Bill Sherdel." SABR BioProject. sabr.org/bioproject.

Wolf, Thomas. *The Called Shot: Babe Ruth, the Chicago Cubs, and the Unforgettable Major League Baseball Season of 1932*. Lincoln: University of Nebraska Press, 2020.

Wood, Allen. *Babe Ruth and the 1918 Red Sox*. Lincoln NE: Writer's Club Press, 2000.

Index

Illustrations are indicated by F *with a numeral; all appear following page 74.*

Aaron, Henry, 178–79
Adams, Sparky, 65
Addams, Jane, 66
Aitken, Albert, 141
Alamac Hotel, 154
Al Capone Stars, 87
Alexander, Aimee Arrants, 58, 63, 178
Alexander, Charles, 169
Alexander, Grover Cleveland "Alex," 4, 15, 129, 180, *F10*; alcoholism of, 58, 64, 149, 177; appreciation day for, 59; contract for, 191n16; described, 54; health problems for, 61, 64, 190n8; Hornsby and, 60, 63, 64–65, 156; House of David and, 177, 181; Lazzeri and, 157; marriage of, 63; McCarthy and, 58, 59, 60, 65; Meusel and, 158; military service for, 62, 63–64, 190n1, 191n19; opening day and, 63; pitching record of, 177; Ruth and, 61, 145, 154, 157, 158, 159, 160, 190n10, 202n14; on Ruth steal attempt, 159; salary for, 62; trade of, 58, 62, 64; workout plans of, 59; World Series and, 144, 145, 150, 152, 153, 154, 156–59; youth of, 60–61
All-Star Game, 204n3
Almendares Blues, 71
Almendares Park, 71
American Association, 20, 21
American League, 3, 4, 17, 18, 19, 46, 52, 100, 111, 118, 130, 131; attendance for, 9–10; New York City team for, 7, 8; standings for, *108*, *133*; Western League and, 9
American Negro League, 176
American Series, 69, 192n14
Angelous Temple, 83, 84
Anthony, Susan B., 66
Anti-Saloon League (ASL), 23, 66, 67
Appel, Marty, 9
Arlington, Lizzie, 92, 195n31
ASL. *See* Anti-Saloon League (ASL)
Atlanta Black Crackers, 123
Atlantic City: Colored World Series and, 165, 166; described, 165
Atlantic City Bacharach Giants, 122, 166, 167, 176, 203n8; Colored World Series and, 164, 165
Atlantic League, 91, 195n30, 196n31
Attell, Abe, 114, 125, 127, 198n8, 198n9

Babe and the Kid (Poekel), 201n3
The Babe Comes Home (movie), 179
Bacharach, Harry, 165
Bacharach Park, Colored World Series at, 165
Bader, Edward, 165
Baker, Frank "Home Run," 16, 17, 56
Baker, Kevin, 37, 74, 192n18
Baker, William, 62
Baker Bowl, 124, 128, 129, 200n4; Colored World Series at, 165
Baldassaro, Lawrence, 91

Baltimore Orioles, 7
Bamberger, Michael, 187n2
barnstorming, 32, 69–70, 71, 72, 98, 116, 123, 193n24, 193n25
Barrow, Ed, 74, 85, 116, 195n30; as business manager, 195n26; described, 91–92; Frazee and, 92; Lazzeri and, 91, 92–93; Ruth and, 92; on Ruth steal attempt, 160
Baseball: the Golden Age (Seymour and Seymour), 111
Bassler, Johnny, 51
Beau James (Fowler), 188n10
Beer and Whiskey League, 20
Bell, Cool Papa, 3, 101, 175
Bell, Herman, 149
Bell, Les, 28, 57, 128, 153; on Alexander's game 7 entrance, 156; hitting by, 55; on Hornsby, 26–27; on Ruth steal attempt, 159; World Series and, 148, 151, 155, 156, 157
Bellows, George, 123, 199n18
Bengough, Benny, 35
Benjamin, Hubert, 75
Bennett, Eddie, 13, 88
Bennett, Floyd, 50
Bentley, Jack, 119
Biden, Joe, 189n1
The Big Fella (Leavy), 74
Bill Brown's Health Farm, 179
Black Sox scandal, 74, 79, 81, 118, 127, 154, 172, 173. *See also* Chicago White Sox
Blades, Ray, 28, 56, 65
Blaisdel, Lowell, 204n21
Blake, Sheriff, 65
Blue Ridge League, 29
Board of Commissioners, Harris and, 105
Boland, Bernie, 77
Bonds, Barry: walks by, 202n15
Boston Braves, 45, 55, 57, 59, 178, 187n4
Boston Red Sox, 16, 18, 42–43, 48, 61, 69, 75, 80, 85, 86, 92, 104, 105, 172, 176; Coolidge and, 182
Bottomly, Jim "Sunny Jim," 28, 42, 150, 153, 155, F7; World Series and, 143, 156
Bottoms Gang, 25
boxing, 36–37, 120, 142; gambling on, 79
Boyd, William, 170
Boyer, Lillian, 185n1
Breadon, Sam, 24, 56, 146; Hornsby and, 129, 171
Brennan, Ollie, 43
Bresnahan, Roger, 15, 22
Brice, Fanny, 75
Brice, Lew, 75
British Open, 121
Britton, Helene Hathaway Robison, 22, 186n6
Broeg, Bob, 29
Brooklyn Citizen, 87
Brooklyn Dodgers, 176
Brooklyn Eagles, 204n3
Brooklyn Robins, 12, 39, 44, 55, 118, 137
Brooklyn Royal Giants, 192
Brooklyn Times-Citizen, 87
Broun, Heywood, 199n22
Brown, Elsie, 162–63, 203n6
Brown, Mordecai "Three Finger," 97
Brown, Warren, 121
Bryan, William Jennings, 2
Bunning, Jim, 190n10
Burke, Edward, 169
Burns, Ken, 196n4
Burns, Sleepy Bill, 114
Bush, Bullet Joe, 17, 51, 106, 107
Bush, George H. W., 189n1
Bush, George W., 189n2
Butler, Samuel, 199n19
Byrd, Richard D., 50

California Winter League, 73, 94, 98, 181, 196n2
Capone, Al, 34, 69, 91, 113, 168, 194n10; baseball and, 87; gang wars and, 203n2; Hoyt and, 86; Ruth and, 195n11
Capone, Deirdre Marie, 87
Capone, Ralph, 69, 87, 195n11
Carraway, Nick, 127
Carter, Jimmy, 188–89n1
Catalina Island, spring training on, 58, 63, 64, 190n2
Chance, Frank, 196n11
Chaney, Lon, 1
Chaplin, Charlie, 1, 13, 124
Charleston, Oscar, 3, 97, 99, 164, 175, 187n8, 196n6
Chase, Hal, 194n6
Chattanooga Black Lookouts, 123
Chattanooga White Sox, 94
Chesbro, Jack, 7, 8
Chicago (musical), 69
Chicago American Giants, 97, 98, 99, 101, 122, 161, 162, 167, 176; championship for, 100; Colored World Series and, 163, 164; domination by, 96; exhibitions and, 100
Chicago Beach, incident at, 99
Chicago Beach Hotel, 100
Chicago Bears, 121
Chicago Cubs, 22, 45, 46, 54, 58, 62, 64, 87, 92, 97, 175, 178; Catalina Island and, 190n2; Ruth and, 195n11
Chicago Defender, 165
Chicago Federal Building, 111
Chicago Giants, 99
Chicago Tribune, 65
Chicago Unions, 96
Chicago White Sox, 7, 21, 45, 46, 76, 80, 81, 97, 98, 132, 172; game-fixing scandal and, 114. *See also* Black Sox scandal
Chicago White Stockings, 66
Christianson, Cuckoo, 130
Cicotte, Eddie, 80
Cincinnati Reds, 14, 27, 35, 45, 56, 59, 62, 81, 90, 114, 124, 128, 140; American Series and, 192n14; as Big Red Machine, 175
Cleveland, Stephen Grover, 60
Cleveland Elites, 122
Cleveland Indians, 45, 57, 75, 76, 109, 131, 169, 181, 193n3; game-fixing scandal and, 168; World Series and, 115
Clinton, Bill, 189n1
Cobb, Amanda, 47
Cobb: A Terrible Beauty (Leerhsen), 48
Cobb, Charlotte, 48, 78
Cobb, Ty, 4, 50, 56, 75, 76, 81, 82, 85, 97, 131, 171, 177, *F18*; career of, 47; Dempsey-Tunney fight and, 124; gambling and, 4, 77, 78, 110, 118, 170; game-fixing scandal and, 109, 126, 168, 169, 172, 173–74; Harding and, 110; hitting by, 176; Johnson and, 111; Landis and, 170, 173, 176; letter from, 78, 80, 118; marriage of, 48; opening day and, 45; retirement of, 169; Ruth and, 47, 49, 51, 52, 105; salary of, 170; style of play of, 49; temper of, 48, 49; vindication of, 174; youth of, 47
Cochrane, Mickey, 187n7
Cole, Bert, 49
Colisimo Café, 197n6
Collins, Pat "Rip," 35, 50, 51, 89, 157
Colored World Series, 4, 100, 122, 164–65, 166, 176; NNL and, 163
Colosimo, Diamond Jim, 113, 197n6
Combs, Earle, 35, 51, 89, 132, 143, 150; World Series and, 144, 155, 157
Comiskey, Charles, 7, 21, 97, 114
Comiskey Park, 87, 98

Committee on Negro Baseball Leagues, 181
Commodore Hotel, 140
Congress Hotel, 72–73
Connelly, Tommy, 106
Connery, Bob, 15, 91
Considine, Bob, 180
Coolidge, Calvin, 3, 102–3, 131, 182, 188n1, *F1*; athletes/sporting events and, 104; Dempsey- Tunney fight and, 124; football and, 121; Harris and, 105; opening day and, 41; speech by, 103, 107; World Series and, 105–6
Coolidge, Grace, 83, 131, 182–83, *F1*; baseball and, 3, 104–5, 107, 130; opening day and, 41; World Series and, 105–6
Cooper, Wilbur, 54
Corbett, Jim, 92
Cotton Club, 69
Coveleski, Stan, 106, 107, 131
Cox, James, 125, 200n27
Creamer, J. C., 34
Creamer, Robert, 193n25; on Ruth steal attempt, 160
Crescent Lake Field, 33; alligators at, 17–18
Crowder, Alvin, 106
Crusinberry, James, 65
Cuban X Giants, 96
Cummings, Chance, 167
Curry, Rube, 101, 165, 166
Cuthbert, Ned, 21

Darrow, Clarence, 2, 113
Dauss, Hooks, 52, 190n10
Davis, Dwight, 131
Dawes, Charles, 41, 42, 124
Dawes Plan, 42
Day, Doris, 178
Dayton Marcos, 122
Deadball Era, 79, 191n8
Dean, Dizzy, 181, 205n13
Del Prado Hotel, 34
Dempsey, Jack, 2, 3, 32, 123–24, 125, 127, 128, 140, 199n16; described, 124; salary for, 126; Tunney and, 199n10; World Series and, 142
Dempsey and Firpo (Bellows), 199n18
Denison Railroaders, 15
Denver Post tournament, 177, 181
Detroit Stars, 101, 162
Detroit Tigers, 12, 45, 47, 51, 52, 75, 85, 92, 97, 109, 170, 172; game-fixing scandal and, 168
Devery, Bill, 10, 11, 12; described, 8–9; New York City team and, 7
Diamond, Neil, 194n4
Dickey, Bill, 187n7
Dillhoefer, Pickles, 62, 63
DiMaggio, Joe, 176, 180–81
Dixon, Phil, 175
Dolan, Cozy, 117, 118
Donaldson, John, 100
Donlin, Mike, 192n10
Donohue, Pete, 38, 59
Donovan, "Wild" Bill, 12, 14, 185n1
Douglas, Shuffling Phil, 84, 117, 118
Douthit, Taylor, 28, 55, 57; World Series and, 143, 145, 149, 153
Doyle, Jack, 140, 143, 145, 153, 154
Doyle Billiard Academy, 140
Dugan, Joe, 35, 46, 51, 73, 86, 89, 153, 194n5; World Series and, 144, 151, 157
Duncan, Isadora, 10
Duval Giants, 203n2

Earhart, Amelia, 1
Eastern Colored League (ECL), 100, 164, 176, 187n8; Colored World Series and, 122
East-West All-Star game, 176
East-West Classic, 204n3

Ederle, Gertrude, 121–22, 198n10, 199n13
Ehmke, Howard: opening day and, 43–44
Eighteenth Amendment, 67–68, 69
Eisenhower, Dwight, 188n1
Elkins Act (1903), 112
Elkus, Gleason and Proskauer (law firm), 11
Engels, Joe, 48
Epstein, Daniel Mark, 84
Erasmus Hall High School, 85, 194n4
Evans, Billy, 171
Evans, Nat (Rachel Brown), 198n9
Evers, Johnny, 196n11
Eynon, Edwin, 81, 109

Farrell, Frank, 8, 12; character of, 9; New York City team and, 7; ownership and, 185n5; Sullivan and, 185n4
Farrell, Luther, 165
Federal League, 98, 99
Feller, Bob, 181, 205n13
Fenway Park, 43, 85; professional gamblers at, 80
Ferrell, Rick, 187n7
Fifth Amendment, 113
Firpo, Luis Angel, 2, 123, 199n16
Fischetti, Charlie, "Trigger Happy," 87, 194n10
Fitzgerald, F. Scott, 70, 127
Fleischmann, Billy, 185n9
Fletcher, Art, 25, 117
Ford, Gerald, 189n1
Foster, Andrew "Rube," 4, 162, 164, 196n4, *F12*; American Giants and, 101; barnstorming by, 98; championship for, 100; Curry and, 101; death of, 180, 196n12; health problems for, 161, 196n10; integration and, 176; Leland and, 96–97; Major Leagues and, 99; McGraw and, 100; Negro Leagues and, 176, 180; NNL and, 100; pitches by, 96; Rogan and, 163; Schorling, 97–98; youth of, 95
Foster, Bill "Willie," 3, 4, 162, 163, 165, 166, 167, *F13*
Foster, Sarah, 161
Foursquare Gospel Church, 83, 182, 205n16
Fowler, Gene, 188n10
Foxx, Jimmy, 107
Frazee, Harry, 86; Barrow and, 92; Ruth and, 69, 192n11
Frisch, Frankie, 44, 105, 117, 179; trade of, 171
Froelich, Ed, 201n16

Galesburg Boosters, 61
Gallico, Paul, 199n22
Gambino, Richard, 91
gambling, 4, 25, 68, 70–72, 74, 76–80, 109–10; on baseball, 113, 115, 118, 140, 153, 154; controlling, 80; in Cuba, 69–70; off-site, 79; spending on, 120
game-fixing scandal, 79, 114–16, 125, 126, 127, 153, 168; allegations in, 109–10, 110–11; hiding, 171
Gandil, Chick, 172, 173
The Gangplank (nightclub), 34, 36, 37
Gardner, Jelly, 167
Gaston, Milt, 17
Gay, Timothy, 79
Gehrig, Lou, 4, 17, 35, 38, 50, 51, 89, 132, 148, *F11*; Dempsey-Tunney fight and, 124; home runs by, 175; nicknames for, 37; Ripken and, 188n7; spring training and, 34; World Series and, 150, 151, 153, 155, 157
Gibson, Billy, 199n24
Gibson, Bob, 30, 188n15
Gibson, George, 53
Gibson, Josh, 175, 187n7

Gibson, Sam, 131
Gilhooley, Frank "Flash," 16
Girard, Joe, 17
Godfather (movie), 195n11
Golden Lion saloon, 20
Gold Rush (movie), 1
Golenbock, Peter, 20–21
Gordon, Joseph, 9
Goslin, Goose, 105, 106, 107, 130
Grand Central Station, 140, 152
Grange, Red, 3, 120, 121, 198n7, 198n8
Great Depression, 176, 181
The Great Gatsby (Fitzgerald), 127
Green, John, 141
Green, Pumpsie, 176
Greenlee, Gus, 176, 204n3
Grier, Claude, 164, 165, 166
Griffith, Clark, 7, 41, 131
Griffith Stadium, 42, 104, *F1*; World Series at, 105
Grimm, Charlie, 54, 65
Groh, Henry "Heine," 62, 105
Grove, Lefty, 4, 107
Guayama Witches, 181

Hafey, Chick, 57, 149, 155
Haines, Bob, 30, 148, 188n15
Haines, Jesse, 29, 30, 53, 54; World Series and, 144, 147–48, 154, 155, 156
Halas, George, 16, 121
Harding, Warren, 110, 188n1
Hargrave, Bubbles, 128, 129
Harpman, Julia, 122, 198n10
Harris, Bucky, 3, 42, 81, 106, 109, 131, 194n12, *F1*; Calvin Coolidge and, 105; Grace Coolidge and, 104–5
Harris, Joe, 42
Harrisburg Giants, 164
Harrison, James, 149, 201n11
Hartnett, Gabby, 54, 187n7
Hayes, Rutherford Birchard, 14
Hearst, William Randolph, 124
Heilman, Harry, 81, 109
Henderson, Rats, 164, 165, 166
Hendricks, Jack, 23
Herrmann, Garry, 114, 140
Herzog, Buck, 48
Heydler, John, 55, 114
Hicks, Rose, 73, 193n30
Hildebrand, George, 48, 157, 202n14
Hill, Pete, 99, 196n5
Hilldale Athletic Club, 29, 197n16
Hilldale Darby Daisies, 29, 100, 122, 164, 187n8
Hilton, Paul, 44, 189n6
Hinckley, John, 200n28
Hines, John, 166
Hite, Mabel, 192n10
Hodgson, Ruth, 189n5
Hoff, Maxie "Boo," 127, 199n24
Holloway, Ken, 50
Holly, Ed, 91
Holm, Wattie, 57, 153
Homestead Grays, 175, 176
Hoover, Herbert, 188n1
Hope, Bob, 188n10
Hornsby, Rogers, 3, 4, 12, 30–31, 53, 55–56, 57, 73, 91, 128, 178, 179, *F2*; Alexander and, 60, 63, 64–65, 156; batting by, 54, 55; Breadon and, 129, 171; dominance of, 137; financial losses for, 187n11; Hendricks and, 23; Huggins and, 15; Keen and, 28; as manager, 23–27, 29, 53, 187n4; McGraw and, 171; as MVP, 55; opening day and, 42; Rickey and, 23–24, 27, 129; Ruth and, 3, 72, 158, 159, 171, 202n16; salary for, 24; Sherdel and, 30; trade of, 171; World Series and, 139, 143, 144, 147–48, 150, 153, 155, 156
horse racing, 20, 24, 25, 71–72, 79, 110, 113, 120, 127

Hotel Adelphia, 60
Hotel Plaza, 71
House of David, 177, 181
House of the Good Shepherd, 19
Hoyt, Waite, 35, 50, 85, 131, 175, 186n3, 194n4, 194n5, *F6*; Capone and, 86; nightlife of, 86; Ruth and, 18; World Series and, 148–49, 149–50, 153, 155
Huggins, Miller, 12, 33, 46, 51, 85, 116, 119, *F11*; on Alexander, 145; on baseball/real estate and, 34; birth of, 14; concerns for, 36; described, 13, 188n4; health problems for, 179; Hornsby and, 15; interview by, 37–38; Koenig and, 107; New York Yankees and, 15, 17, 23; as player-manager, 15, 22; rebuilding by, 34–35; Ruppert and, 13, 14, 198n2; Ruth and, 3, 18, 19, 34, 49, 92, 151; on Ruth steal attempt, 160; trade of, 22; World Series and, 137, 142, 143–44, 147, 151, 152, 153
Huggins, Myrtle, 13, 14
Hunt, Marshall, 19, 72–73
Hunter, Catfish, 190n10
Huston, Tillinghast "Til," 10, 12, 185n8, 185n9

The Importance of Being Earnest (play), 69
Indianapolis ABCs, 99
Indianapolis Freeman, 97
In the Service of the King (McPherson), 182

Jackson, Sanford, 101, 163
Jackson, Shoeless Joe, *F18*
James, Bill, 196n6, 203n6
Jazz Age, 37
Jefferson, Thomas, 197n7
Jeffries, James, 91
Johns, Augie, 51, 190n9
Johnson, Ban, 10, 12, 75, 76, 82, 100, 114, 154, 169, *F20*; Cobb and, 111; Devery/Farrell and, 9; game-fixing scandal and, 98–99, 109–10, 171; health problems for, 111; influence of, 182; Landis and, 111, 118, 173–74; Leonard and, 80, 81; New York City team and, 7, 8; secret meeting of, 109; Speaker and, 111; speech by, 148
Johnson, Home Run, 97
Johnson, Jack, 95
Johnson, Judy, 29, 175
Johnson, Lyndon, 188n1
Johnson, Sylvester, 27
Johnson, Walter, 3, 41, 42, 64, 105, 106, 107, 131, 187n8
Jones, Bobby, 121
Jones, James C., 22
Jones, Sad Sam, 43, 86
Judge, Joe, 105, 106, 107, 130

Kankakee State Hospital, 161, 180
Kansas City Monarchs, 100, 101, 122, 162–63, 167, 181
Karst, Gene, 27
Keaton, Buster, 72
Keeler, Willie, 7, 8
Keeley Institute, 58, 190n1
Keen, Vic, 28, 29, 53, 55, 187n98; trade of, 27
Keller, Helen, 72
Kellogg, Frank, 131, *F1*
Kelly, Alvin "Shipwreck," 2
Kelly, George, 105, 117, 118
Kendrick, W. Freeland, 124
Kennedy, John F., 188n1
Kennedy, Minnie, 83, 84
Kenny, Arthur, 189n6
Kentucky Derby, 121
Keyes, Asa, 182
Khan, Roger, 194n4

Kiernan, John, 138
Killefer, Bill, 28, 31, 53, 63, 65; trade of, 62
Killilea, Henry, 81, 109, 110
KKK. *See* Ku Klux Klan (KKK)
Knights of Pythias band, 165
Koenig, Mark, 36, 38, 46, 50, 89, 189n3; errors by, 107, 149; Ruth and, 48; World Series and, 144, 148, 150, 151, 155, 157
Krichell, Paul, 91
Ku Klux Klan (KKK), 2, 66, 90, 99

Landis, Kenesaw Mountain, 19, 55, 74, 146, 154, 204n21, *F21*; Black Sox verdict and, 115–16; Cobb and, 170, 173, 176; as commissioner, 115–16, 181–82; Dempsey-Tunney fight and, 126; described, 111; exhibition games and, 100; gambling and, 115; game-fixing scandal and, 74, 111, 172; investigation by, 168; Johnson and, 111, 118, 173–74, 174–75; Leonard and, 118, 168–69; McGraw and, 117, 192n15; Rockefeller and, 112, 113; Rothstein and, 127; Ruth and, 116–17, 193n24; Standard Oil and, 112–13; Stoneham and, 192n15; White Sox and, 114; World Series and, 140, 142, 152
Lardner, Ring, 199n22
Last Call: The Rise and Fall of Prohibition (Okrent), 67
Law, Ruth: Stengel and, 138–39
Lazzeri, Tony, 4, 36, 38, 46, 50, 51, 124, 180, 195n20, *F9*; Alexander and, 157; background of, 89, 91; Barrow and, 91, 92–93; confidence of, 90; death of, 205n9; Dempsey-Tunney fight and, 124; health problems for, 90; Italian Americans and, 91, 93; nicknames for, 37; stolen bases by, 203n25; World Series and, 144, 148, 150–51, 153, 155, 156, 157
Leavy, Jane, 74
Leeke, Jim, 191n19
Leerhsen, Charles, 48
Leland, Frank, 96–97
Leland Giants, 98
Leonard, Dutch, 51, 61, 75, 76, 126, 194n12, *F17*; death of, 177; gambling and, 77, 170; game- fixing scandal and, 109, 111, 171, 172; Johnson and, 80, 81; Landis and, 118, 168–69; letters and, 81, 170; retirement of, 177; revenge of, 81–82
Leuchtenburg, William, 120
Lewis, Duffy, 89
Lexington Hotel, 86
Lieb, Fred, 19
Linares, Abel, 70
Lincoln, Abraham, 84, 86
Lindbergh, Charles, 2, 142
Lindstrom, Freddie, 27, 119
Lippman, Walter, 102
Lloyd, John Henry "Pop," 97, 164, 196n5, 203n6
Lockhart, Hubert, 167
Lombardi, Ernie, 187n7
London Evening News, 18
Lowenfish, Lee, 23
Lucas, Red, 59, 128
Luderus, Fred, 61
Lundy, Dick, 164, 165, 203n6
Luque, Dolf, 38, 128, 130

Mack, Connie, 4, 96, 140; Cobb and, 176; World Series and, 142
Mackey, Biz, 187n7, 187n8
Maharg, Billy, 114
Major Leagues, 3, 123, 166, 176, 194n6; attendance for, 68; integration and, 100; standings for, *108, 133*; transition for, 4; World War I and, 63

Malamud, Bernard, 194n4
Malarcher, Dave, 161–62, 163, 165, 167, *F16*
Mallory, Molla Bjurstedt, 121
Malone, Pat, 59
Manley, Abe, 204n3
Manley, Effa, 204n3
Mann, Les, 117
Maranville, Rabbit, 53
Marberry, Firpo, 106
Maryland Park, Colored World Series at, 165
Matthewson, Christy, 63, 96
Matthewson Park, 119
Maugham, Somerset, 199n19
Mays, Carl, 38, 75, 86, 192n16
Mays, Willie, 196n6
McCarthy, Joe, 53–54, 189n2; alcoholism of, 64, 191n23; Alexander and, 58, 59, 60, 65; opening day and, 45
McGeehan, W. O., 199n22
McGill, James, 186n7
McGovern, Artie, 32, 33
McGraw, Blanche, 119
McGraw, John, 4, 8, 15, 44, 85, 96, 105, 106, 109, 116, 120, 128, 141; barnstorming and, 69–70; Dempsey-Tunney fight and, 124; Foster and, 100; Hornsby and, 171; Huggins and, 14; Landis and, 117; as manager, 197n9; racetrack/casino and, 71, 72, 119, 192n15; trade by, 56–57
McGraw-Pennant Park Corporation, 119
McNamee, Graham, 106, 153; Dempsey-Tunney fight and, 124; World Series and, 142, 158, 159
McNeely, Earl, 130
McPherson, Aimee Semple, 2, 182, 194n1; disappearance/reappearance of, 84–85, 119; rise of, 83–84
Mellon, Andrew, *F1*
Memphis Red Sox, 101
Mendez, Jose, 101
Merriwell, Frank, 44
Meusel, Bob, 17, 35, 48, 72, 73, 86, 89, 90, 132, 194n5; Alexander and, 158; barnstorming and, 116, 193n24; stolen bases by, 203n25; World Series and, 143, 144, 148, 151, 153, 155, 157, 158
Meusel, Irish, 105, 119
Mexican League, 178
Miller, Victor, 146, 147
Milwaukee Braves, 179
Mix, Tom, 124
Moore, Dobie "Black Cat," 101, 203n6; shooting of, 162–63
Moore, Frank, 25
Moran, Charlie, 65
Morrison, Johnny, 59
Mueller, Heinie, 28; batting by, 54, 55; trade of, 56, 57
Murderers Row, 148, 175, 204n1
Murlin, James, 169
Myer, Buddy, 130
Myers, Elmer, 77

Nast, Conde, 124
Nation, Carrie, 67
National Baseball Hall of Fame, 29, 187n7, 196n5, 196n6
National Football League, 16, 121
National League, 22, 23, 24, 28, 53, 58, 62, 114, 173; alcohol and, 20; attendance for, 9–10; establishment of, 111; New York City teams of, 7; standings for, *108*, *133*; Van der Ahe and, 21
National Origins Act (1924), 2, 90
Navin, Frank, 81, 109, 169
Navin Field, 48, 76
Negro Leagues, 3, 4, 29, 122–23, 163, 187n7, 192n21, 195n11, 204n3; Foster

Negro Leagues (*continued*) and, 176, 180; great teams from, 175; World War I and, 63
Negro National League (NNL), 100, 101, 162, 164, 165; Colored World Series and, 122, 163; organization of, 99
Negro National League (NNL) Championship, 163
Negro Southern League, 94, 123
Neum, Johnny, 51
Newark Eagles, 204n3
New York City Police Department, 141, 192n13
The New York Daily News, 198n10
New York Evening Sun, 7
The New York Game (Baker), 74
New York Giants, 10, 27, 38, 44, 54, 57, 59, 62, 85, 96, 106, 117; barnstorming and, 69–70
New York Lincoln Giants, 164
New York Palace, 72
New York Times, 50, 131, 137; on Coolidge, 103; on gambling/baseball, 79
New York Yankees, 15, 42–44, 46, 48, 51, 69, 75, 86, 87, 89, 121, 122; American League crowns/World Series titles for, 175–76; dominance of, 17, 107, 109, 131; as greatest baseball team of all time, 175; ownership of, 10–11; sale of, 185n9; World Series and, 132, 137, 152
Nineteenth Amendment, 1
Nixon, Richard M., 188n1
NNL. *See* Negro National League (NNL)

Obama, Barack, 189n1
O'Connell, Jimmy, 117–18
O'Farrell, Bob, 128, 187n7, *F15*; described, 139; as MVP, 28; on Ruth steal attempt, 159; World Series and, 144, 145, 148, 149, 151, 155, 156, 158
Ohio State League, 57
Okrent, Daniel, 67
O'Rourke, Frank, 50
Owens, Brick, 48

Pacific Coast League (PCL), 27, 36, 90, 189n3
Paige, Satchel, 3, 94, 175, 177, 180, 205n4, 205n13, 205n15, *F5*; barnstorming by, 123, 181; named pitches of, 94, 196n1
Paschal, Ben, 151
Patten, Gilbert, 44
PCL. *See* Pacific Coast League (PCL)
Peckinpaugh, Roger, 15, 16, 17
Pegler, Westbrook, 198n10, 199n22
Pennant Park, 119
Pennock, Herb, 35, 50, 52, 73, 85, 86, 139, 175, 194n5; described, 87; trade of, 87; World Series and, 142–43, 147, 150, 151, 155, 157
Penn State League, 85
Pennsylvania Station, 33
Pesky, Johnny, 180
Petty, Jesse, 44
Petway, Bruce, 97
The Phantom of the Opera (movie), 1
Philadelphia Athletics, 41, 42, 62, 74, 104, 132, 140, 142
Philadelphia Giants, 95, 96
Philadelphia North American, 114
Philadelphia Phillies, 45, 54, 61, 62, 71, 96, 117, 124; attendance for, 200n4
Pinstripe Empire (Appel), 9
Pipp, Wally, 16, 35, 38, 128, 130; Ruth and, 48
Pittsburgh Courier, 204n3
Pittsburgh Crawfords, 175, 176, 181, 204n3

Pittsburgh Pirates, 38, 57, 97, 106, 107, 179
Plank, Eddie, 16, 29
Poekel, Charlie, 201n3
Polo Grounds, 2, 8, 10, 44, 63, 123, 128
Pomrenke, Jacob, 79
Ponzi, Charles, 1
Portsmouth Cobblers, 57
Posey, Cum, 204n3
Powell, Willie, 166
Pratt, Del, 15, 16
Prendergast, Mike, 62, 63
Prohibition, 1, 23, 37, 66, 73, 83, 113; defiance of, 2, 67–68; as legal/social issue, 68
Putnam, Charlie, 48

Reagan, Nancy, 200n28
Reagan, Ronald, 178, 200n28
Red Cross, 104
Red Scare, 1
Red Summer (1919), 99
Reilly, Tommy, 124, 125
Rhem, Flint "Big Smokey," 29, 54, 55, 128, 187n10; alcoholism and, 149; opening day and, 42; World Series and, 144, 148–49, 156
Rice, Grantland, 48, 199n22
Rice, Sam, 105, 106, 107
Rickey, Branch, 30, 56, 60, 117, 146; Hendricks and, 23; Hornsby and, 23–24, 27, 129; Keen and, 28; St. Louis Cardinals and, 22–23; trade by, 56, 58
Ring, Jimmy, 171
Ripken, Cal: Gehrig and, 188n7
Risberg, Charles "Swede," 171, 173
Rixey, Eppa, 38, 130
Robinson, Jackie, 176
Robinson, Wilbert, 12, 38, 142, 150; column by, 137, 139, 147, 154; Dempsey-Tunney fight and, 124; described, 137–38; Stengel and, 138; World Series and, 140, 141
Robison, Frank, 21, 22
Robison, Stanley, 21, 22, 186n6
Rockefeller, John D., 112, 113
Rogan, Bullet Joe, 4, 100, 101, 162, 167; Foster and, 163
Rogers, Will, 142
Rogers Hornsby Day, 55–56
Rommel, Eddie, 30, 42
Roosevelt, Franklin Delano, 84, 188n1, 200n27
Roosevelt, Theodore, 112
Root, Charlie, 54
Root, Elihu, 13
Rothstein, Arnold, 114, 198n8, 199–200n24; Dempsey-Tunney fight and, 125, 126; Landis and, 127
Roush, Edd, 38, 129
Rousseau, Jean Jacques, 197n7
Ruel, Muddy, 130
Ruether, Dutch, 106, 147
Runyon, Damon, 13, 82, 199n22
Ruppert, Jacob, 10, 11, 12, 19, 119, 122, 186n3, 199n13; Dempsey-Tunney fight and, 124; described, 13–14; Huggins and, 13, 14, 198n2; Huston and, 185n9; lifestyle of, 186n6; Walker and, 36–37; World Series and, 142
Ruppert Beach Development Company, 119
Russ, Pythias, 101
Ruth, Babe, 2, 35, 46, 50, 75, 80, 86, 89, 90, 121, 132, 140, 170, *F11*; Alexander and, 61, 145, 154, 157, 158, 159, 160, 190n10, 201n14; alligators and, 17–18, 33; antics of, 71–73, 74; attendance increase and, 68; barnstorming and, 32, 71, 116,

Ruth, Babe (*continued*)
193n24, 193n25; Barrow and, 92; called shot by, 189n3; Capone and, 195n11; Cobb and, 47, 49, 51, 52, 105; comeback by, 4; criticism of, 17–18; Dempsey-Tunney fight and, 124; dominance of, 137; endorsements by, 179; gambling by, 70–71, 71–72, 74; health problems for, 3, 19; home runs by, 16, 175; Hornsby and, 3, 72, 158, 159, 171, 202n16; Hoyt and, 18; Huggins and, 3, 18, 19, 34, 49, 92, 151; Hunt and, 19, 72–73; Landis and, 116–17, 193n24; legal problems for, 43–44; marriage of, 48; McGovern and, 32, 33; physical resilience of, 74, 107; on prostitutes, 19; salary of, 24, 116, 192n16; sale of, 16, 69, 192n11; spring training and, 17–18, 32; stolen bases by, 203n25; style of play of, 49; temper of, 48; Torriente and, 71, 193n21; vaudeville and, 72, 73, 179; World Series and, 139, 143, 144, 147–51, 153–55, 157, 158, 160; youth of, 47
Ruth, Claire, 192n19
Ruth, George, 47
Ruth, Helen Woodford, 31, 48, 192n19

Sacco, Nicolo, 1, 91
Salt Lake City Bees, 89, 90, 93
Sand, Heinie, 117
Santa Clara Leopards, 181
Santop, Louis, 29, 187n7, 187n8
Sarazen, Gene, 32
Sargent, John, *F1*
Schalk, Ray, 187n7
Schorling, John, 97–98, 196n12
Schorling Park, 99, 166
Scopes, John, 2
Scott, Everett, 35
segregation, 94, 98, 99, 176, 181
Selective Service Act, 62
Seminick, Andy, 187n2
Severeid, Hank, 144
Sex (play), 1, 69
Seymour, Harold and Dorothy, 111
Shakespeare, William, 124, 199n19
Sharkey, Jack, 126
Shawkey, Bob, 35, 51, 107, 131–32, 190n9, 192n16; opening day and, 43; World Series and, 153
Sherdel, Bill "Wee Willie," 29–30, 54, 55, 56, 129, 139, 188n15, *F4*; World Series and, 143, 150–51
Shibe Park, 104
Shocker, Urban, 35, 43, 51, 85, 131, 175, 180; health problems for, 88–89; spitballs and, 87–88, 201n15; trade of, 15–16, 17; World Series and, 143–44, 145, 153
Shore, Ernie, 61, 75
Sisler, George, 47, 71, *F3*
Skipper, John C., 64
Sloppy Joe's Bar, 71
Smith, Earle, 53
Smith, Red, 180
Smith, Wendell, 204n3
Soldier Field, 126
South Side Park, 98
Southworth, Billy, 65, 105, 128, 129, 178–79, *F14*; trade of, 56–57, 58; World Series and, 143, 145, 147, 149, 151
Souza, John Phillips, 32
Spanish-American War, 10, 185n8
Spatz, Lyle, 199n13
speakeasies, 1, 2, 34, 68, 86, 120
Speaker, Tris "the Grey Eagle," 4, 56, 75, 76, 79, 81, 82, 131, 177, *F19*; gambling and, 4, 77, 110, 118; game-fixing scandal and, 109, 126, 168, 169, 170, 171, 172, 173–74; Johnson and, 111; opening day and, 45; retirement of, 169

Spillane, Mickey, 194n4
spitballs, outlawing, 87–88, 201n15
Sportsman's Park, 42, 55, 56; World Series at, 146
spring training, 17–18, 26, 32, 35–38, 58, 63, 64, 190n2
Standard Oil, 112–13
Stearnes, Turkey, 101
Steinberg, Steve, 88, 199n13
Stengel, Casey: Law and, 138–39; Robinson and, 138; storytelling by, 200–201n4
Stevenson, Riggs, 54
St. Louis Browns, 15, 17, 20, 22, 35, 45, 106, 132, 178, 181; American Association and, 21; Paige and, 205n15
St. Louis Cardinals, 3, 12, 24, 53, 54, 64, 117, 179, 187n4, 201n3; establishment of, 22; National League crowns/World Series titles for, 175; parade for, 146; pennant for, 128; sale of, 20; spring training for, 26; World Series and, 132, 137, 146, 147, 159
St. Louis Stars, 101
Stoneham, Charles, 199n24; barnstorming and, 69–70; racetrack/casino and, 192n15
"Story of My Life" (McPherson), 182
St. Petersburg, 34, 37, 119; spring training in, 17–18, 32, 33
Street, Gabby, 138
Streisand, Barbara, 194n4
Stroud, Lizzie (Lizzie Arlington), 195–96n31
St. Vincent hospital, 18, 179
Sullivan, Big Tim, 185n4
Sullivan, John L., 91
Sullivan, Sport, 80, 114, 154, 194n10, 198n9
Sunday, Billy, 2, 66, 70, 83, 172; on Prohibition, 67
Sutherland, Howard, 131
Sutherland, Mary Elizabeth, 131
Suttles, Mule, 101, *F8*
Sweatt, George, 101
Sylvester, Johnnie, 148, 149, 201n3

Taft, William Howard, 41, 188n1
Talmadge, Norma, 124
Tammany Hall, 7, 8, 9, 36, 185n4
Taylor, Ida Estelle, 123, 125, 142
Taylor, Nellie, 1
Teapot Dome, 1
Tenace, Gene: walks by, 202n15
Tennes, Mont, 113, 114
Terrell Wood, spring training at, 26
Terry, Bill, 4, 105, 128
Thevenow, Tommy, 28, 56, 128; World Series and, 145, 148, 149, 153, 155, 156
Thomas, Myles, 52
Thompson, Sandy, 163, 167
Toporcer, George, 128, 149
Torriente, Cristobal, 97, 101, 192n21, 196n6, 197n17; home runs by, 193n21; Ruth and, 71
Torrio, Johnny, 34, 87, 113
Traynor, May, 19
Truman, Harry, 205n5
Trump, Donald, 189n1
Tunney, Gene, 123, 125, 127, 128, 140, 199n19, 199n24, 200n25, 200n27; Dempsey and, 199n10; described, 124; salary for, 126
Twain, Mark, 10

U.S. Cavalry Band, 105
U.S. Constitution, 67
U.S. Open (golf), 121
U.S. Open Tennis, 121

Vance, Dazzy, 38
Vanzetti, Bartolomeo, 1, 91

vaudeville, 72, 73, 75, 85, 179, 191–92n10
Veeck, William, 53, 54, 91
Vera Cruz Blues, 178
Vick, Sammy, 16
Vila, Joe, 7, 202n6
Volstead Act, 67
Von der Ahe, Chris, 20, 186n3

Waco Yellow Jackets, 95
Waddell, Rube, 96, 196n4
Wagenheim, Kal, 193n25
Wagner, Honus, 91, 196n6
Wagner, Robert, 142, 201n13
Watkins, Maurine Dallas, 69
WEAF (radio station), 142
Weaver, Buck, 80
Weegham, Charles, 62, 114, 186n7
Weiss, Hymie, 168
Weissmuller, Johnny, 37
Wells, Willie, 203n6
West, Fred, 76, 77, 170
West, Mae, 1, 69, 83
Western Association, 15
Western League, 9, 99, 111, 186n7
Wharton, Edith, 10
White, Chaney, 167
Whitehill, Earl, 131
Whiteman, Paul, 32
White Pine Camp, 103
Wilde, Oscar, 69
Willard, Jess, 123, 199n16
Williams, Charlie, 101
Williams, Smokey Joe, 97, 196n5
Wilson, Hack, 4, 54, 59, 105
Wilson, Woodrow, 62, 188n1
Wingo, Al, 51
The Winning Team (movie), 178
Witt, Lawton, 62
Waldorf Hotel, 62
Walker, Curt, 129
Walker, Jimmy, 188n10; Dempsey-Tunney fight and, 124; Ruppert and, 36–37; World Series and, 142
Walsh, Christy, 179
Waner, Paul, 4
Washington, George, 86
Washington Monument, 138
Washington Nationals, 3, 4, 8, 46, 51, 81, 85, 88, 104, 130, 138, 177; opening day and, 41, 42; World Series and, 105–6
Wolcott Hotel, 10
Wolfsheim, Meyer, 127
Wood, Smokey Joe, 75, 109, 173–74; gambling and, 77, 78, 170; letter from, 77–78, 80, 118
Woods, Doc, 143
World War I, 1, 12, 42, 79, 99, 162, 186n1
Worth, Muriel, 74
Wrigley, William, 195n11; Catalina Island and, 58, 190n2
Wrigley Field, 59, 63, 189n3

Yankee Stadium, 47, 52, 131; attendance at, 51, 68; Paige-Feller matchup at, 205n13; World Series at, 4, 132, 140, 142, 151, 154, 156, 166
Young, Cy, 22, 194n10
Youngs, Ross, 56, 105, 117

Zachery, Tom, 106
Zelcer, David, 198n9
Zork, Carl, 198n9